Scum of the Earth

When World War II started, Arthur Koestler was living in the South of France, working on his great novel, *Darkness at Noon*. He continued writing it for the next two months in Paris, until he was arrested and interned, along with the other anti-Nazis, the men and women who had already fought a round with the Gestapo, the refugees from persecution. These were the 'scum' whom the French imprisoned, and released, and re-arrested, and—in all too many tragic cases—finally handed over to their Nazi executioners. Koestler tells the story of his own imprisonment and final escape without heroics, with humanity and even with humour; but it is set squarely in the sombre context of what happened to the less fortunate of his fellow prisoners.

Certificate of demobilisation, dated August 31, 1940,
of Albert Dubert, the name under which Arthur Koestler
served in the Foreign Legion.

ARTHUR KOESTLER

Scum of the Earth

With a new Preface
by the author

THE DANUBE EDITION

HUTCHINSON OF LONDON

HUTCHINSON & CO (*Publishers*) LTD
178–202 Great Portland Street, London W1

London Melbourne Sydney
Auckland Bombay Toronto
Johannesburg New York

★

First published by Cape September 1941
Re-published by Collins with Hamish Hamilton April 1955
New English Library paperback edition 1958
Danube Edition 1968

This book has been set in Baskerville, printed in Great Britain
on Antique Wove paper by Anchor Press, and
bound by Wm. Brendon, both of Tiptree, Essex

09 087280 0

Contents

Author's Note to First Edition

This book was written in January–March 1941, before the German attack on Russia; yet the author sees no reason to modify his observations on the psychological effects of the Soviet-German pact of August 1939, or his opinion on the policy of the Communist Party in France. To smuggle in elements of a later knowledge when describing the mental pattern of people in an earlier period is a common temptation to writers, which should be resisted.

August 1941

Preface to the Danube Edition

Scum of the Earth was the first book that I wrote in English. It was written in January–March 1941, immediately after I had escaped from occupied France to England. My friends were either in the hands of the Gestapo, or had committed suicide, or were trapped, seemingly without hope, on the lost continent. The agony of the French collapse was reverberating through my mind as a scream of terror echoes in one's ear. Within the previous four years I had been imprisoned in three different countries: in Spain during the civil war; as an undesirable alien in France; finally, having escaped to England with false papers at the height of the Fifth Column scare, I was locked up, pending investigation, in Pentonville prison. The book was written in the blacked-out London of the night-blitz, in the short breathing space between my release from Pentonville and enlistment in the Pioneer Corps. Not only was time short, but money too. Having lost all my possessions in France, I arrived in England penniless, and had to live on the advance which the original publishers of the book paid me: five pounds a week during the ten weeks which it took to write, plus an additional ten pounds on delivery of the manuscript, minus the cost of hiring a typewriter and sundry other expenses deducted from the weekly five pounds.

Re-reading the book after all these years, I find these outer and inner pressures reflected in its apocalyptic mood, its spontaneity and lack of polish. Some pages now appear insufferably maudlin; others are studded with clichés which at the time, however, seemed original discoveries to the innocent explorer of a new language; above all, the text betrays the fact that there had been no time for correcting proofs. To remedy these faults would mean to re-write the book, and that would be a pointless undertaking—for, if this story has any value, it is in its documentary period character. I have confined myself to correcting only the most glaring gallicisms, germanisms and grammatical slips—and to throwing out a few purple patches here and there.

The period character of the book is particularly evident in its political outlook. It is the romantically and naively Leftist outlook of the Pink Thirties. I had been a member of the Communist Party for seven years; I had left it in disgust in 1938, but certain illusions about Soviet Russia, and 'the international solidarity of the working classes as the best guarantee of peace', lingered on, and are reflected throughout the book. That again is typical of the time—a time when my late friend George Orwell, who was of a less romantic disposition than I, could write that :

'. . . the war and the revolution are inseparable . . . We know very well that with its present social structure England cannot survive . . . We cannot win the war without introducing Socialism. Either we turn this war into a revolutionary war or we lose it.'[1]

If all this is dated, other aspects of the story have, alas, remained painfully topical. The sickness of the French body politic, which led to the débâcle of 1940, is expressed today in a different form, but it once more threatens to disrupt the unity of the Western world.

To protect the personages who appear in the book from Gestapo persecution, I had to camouflage them; for similar reasons certain episodes had to be passed over in silence. The

[1] George Orwell, *The Lion and the Unicorn* (London 1941).

friends who were hiding me from the French police in Paris
(p. 185) were the late Henri Membré, Secretary of the
French PEN Club, and that admirable woman of letters,
Adrienne Monnier. The real name of 'Père Darrault' is Père
Pieprot, O.D., at present Secretary General of the International Congress for Crimonology. 'Albert' was the
German-American author Gustav Regler. Among the
various characters in Hut No. 33 of the concentration camp
at Le Vernet, who are only referred to by initial letters, were
the German Communist leaders Paul Merker and Gerhardt
Eisler. Finally, there is 'Mario' about whom I must say a
little more.

His real name is Leo Valiani. He was not quite thirty
when we met, but he had already spent nine years in prison
as a member of the anti-Fascist underground. He escaped
from Le Vernet in October 1940, and in 1943 returned to
Italy with British help, to join the Resistance. In 1945 he
was one of the three members of the Central Insurrectional
Committee which organised the rising against the Nazis and
ordered Mussolini's execution. In 1946 he was elected to the
Constituent Assembly. Three years later he retired from
politics, published his memoirs of the Resistance and a number of books ranging from a History of the Socialist Movement to a critical evaluation of the philosophy of Benedetto
Croce. He has remained one of my closest friends throughout the years.

The narrative of *Scum of the Earth* ends in August 1940
with my arrival at the Headquarters of the Foreign Legion
in Marseilles, disguised as Legionnaire Albert Dubert. There
I joined forces with three British officers and a staff sergeant,
who had escaped from German captivity and had been interned by the French in the Fort St. Jean. For reasons of
security the story of our escape via Oran to Casablanca, then
by fishing boat to Lisbon and thus eventually to England,

could not be told at the time; and there would be no point in enlarging on it now. It is an escape story like dozens of others that have been told since, except in one respect. This concerns a member of the British Intelligence Services, with whom we made contact in Casablanca and whom we knew by the name of Mr. Ellerman. It was due to his genius for improvisation that the four of us, plus some fifty other escapees, were able to board that fishing boat, which in four days somehow managed to roll and toss us past the German submarines into the neutral harbour of Lisbon.

We all agreed that our rescuer was the most mysterious and impressive character we had ever met. Whatever one's idea of a Military Intelligence officer may be, he did not fit it. He was in his late forties, tall, elegant, dignified, charming, sophisticated and aristocratic. He could have been invented by Evelyn Waugh or Nancy Mitford, but never by Ian Fleming. Regarding politics he was surprisingly naive; his main interests seemed to be archaeology, poetry, gastronomy and the fair sex. In a word, our Ellerman belonged to an extinct species like the fabulous unicorn: he was a European grand seigneur. I say European because he spoke five or six Continental languages accent-free, and also Hebrew and Arabic.

I knew that Ellerman was not his real name. Ever since we parted in Lisbon I tried to discover his identity in order to contact him, but the powers that be were not co-operative. At some stage I was given to understand that he was killed on a mission, so I gave up. In May 1967, twenty-six years after the event, I read the following item in the Diary of the London *Times*:

Envoy's brother was our spy

The astonishing story may soon be told for the first time of a member of one of pre-war Germany's leading families who became so disgusted with the Hitler regime that he gave up everything—successful career, wealth and fame—to become a British agent. Baron

Rüdiger von Etzdorf, elder brother of Dr. Hasso von Etzdorf, ambassador to Britain from 1961 to 1965, died in London three weeks ago, aged 72, unknown and unsung . . .

Von Etzdorf—he dropped his German title when he took British nationality in 1946—was in the German navy in the first world war and fought at Jutland. His father was a close friend of the Kaiser and he had visited Sandringham in the days of King Edward VII. His extraordinary story begins in 1935, when he was approached in London by British Intelligence and asked if he would work for them.

By this time he had become something of a globe-trotter, after warning his brother Hasso that Hitler was heading straight for war— and being told not to be ridiculous.

One of his first assignments was in Italy, sending to London information on relations between Italy and Germany. When war broke out he was in Tripoli and organised an escape route for British soldiers after the fall of France. One person brought out in this way was Arthur Koestler . . .

In one convoy across the Atlantic, his was the only ship to come through unscathed. Before the war he was introduced several times to Hitler and, says Mrs. von Etzdorf, 'he found everything about the little Nazi unpleasant'.

After the war, life was not easy for von Etzdorf. Relations with his family were somewhat cool, although he did see his brother while he was ambassador in London . . . But, says a friend at the German embassy, he was never bitter—'a man of great courage and determination—one of the last genuine gentlemen'.[1]

After being congratulated on our escape by the British authorities in Lisbon, my four companions were flown the next day to England, whereas I was informed I could not go as I had no valid papers and no entry permit. I waited for two months, but the permit was never granted; 'Ellerman' tried to help, but was powerless against Government red tape. In the end I decided to get to England without a permit—although I was warned that in view of the Home Office's refusal and the Fifth Column scare this would mean another period of imprisonment or internment. Nevertheless, with the connivance of the British Consul General in

[1] *The Times,* May 25, 1967.

Lisbon, Sir Henry King, and the help of the correspondent of *The Times*, Walter Lucas, I managed to board a Dutch aeroplane to England. In Bristol, where we landed, I handed the Immigration Officer a written statement explaining my case—and was, as I had expected, promptly arrested. I spent one night at a Bristol police station, was taken under escort to London and spent six weeks in Pentonville prison in solitary confinement during the blitz. It was not a pleasant sojourn, but I knew that every one of my friends trapped on the occupied continent would gladly have changed places with me.

I was released from Pentonville a few days before Christmas 1940, and started to write this book.

A.K.

London, Spring 1968

To the memory of my colleagues, the exiled writers of Germany who took their lives when France fell :

WALTER BENJAMIN	CARL EINSTEIN
WALTER HASENCLEVER	IRMGARD KEUN
OTTO POHL	ERNST WEISS

And for

PAUL WILLERT

without whose help this book could not have been written.

AGONY

I

SOME time during the last years of Queen Victoria's reign, the Prince of Monaco had an anglicised mistress who wanted a bathroom of her own. He built her a villa, with a real bathroom, with parquet flooring, and colour prints of knights in armour and ladies in bustles fed on Benger's Food adorning all the walls. He built it at a prudent distance from his own residence in Monaco : about fifty miles up the valley of the Vésubie and only ten miles from the Italian frontier, in the parish of Roquebillière, *département des Alpes Maritimes*. With the march of time and the dawn of the twentieth century, the refined courtesan became a respectable old *rentière*, let the bathroom decay, planted cabbage in her garden, and eventually died. For some twenty years the house stood empty and the garden ran wild.

Then in the late nineteen-twenties a landslide occurred in the valley of the Vésubie which destroyed about fifty of the hundred houses of Roquebillière and killed sixty out of its five hundred inhabitants. As a result, ground rents in Roquebillière went down, and in 1929 Maria Corniglion, wife of Corniglion-upon-the-Bridge, talked her husband into buying the villa with the bathroom from the defunct lady's heirs.

Ettori Corniglion was a peasant who still cultivated his five acres of land himself with a primitive plough and a yoke of oxen, but Maria Corniglion was an enterprising woman who had brought him a respectable dowry. The Corniglions-upon-the-Bridge were well-to-do people—more so than

B

Corniglion-the-Grocer or Corniglion-the-Butcher. Mme.
Ettori Corniglion was herself born a Corniglion—for an
area extending about twenty miles down the Vésubie from
St. Martin one-third of the population were Corniglions.
They intermarried frequently, producing a remarkable rate
of cripples and idiots, and had the most imposing marble
tombstones and family vaults in the graveyards of old
Roquebillière, new Roquebillière, and St. Martin. The only
son of Ettori and Maria Corniglion was lame; he was a
schoolteacher at Lyons; during the holidays, which he spent
at home, he spoke hardly a word, and read Dostoievsky and
Julian Green. Their daughter was also a schoolteacher;
she was about thirty, but rapidly turning into an elderly
spinster. The fact that both the Corniglion children had
become members of the *corps d'enseignement* bore testi-
mony to Mme. Corniglion's ambitious character. She gave
another proof of it when, in the year before the landslide,
she had fixed to their farmhouse gate a notice with the inscription, 'HOTEL ST. SÉBASTIEN'. Her third remarkable
achievement was the purchase of the villa. But there old
Ettori put a stop to her extravagance: he would not hear of
repairing and refurnishing the villa. He planted the better
part of the garden with various kinds of salads and vegetables, and installed a pig in the summer-house. The villa
itself was not touched, and stood empty for another ten
years. It was altogether thirty years since the proprietress
had died, and the original rats and mice had been succeeded
by the three hundred and sixtieth generation of their grandchildren, when we turned up.

There were three of us: Theodore, G., and myself. We
had searched the Riviera during the past three weeks, from
Marseilles to Menton and up the valleys of the Basses-Alpes
and of the Alpes Maritimes, for a suitable house to live in.
Although our requirements were modest, we had not yet
found the house we wanted. We wanted a house with a

bathroom. G. is a sculptor; she wanted a room suitable as a studio, with windows which would fulfil certain conditions of lighting. She also wanted the house to be quiet, with no neighbours, and no wireless within five hundred yards, as she intended to make all the noise herself with her hammer and chisels. I wanted to finish the writing of a novel, to be called *Darkness at Noon*, so the house had to be old with thick, solid walls, which would stifle the sound of G's hammering; my room was to be furnished very simply and soberly, like a monk's cell, yet with a certain touch of homely comfort. Then we wanted an abode for Theodore. Theodore was a Ford born in 1929 and with a noble pedigree of eight previous owners. The third owner had fitted him with a new body, and the fifth owner with a new engine. If it is true that a human being is completely renewed every seven years by the continuous discarding and replacing of the cells constituting its vital organs, Theodore was a new car. The only inconvenience with him was that we had always to carry two gallons of water in the dickey, for he was unable to contain his water in the radiator—it escaped partly skywards in steam and froth and partly earthwards through sundry leaks. Hence the garage in the house which we were looking for had to have an easy access, which would spare Theodore those jerky leaps backward and forward which particularly annoyed him—after the third change of gear he would get a fit of megalomania, and blow white steam, believing himself to be a locomotive. Besides, the exit to the garage had to be on a slope to help start the engine, for Theodore's only response to the starter-knob was a few chuckles and hiccoughs, as if the knob tickled him. We loved Theodore very much; he was still rather good-looking, especially in profile.

We arrived at the Hotel St. Sébastien one morning at about 2 a.m. Everything was very dark and very quiet. We sounded our horn for some time and Theodore roared into the night like a hungry lion, until finally Mme. Corniglion appeared. Our acquaintance started with a mutual misunderstanding: we took the St. Sébastien for a real hotel and Mme. Corniglion took us for rich summer tourists. But next morning, when she saw Theodore, a sudden cunning look came into her old peasant eyes. She sat down at our breakfast table, and after some preliminary beating about the bush, and a furtive look round as if to make sure nobody was listening, she offered to let us a villa with a garden, a bathroom, a large barn as garage, an unused reception-room as a studio, and a quiet little attic in which the gentleman could write his poetry, and all modern conveniences. Of course, she would need a few days to clean it and arrange it, as the house had stood empty for a few weeks, owing to the illness of an aunt in Périgueux. We had a look at the house and liked it at once. It was exactly what we had been looking for.

We agreed that we would move into the house in three days. We were to have our lunch and dinner at the Hotel St. Sébastien, breakfast would be brought by a maid who would come every morning to clean up for us. We were to pay 30 francs per head a day, or £5 a month, for villa, garden, meals, service and *vin à discrétion*—as much as we liked or were able to stand.

We intended to stay three or four months, and work and drink *vin à discrétion*. We were very happy. We moved into the house in the beginning of August, 1939, about the time when the puppet Senate of Danzig decided to join Hitler's Reich.

II

A company of shabby French soldiers was sitting in the sun on a wall covered with wild vine, dangling their legs. They rolled cigarettes and threw stones for a black mongrel dog. It was a funny little dog and they called it Daladier. '*Vas-y, Daladier*,' they said, '*dépeche-toi. Cours, mon vieux, faut gagner ton bifteck*.' When we turned up in the car, they did not seem embarrassed. They made some joking remarks about Theodore, steaming and spitting as usual after the brisk ascent, and then went on urging Daladier to run and earn his daily *bifteck*. They spoke French to us and to the dog, but amongst themselves they spoke a kind of Italian dialect, the *patois* of the region.

All the sleepy, age-old mountain villages of the Maritime Alps north of the Riviera were now packed with soldiers—grumbling, drinking red wine, playing belotte, and bored. We were on the road again, waiting for our house to be prepared for us; with poor Theodore, we climbed the tortuous by-roads indicated on the Michelin map by a dotted line with a green border—the dotted line meant 'danger' and the green border 'picturesque view'. There was Gorbio and St. Dalmas and St. Agnès and Valdeblore and Castellar —they all looked the same; eagle nests on bare rocks, carved out of the rocks, built of the products of the decaying rocks, stone and clay. The houses, with stone walls as thick as mediæval fortresses, were built on different levels, the ground floor of one row on a level with the upper floor of the row across the street, and some of the streets were actually tunnels, carrying enormous vaults, cool and dim in the blazing sunshine, like Arabian *shuks*. But no one walked through these streets except a furtive cat, a herd of goats, or a very old woman in black, dry and twisted like the dead branches of an olive tree. When one climbed to the top of the village, one saw the neck-breaking serpentine road by which one had just come, and, 2,000 feet below, the valley; and far behind the decreasing mountains, the sea with Nice and the Cap d'Antibes and Monte Carlo, veiled by the mist. There lay the Shore of Vanity, and here was the realm of the Sleeping Beauty; but of an Italian Sleeping Beauty of the mountain, lying hidden behind a rock, bare-footed, with dry mud between her toes, with tangled, black gypsy hair straggling over her young and yet wrinkled face, and a goat's-skin bottle of acid red wine warming on the hot rock within reach. Thus had we found St. Agnès and Gorbio and Castellar a year before; but now the soldiers had invaded the mountains, they had stretched barbed wire across the pasture and installed machine-guns and field-kitchens on the olive-tree terraces. And they had woken the Sleeping Beauty by telling her that the French were going to fight the Italians because the Germans wanted a town in Poland. But, as she did not believe it, they offered her red wine and tickled her bare heels to pass the time.

We talked to many of the soldiers. They were sick of the war before it had started. They were peasants, and harvest time was approaching; they wanted to go home and did not care a bean for Danzig and the Corridor. The majority of them came from the Italian-speaking districts of the frontier region. They had become, in their habits of life, more French than they were consciously aware of; they thought that Mussolini with his big *gueule* was a rather ridiculous figure and that all that Blackshirt business which began just beyond the next mountain ridge was a sort of comic opera. They rather liked La France, but they did not actually love her; they rather disliked Hitler for all the unrest he created, but they did not actually hate him. The only thing they really hated was the idea of war—and of any sort of political creed which might lead to war. And this was the point where these descendants of Italian emigrants had become most strikingly French : they had acquired very quickly the average Frenchman's conviction that politics were a racket, that to become a Deputy or Minister was only a form of earning one's *bifteck* and rather a fat one; that all political ideals and 'isms' were a matter of salesmanship and that the only thing a sensible man could do was to follow the advice of Candide and cultivate his little garden.

Why, for what reason on earth, should they die for Danzig? The newspapers which they read—the *Eclaireur du Sud-Est* and *Paris Soir* and *Petit Parisien*—had explained to them during all these years that it was not worth while to sacrifice French lives for the sake of the Negus or for the sake of some Schuschnigg or some Negrin or Dr. Benes. The newspapers had explained to them that only the warmongers of the Left wanted to precipitate France into such an abyss. They had explained to them that Democracy and Collective Security and the League of Nations were all beautiful ideas, but that anybody who wanted to stand up for these ideas was an enemy of France. And now the same newspapers all of a sudden wanted to convince them that their duty was to fight and die for things which only yesterday had not been worth fighting for; and they proved it with exactly the same arguments which only yesterday they had ridiculed and abused. Fortunately, the soldiers only read the crime and sporting pages. They had learned long ago that everything in the editorials was tripe and eyewash.

I wonder whether the French Command knew much about the morale of their troops. Perhaps they preferred not to investigate too closely, and thought things would be all right once the actual fighting started. I have lost my diary with everything else in France, but I remember writing in it on the day when the invasion of Poland began: 'This war starts in the moral climate of 1917.'

There was only one consideration which prevented the average French soldier from looking at the war as complete madness and which gave him at least a vague notion of what it was about: it was summed up in the slogan, '*Il faut en finir*'. His ideals had been gutted during the disastrous years of Bonnet-Laval-Flandin statesmanship; the cynicism of the Munich era had destroyed any creed worth fighting for; but he had been mobilised three times during the past few years and he was sick of having to leave his job and his family every six months and to return after a few weeks, feeling ridiculous and cheated. It was time '*pour en finir*'— to put an end to it once and for all. '*Il faut en finir*' was the only popular slogan, but it carried no real conviction. It was the grumbling of an utterly exasperated person rather than a programme for which to die. To fight a war only for the purpose of ending the danger of war is an absurdity —as if a person condemned to sit on a powder-barrel should blow himself up deliberately, out of sheer annoyance at not being allowed to smoke his pipe.

And on top of all this they did not, of course, believe that there really would be a war. It was just another bluff, and in due time there would be another Munich. The newspapers would again do a complete about-turn, and nicely explain that it was not worth while to die for Danzig. Marcel Déat had already done so in *L'Œuvre*. And so another lump of Europe's bleeding flesh would be thrown to the monster to keep him quiet for six months—and another lump next spring and another next autumn. And, for all one knew, in due time the monster might die a natural death by indigestion.

So far France had not fared too badly by sacrificing her allies. '*Tout est perdu sauf l'honneur*,' a noble Frenchman had once said. Now he could say : '*Nous n'avons rieu perdu sauf l'honneur*.'

III

We moved into our house. It was a complete success.

At seven o'clock in the morning Teresa, the maidservant at the Hotel St. Sébastien, would bring us our breakfast. She was a dark and stolid young woman who worked sixteen hours a day for a salary of 50 francs, or 5s. 6d., a month. Sometimes Teresa was too busy, and our breakfast would be brought by the Corniglions' daughter, the schoolmistress. After breakfast we went to watch Teresa feed the pig in the summer-house. It was so narrow that the pig could hardly turn round; just eat and digest and sleep. We had never seen such a fascinatingly disgusting pig. Then we walked knee-deep through the wet grass on the lawn and inspected our fig-tree. There were seventeen figs on the tree in different stages of ripeness, mostly on the topmost branches; we kept an eye on them and shot them down with stones when we judged them nearly ripe, before Mme. Corniglion, who also had her eye on them, had time to collect them. Then we worked until noon, and walked down to the hotel for lunch and *vin à discrétion*. Then came the siesta, and work again until the hour of the *apéritif*. Theodore was allowed a long rest and slept peacefully in his barn; his tyres were deflated and he looked shrunken, as very old people do; from time to time we would sound the claxon to see whether he were still alive.

We were very happy. All was quiet in the country of the Sleeping Beauty. True, those noisy garrisons had woken her, but she was still drowsily rubbing her eyes and yawning and stretching, and just put out her tongue at the growling monster. No, there would be no war. We would sacrifice another piece of our *honneur*—who cares for *honneur*, anyway?— and go on playing belotte. And writing novels and carving stones, and cultivating our garden, like sensible people should do during their short stay on this earth. Besides, Hitler couldn't fight against the Soviets and the West simultaneously. And if the West made a firm stand this time, the Soviets would come in at once. There would be no war. You had only to repeat it sufficiently often, until you were sick of hearing yourself say it.

And all the time we knew that this was our last summer for a long time, and perhaps for ever.

By the middle of August green-and-yellow posters appeared on the town hall of Roquebillière, calling up the men of Categories 3 and 4 to join their regiments within forty-eight hours. Little groups of people collected in front of the posters, and the younger women appeared at the village shop with swollen eyes, and the older women, the widows of 1914, walked down the street in their black clothes with a gloomy and triumphant look.

Then the annual fair in honour of the local patron saint was cancelled. The dancing-floor was dismantled and the flagpoles pulled down.

And one Sunday morning a persistent cloud of dust hung in the air and a continuous confused noise of bleating and lowing and barking came down the hillside; the sheep and goats and cattle were returning from their pastures on the Italian frontier. The whole village gathered at the bridge to see them pass. It was a long procession, with tired, cursing shepherds, and sheep bleating incessantly, pushing and jostling each other in a general and senseless panic. The people at the bridge looked as if they were watching a funeral procession.

And yet there would be no war. We had to reassure, not only ourselves, but also the Corniglions and the village people who asked us our opinion; for, being foreigners and educated people, we must know. Our presence alone was a reassurance for them; if there had been a real danger of war, we would have gone home. Every morning, after bringing us our breakfast and feeding the pig, Teresa had to report to the butcher whether we really were still in the villa. We had become a sort of talisman for the people of Roquebillière.

The days passed. We tried to work. Telephone calls came from friends on the Riviera: they were leaving; everybody was leaving. We jeered at the *paniquards*. Last year at the time of Munich, G. had cut short her stay in Florence and I had cancelled a newspaper assignment to Mexico at the last minute. This time we would not let ourselves be fooled.

There were still five or six guests at the Hotel St. Sébastien, who packed and unpacked their suitcases according to the latest news on the wireless : an asthmatic priest from Savoy, gloomy and congested-looking, who reminded one of those mediæval mountain *curés* in the uncanny novels of Georges Bernanos. Then an Italian wine-merchant from Marseilles and a petty-officer's widow from Toulon with three plain but coquettish daughters, the eldest liable to fits of hysterics. They all had their meals together at a long table in the dining-room; we preferred to eat on the terrace, even when it rained, to escape their company.

But we could not avoid the inmates of the asylum on the road below our villa. It was the regional asylum for the aged paupers, cripples, village idiots, and harmless lunatics of the district. It stood on our way to the hotel, and some of its inmates were always sitting in front of the institution on a wooden bench under a painted crucifix. There was Aunt Marie, knitting an invisible jumper with invisible wool; and the other old woman, wagging her shrunken head, not much larger than a grape-fruit; and a third one, making faces and telling a funny story to which nobody listened; and a silent, always neatly dressed man with beautiful hands and a noseless death's head. We had to pass them four times a day, on our way to the St. Sébastien and back, and they always stared at us in visible disgust. During daytime we tried not to notice; but we did not like walking past the asylum at night.

It was a strange place, Roquebillière. The houses destroyed by the landslide in 1926 had never been rebuilt and the débris had not been cleared away. Although the disaster had happened thirteen years before, half of the village consisted of the empty shells of abandoned houses and heaps of rubbish. They said there was no money to reconstruct it and to clear away the rubbish, but they had erected a large marble slab, like a war memorial, at the entry of the village, with all the names of the victims carved on it, mostly Corniglions.

They seemed to cherish the memory of *la catastrophe*. When we were still new to Roquebillière and heard the standard expression, '*Il a péri pendant la catastrophe*', uttered with a certain pride, we thought they meant the War of 1914. The inscription on the marble slab was composed in a tone of patriotic reproach. They felt that God had assumed a debt towards Roquebillière, and that he alone could be expected to do something about it.

In the year after the landslide, however, some of the younger men of Roquebillière embarked upon a truly extraordinary enterprise. They had heard of the rain of gold pouring down on the Riviera; and they wondered why the same thing should not happen in the valley of the Vésubie. They had received a fair sum from departmental and Government relief funds; so, instead of rebuilding Old Roquebillière, they decided to build a New Roquebillière a mile or so across the valley on the other side of the Vésubie, and to make it a fashionable holiday resort, a kind of Juanles-Pins or Grasse. They found some estate agents to back them up, and got to work. Two years later new signposts appeared all along the road from St. Martin du Var up the Valley :

TOURISTES !

VISITEZ LA NOUVELLE ROQUEBILLIÈRE,
LA PERLE DE LA VÉSUBIE—*à 4 Klm.*

The Pearl of the Vésubie had about 150 inhabitants, but accommodation for 500 tourists. There were three hotels and an American bar, two fancy shops and another shop for souvenirs, and a town hall with an electric clock like a railway station. Everything was ready for the tourists, but the tourists did not come. They waited for them, first hopefully, then with growing despair, and finally they resigned themselves. Some of the pioneers went back to Old Roquebillière, the others just stayed on. Like ghosts in a deserted gold-digging town of Alaska, they shuffled through the asphalt streets, past the closed American bar and the closed fancy shops. They had as much use for the pretentious town they lived in as a miner's wife for an evening dress; but it had swallowed up all their money and there was none left to tidy up the débris of their former home; so they put their last pennies together and erected the marble memorial as a double reproach to Fate.

It took us quite a time to discover that the main reason for the misfortunes of Roquebillière was its climate. The mornings were radiant, but at about four in the afternoon the sky over the valley would become grey and leaden. The atmospheric tension made us tired and irritable; once a week a crashing thunderstorm would clear the sky, but usually all the promising thunder and lightning ended in a miscarriage and the oppression remained.

Perhaps it was all the fault of the ogre—an enormous dark mountain on the other side of the valley, obstructing and dominating it and bending over it, as if to watch malevolently from above the clouds what was going on down below. The ogre had a strange outline; a large crack in the rock had thrown open its huge, man-eating mouth, with a single jagged tooth sticking out of the gaping lower jaw. We could escape the newspapers, switch off the wireless, and turn away our eyes when we passed the lunatics—but the ogre was always there, especially at night, watching us and watching the valley.

This Roquebillière had become a sinister, depressing place. Perhaps it had always been so, but now we saw it with different eyes. We knew it was our last summer, and everything around us assumed a dark, symbolical meaning. Yet it was still August, and the sun was still vigorous and bright, and the figs still went on ripening in our garden. We had never loved France as we loved it in those late August days; we had never been so achingly conscious of its sweetness and decay.

IV

I am definitely Continental : that is, I always feel the urge to underline a dramatic situation by a dramatic gesture. G. is definitely English : that is, she always feels the urge to suppress the original urge; and usually this second reflex precedes the first.

When, on August 23rd, I saw the inconspicuous Havas message on the third page of the *Eclaireur du Sud-Est*, saying that a treaty of non-aggression had been signed between Germany and the Soviet, I began beating my temples with my fist. The paper had just arrived. I had opened it while we were walking down to the St. Sébastien for lunch. 'What is the matter?' said G. 'This is the end,' I said. 'Stalin has joined Hitler.' 'He would,' said G., and that was all.

I tried to explain to her what it meant—to the world in general and to me and my friends in particular. What it meant to that better, optimistic half of humanity which was called the Left because it believed in social evolution and which, however opposed to the methods employed by Stalin and his disciples, still consciously or unconsciously believed that Russia was the only promising social experiment in this wretched century. I myself had been a Communist for seven years; I had paid dearly for it; I had left the Party in disgust just eighteen months ago. Some of my friends had done the same; some were still hesitating; many of them had been shot or imprisoned in Russia. We had realised that Stalinism had soiled and compromised the Socialist Utopia just as the Mediæval Church had soiled and compromised Christianity; that Trotsky, although more appealing as a person, was in his methods not better than his opponent; that the central evil of Bolshevism was its unconditional adoption of the tenet that the End justifies the Means; that a well-meaning dictatorship of the Torquemada-Robespierre-Stalin ascendancy was even more disastrous in its effect than a naked tyranny of the Neronian type; that all the parties of the Left had outlived their time, and that one day a new movement was to emerge from the deluge, whose preachers would probably wear monks' cowls and walk barefoot on the roads of a Europe in ruins. We had realised all this and had turned our backs to Russia, yet wherever we turned our eyes for comfort we found none; and so, in the back of our minds there remained a faint hope that perhaps and after all it was we who were in the wrong and that in the long run it was the Russians who were in the right. Our feelings towards Russia were rather like those of a man who has divorced a much-beloved wife; he hates her and yet it is a sort of consolation for him to know that she is still there, on the same planet, still young and alive.

But now she was dead. No death is so sad and final as the death of an illusion. The first moment after receiving a blow one does not suffer; but one knows already that soon the suffering will start. While I was reading that Havas notice, I was not depressed, only excited; but I knew that I would be depressed tomorrow and the day after tomorrow, and that this feeling of bitterness would not leave me for months and perhaps for years to come; and that millions of people, representing that more optimistic half of humanity, would perhaps never recover from this depression, although not consciously aware of its reason. Every period has its dominant religion and hope; only very rarely, in its darkest moments, has humanity been left without a specific faith to live and die for. A war was to be fought. They would fight, the men of the Left, but they would fight in bitterness and despair; for it is hard for men to fight if they only know what they are fighting against and not what they are fighting for.

This is what I tried to explain to G., who was born in the year of the Treaty of Versailles and could not understand why a man of thirty-five should make such a fuss at the funeral of his illusions—belonging, as she did, to a generation with none.

Next morning, August 24th, the news had spread from the third to the front page. We were spared none of the details. We read about von Ribbentrop's lightning visit to Moscow and about his cordial reception—and I remembered what fun our Party papers had made of the ex-commercial traveller in champagne who had been promoted chief diplomatic salesman of Genuine Old Red Scare, bottled in Château Berchtesgaden. We learned all the picturesque details of how the swastika had been hoisted over the Moscow aerodrome and how the band of the Revolutionary Army had played the Horst Wessel song—and I remembered the whispered explanations of the Party officials after the execution of Tukhachevsky and the other Red Army leaders. The official explanation (Version A, for the pious and simple-minded) stated that they were ordinary traitors; Version B (for the intelligentsia and for inside use) informed us that, although not exactly traitors, they had advocated a policy of understanding with the Nazis against the Western Democracies; so, of course, Stalin was right to shoot them. We learned of the monstrous paragraph 3 of the new treaty,[1] a direct encouragement to Germany to attack Poland—and I wondered how this time the Party was to explain this latest achievement of Socialist statesmanship to the innocent masses. Next morning we knew it: *Humanité*, official organ of the French Communist Party, explained to us that the new treaty was a supreme effort of

[1] The classical form for non-aggression treaties had been so far to promise neutrality should the partner be *attacked* by a third Power: in the Soviet-German Treaty for the first time neutrality was promised should the partner be *involved* in a war.

Stalin to prevent the threatening imperialist war. Oh, they
had an explanation ready for every occasion, from the extension of capital punishment to the twelve-year-old to the
abolition of the Soviet workers' right to strike and to the
one-party-election-system; they called it 'revolutionary dialectics' and reminded one of those conjurers on the stage
who can produce an egg from every pocket of their frock-
coats and even out of the harmless onlooker's nose. They
explained everything so well that old Heinrich Mann, at one
time a great 'sympathiser', shouted to Dahlem, leader of the
German Communists, during a committee meeting : 'If you
go on asking me to realise that this table here is a fishpond,
then I am afraid my dialectical capacities are at an end.'

Poor old Heinrich Mann—and André Gide and Romain
Rolland and Dos Passos and Bernard Shaw : I wondered
how they would react to the news. How clever those conjurers had been to produce eggs out of the noses of the intellectual *élite* all over the world. And all the old workers of
Citroën and the young workers in the dungeons of the
Gestapo and the Members of the Left Book Club in Bir-
mingham and the dead in the mass-graves of Spain—we
had all been taken in all right in the greatest farce the world
had ever seen.

It was a bright, sunny day, this August 24th, 1939. I
read the paper as usual while we were walking down to the
St Sébastien for lunch. I gesticulated and spoke very loudly.
Aunt Marie, sitting in the sun and knitting busily her invisible jumper, gave us a shocked look as we passed the
asylum.

v

There was an exhibition of Spanish paintings in the
Musée Nationale in Geneva. It consisted of the works from
the Prado which had been sent to Switzerland by the
c

Spanish Government during the civil war. The exhibition was to be closed on August 31st; G. wanted to see it. I tried to persuade her that it was foolish to go abroad when the war might start from one day to another. But she said : Just because of that; it was perhaps her last chance to see the works from the Prado, and nothing should prevent her doing it. So she left—on Friday, August 25th, exactly one week before the Germans invaded Poland. She was probably the only person in Europe at that time who went abroad to see the exhibition in Geneva.

I saw her to the cross-country bus for Nice, which was packed with panic-stricken people evacuated from the frontier zone; I shoved her small suitcase on top of the heap of mattresses, frying-pans and canary cages on the roof; then the bus left.

It was five o'clock in the afternoon; I walked slowly back to our villa. So far G.'s presence had protected me from becoming fully conscious of what was going on. She had the post-Versailles generation's typical way of taking for granted that this world was a hopeless mess; but this innate lack of illusions, instead of making her cynical, produced a sort of cheerful fatalism which made me, with my chronic political despair, feel like a sentimental, middle-aged Don Quixote. She had ridiculed me for drugging myself by buying all available newspapers and listening to all available stations on the wireless; and this fear of appearing ridiculous had a rather sedative effect. But now I was left alone and fell back into the grip of the drug.

On Saturday, August 26th, new posters appeared on the town hall: Categories 2, 6 and 7 were called up simultaneously. This meant practically general mobilisation; there was but one category of reservists left. I spent nearly the entire day in the Corniglions' kitchen, where the wireless set was installed next to the large, old-fashioned kitchen range. The widow with the three daughters and the wine merchant and the asthmatic priest had all left the day before; the St. Sébastien had ceased to be an hotel and had become a farm-house again. Teresa had taken off her shoes and stockings, and the wireless had returned to the kitchen. While Mme. Corniglion cooked on the kitchen range and old Ettori drank his pint of wine, I translated to them the news from Berlin and London; the odds for peace and war seemed now to change from hour to hour, and old Ettori said it reminded him of the way his grandmother used to cure his chilblains by making him put his feet alternately in a bucket of cold and in a bucket of hot water. In the afternoon more evacuees came from the frontier, in packed cars, lorries and mule-carts; their luggage consisted mainly of mattresses and frying-pans, as if to demonstrate that humanity was going to be reduced to the mere satisfaction of her two primary needs. Late in the evening a telegram from G. came from Geneva, announcing her return for tomorrow, Sunday, night. I was relieved and had at the same time a feeling of mild I-told-you-so superiority: the telegram sounded neither fatalistic nor cheerful.

I had given up all efforts to force myself to work. Curiously enough, the novel which I was writing had its setting in Russia, more exactly in a Soviet prison; a few days before I had just finished a long dialogue, in the course of which Gletkin, the G.P.U. interrogator, says:

'We did not recoil from betraying our friends and com-promising with our enemies, in order to preserve the Bas-tion. That was the task which history has given us, the representatives of the first victorious revolution'.

It was no coincidence—just the hidden logic of events. Yet I wondered whether Cassandra felt any happier when the logic of events actually brought the Greeks to Troy.

So I spent most of the next day—Sunday, the 27th—in

the Corniglions' kitchen. Old Corniglion, too, for the first time since days immemorial, had not gone out to work in his fields; he sat next to the hearth, looking miserable and oddly out of place. I had become part of the family; we sat mostly in a mournful silence, a gathering of casualties of the *guerre des nerfs*.

After dinner I started up our weary Theodore to go and fetch G. from the railway station in Nice. I had plenty of time; the train was only due to arrive at about midnight; so I chose a secondary road over a mountain pass which we had always intended to explore. It was a moonlit night, the road utterly deserted, and the villages I passed already asleep, with only an occasional window lit by an oil lamp inside. I stopped Theodore on the top of the pass and let the moonlight and the silence and the mountain air envelop us like a cool and soothing bath; and I remembered nights like this driving home to Malaga from the Andalusian front; and I wondered how soon we all would again curse the full moon and the stars, and pray for nights with fog and rain to hide the men of the earth from the men prowling between the clouds.

Eventually we descended on Nice about midnight. I had to wait for nearly an hour for the train, which was, of course, late—I think trains always rejoice in wars, which provide them with an excuse to shake off the wearisome fetters of the time-table and proceed at last at their leisure. There was an elderly Riviera-Englishman on the platform, waiting for his wife and children to arrive; after pacing up and down for half an hour past one another, we had a drink together at the buffet. He was as depressed as I, and confessed that, although for years he had been furious because we didn't make a stand against the Axis, now that we were at last going to do it, he could hardly suppress a shameful wish to go on with the old, disastrous muddle. 'I know it is idiotic and criminal, yet I almost want to say: For God's sake give that bastard all he asks for—Danzig and Eupen and colonies and what not, and let us hear no more about him.' I confessed that I was afraid most of us were liable to the same sort of suicidal temptation :

'It is the old story of going to the dentist to have a tooth extracted—at the moment of ringing the bell it stops aching, and all of a sudden one wonders whether it is worth while suffering the agony of the operation. Yet if we do not, the infection will gain the jaw, and eventually the whole body.' I thought it was quite a good metaphor, but it did not sound convincing.

Eventually G. arrived, and on the way back we decided to stop pretending and go home to Paris next day. She had travelled about thirty-six hours to Geneva and back, and had only been able to spend two or three at the Exhibition —yet she didn't regret the trouble and was quite content to have at least had a sight of the Prado treasures. For me, in her place, the pleasure of seeing what I could see would have been poisoned by the regret of missing what I couldn't.

VI

And so, after all, we too started packing.

It took us all the next day, and it was a melancholy business. G. had portrayed me in clay, and the life-sized head had to be stowed with much care and fuss in the depths of Theodore, and secured against the impact of the rest of the luggage. We eventually brought it safely to Paris with only one ear missing and the lips smeared together into a Mephistophelian grin—and it was grinning still when the Gestapo took it away in a removal van ten months later, together with my manuscripts, books, and furniture, rugs and lamps included, from my Paris flat.

We dawdled over our packing, still hoping that some

miracle might happen at the last minute, which would allow us to unpack again. How many people in Europe turned on the wireless on that Tuesday morning, August 29th, in the secret hope that overnight a benevolent stroke had killed the man whose disappearance would perhaps enable them to carry on with their mediocre and, in retrospect, oh, so pleasant existence? Instead, they were admonished in every language of the world to gird up their loins. They sighed, incredulous; they had lived so long under the Sign of the Umbrella that they found it difficult to believe that the Age of the Sword had come.

We finally left on Tuesday evening, when all pretexts to postpone our departure had been exhausted.

There were still three figs left on the tree in our garden. When we had manœuvred through the gate and turned our heads, the villa looked already as though no one had ever lived within its walls. We passed the asylum, but the bench under the crucifix was empty; Aunt Marie and the man with the death's head had gone inside. We rolled over the bridge and waved to the Corniglions, but they did not see us; they were probably gathered for dinner in the kitchen, sitting by the hearth. The street was empty and none of the people of Roquebillière were there to wave us good-bye.

I stepped on the gas and we sped out of the village, feeling like deserters. While I write these lines, the Blackshirts are sitting in the garden of the Prince's late mistress; they have probably killed the pig and picked the figs from the trees and put Teresa in the family way.

We passed the night in a deserted hotel in a deserted Nice; and all through the night we heard the plaintive neighing of horses which had been requisitioned for the Army and stood crowded together under the archways of the Casino Municipal. We had intended next day to push on our homeward way as far as Avignon; but early in the morning I went down to buy the *Eclaireur du Sud-Est*, and when I had finished reading the editorial I ran up the stairs like a madman to break to G. the news that there would be no war.

The *Eclaireur* was one of the important provincial newspapers of France, outspokenly sympathetic towards the La Rocque and Doriot movements and supported the policy of Bonnet (who was still Minister of Foreign Affairs). In the previous weeks, during the dramatic crescendo of the European crisis, it had taken a line of uncompromising firmness towards Hitler's Polish demands—according to the *mots d'ordres* from the Quai d'Orsay. In times of emergency, the Quai d'Orsay always exercised a kind of silently accepted dictatorship over the Press, which showed in such moments a considerable capacity for national discipline.

And now on this Wednesday, August 30th, when the German ultimatum to Poland was already on its way, the *Eclaireur du Sud-Est* suddenly advocated peace at any price. There was nothing in the German demands, it said, which could not be settled by peaceful negotiation. I remember particularly one sentence which said that it was time to abandon a certain number of outworn conceptions and alliances, and 'dig deep in our pockets' if we wanted to ensure a really lasting peace. And so on over two columns, in heavy type, large spacing, front page.

It seemed impossible that the editorialist of the paper had dared to write this off his own bat, at the climax of the crisis. Something must have happened during the night; the article was obviously inspired from high quarters. The Paris morning papers would not arrive until late in the evening and the wireless gave only news bulletins without commentary. Had I not been a journalist, I would probably not have paid much attention to that article; but as I knew how carefully a sensational statement of this sort would be concocted in the Editor's office, I was convinced that Bonnet had once more sacrificed the *honneur* of France and that the war was called off.

Twenty-four hours later the *Eclaireur* published a tortuous apology, and became firm and patriotic again. As to its readers, I wondered how M. Dupont was going to die, if he was to die, in the defence of liberty, after this kind of moral preparation. It was only after the collapse of France, when a stupefied world learned how France's Minister of Foreign Affairs had tried to double-cross his Allies and his own Premier in the very last six hours before he declared war, that I realised the meaning and the background of that typical episode.

Anyhow, the *Eclaireur* had provided us with a pretext to linger for another couple of days on the Mediterranean; so, instead of leaving for Paris, we went in the opposite direction, toward Menton, to pay a visit to a friend—a vaguely Turkish princess who had married an ex-croupier of the Casino in Monte Carlo and ran a second-rate hotel on the Cap Martin. We arrived about tea-time to find the last guest gone, and the princess and M. Robert, the ex-croupier, quarrelling hysterically. In the course of the discussion, it transpired that they were never married, that the Turkish princess apparently had an Italian passport and, fearing internment, had threatened M. Robert to leave for Italy if he didn't marry her on the spot, after having for fifteen years lived peacefully in sin. Eventually the discussion was postponed and we all listened to the wireless. For dinner a friend of M. Robert's turned up, a M. de Something, who had been mobilised a few days before and was posted in one of the frontier forts near by. He wore a crumpled lieutenant's uniform, and was unshaven and bad-tempered. He complained of the *pagaille*—muddle—in the fortress, the dampness of the concrete, which gave the men rheumatic pains, and told us an incredible story to the effect that more than half of the shells in the munition depot were the wrong size and did not fit the guns. At that time I did not believe it, but later on I heard several stories of the same kind, particularly about the block-houses of the so-called Extended Maginot Line.

After a few glasses of wine, the lieutenant cheered up a little and explained to us that, in the event of Italy remaining neutral, she would be presented with an ultimatum to let the French troops pass for an outflanking attack on Germany. He said he knew this from a most reliable source; and he had even heard of a witty *bon mot* by Gamelin himself :

'To force my way through a hostile Italy,' the Generalissimo had said, 'I need ten divisions. To secure the frontier against a neutral Italy, I need fifteen divisions. To help an allied Italy out of the mess, I need twenty divisions. So let's declare war on them.'

Next morning the Gendarmerie at Cap Martin was pasted all over with posters on black-out regulations and air-raid precautions. I drove to a garage and had the headlights painted blue. Poor Theodore looked like a blind old man with blue spectacles out of *The Beggar's Opera*.

The Cap Martin, a tongue of land stretched towards the Italian shore, was buzzing with troops, lorries, and armoured cars. Six light tanks stood tidily parked on the parking place in front of the Hotel Splendide, looking like wolves in a sheep-pen. The elegant sheep of the mechanical fauna had mainly disappeared, requisitioned for the Army.

At lunch we learned the details of the German ultimatum. Then we got hold of the *Eclaireur*. It was eating its words of the previous day and bursting with *gloire* and bellicosity. So now it really was time to leave. We said good-bye to the princess and M. Robert, and set out on the road to Paris.

The night from Thursday to Friday we had to spend in St. Tropez, owing to a series of punctures. Next morning we went on and stopped for lunch in Le Lavandou. We found a place called 'Le Restaurant des Pêcheurs'—one of those enchanting little inns which make one remember meals in France like gaily-coloured landmarks of the past. We had a *bouillabaisse* with mussels and *langouste* and saffron, and an *omelette aux fines herbes* which made one smell the wet grass of an Alpine meadow in the sunshine; and then the waitress came in with the *entrecôte*, and said in a flat voice, while arranging the dishes on the table : 'They have just announced on the wireless that early this morning the Germans opened fire on Poland. The Government has decreed general mobilisation.'

There was only an old couple in the restaurant apart from us, sitting at a neighbouring table. They were both in black, and the woman, with protruding, red-veined eyes, nodded to us in mournful reproach. She had eaten and drunk an enormous amount without losing her mournful look—the type of Frenchwoman who already as a bride has the future widow written on her face. She went on nodding at us in silence, and it seemed to me that with her appraising eyes she tried to divine what G. would look like with a black veil. One felt that a great time began for her now, a sort of Indian summer blooming, nourished by the black saps of general despair.

It was at that moment—at 1 p.m. on Friday, September 1st, 1939, at the Restaurant des Pêcheurs at Lavandou—that the war began for us. In my memory that hour is marked as a thin black line, like the Equator on a map, separating the sphere of the pleasant and trivial Past from the age of the Apocalypse, which is still the Present.

VII

We arrived at Toulon in the afternoon, its narrow, tortuous streets in hectic effervescence. In the hall of the Havas building a crowd had gathered to read the latest news, but there was very little discussion and nothing in the atmosphere which could be compared with that of the drunken

crowds of the August days of 1914. We drove to a garage
to buy a new tyre, and there the patronne told us trium-
phantly that France had presented a short-termed ultimatum to Italy, that French troops had penetrated twenty
miles into Italian territory, that King Victor Emmanuel had
abdicated in favour of Prince Umberto, obviously with the
view of removing Mussolini from his post. The news came
from a so-to-speak official source: the *adjudant* from the
Gendarmerie, a friend of her husband's, had just told her.
At first we were rather incredulous; but she told the story so
convincingly and with such matter-of-fact details, that
finally I too was convinced. So, at last, after seven years of
humiliation and disgrace, the hour of the Democracies had
come: they had struck—and with what speed, with what
efficiency! I became quite drunk with joy and explained
solemnly to G. that this was more than a strategic move—it
was a turning point in history, the renaissance of the era of
Liberalism. I was annoyed when she remained sceptical.

My illusions lasted until Aix-en-Provence, where we arrived just in time to hear the trite, colourless communiqués
of the eight o'clock news. It was very depressing. For the
first time in this war I had been taken in by a *bobard*—a
false rumour—and, in spite of the professional caution of
one who had been a newspaper correspondent since the age
of twenty, it happened several times again; the last time was
shortly after the fall of Paris, when for a few hours people all
over France believed that the longed-for miracle had come
to pass and Russia had declared war on Germany. Each
time the *bobard* was set rolling so cleverly, at a psychological moment so well chosen, and so devastating was the
effect on morale of the subsequent disappointment, that the
assumption of deliberate Fifth Column work was hard to
dismiss, even for people with no fondness for spy stories.

The cafés in Aix were crowded; there were a lot of soldiers about and quite a number of them were drunk; they

looked, in their unbecoming uniform, made of a very inferior material, and with their traditionally unshaven faces —hence the word *poilu*—as if they had already been in the forefront of the battle. We sat down on a *terrasse*, but to hear the news bulletin I had to go to the manager's office; it was surprising that nobody else had the same idea. On the *terrasse* of the next-door café there was a loudspeaker, but nobody listened to it; the news was drowned in the general chattering; and this at a time when France's declaration of war was to be expected from hour to hour. Apparently people had given up hope of learning anything from M. Giraudoux's lamentable news service, and they were sick of listening to those futile, tortuous communiqués and lame speeches, in which they were constantly admonished in a schoolmasterly, wrangling tone to trust their leaders (including M. Bonnet), and not to ask silly questions.

We found in Aix some new and partly contradictory posters concerning the requisitioning of cars, freshly pasted on the walls, and we had to drive all around the town until finally we found the requisitioning commission sitting at the Cavalry Barracks; but when they had had a look at Theodore, they said with a shudder that we could continue on our way to Paris, and report to the commission there.

So we drove off to Avignon in the dark with our completely blind headlights. In those prehistoric days the more refined devices for dimming the lights did not yet exist, but we were now in a nervous hurry to get to Paris, and thence on to London, where I was to enlist in the Army; I felt in a way guilty about all that dawdling of the last few days, and drove at the relatively neck-breaking speed of thirty miles an hour.

But from Avignon onwards, next morning, we met a practically uninterrupted stream of Army transports, and could only advance in jumps and jerks. For miles on end we passed a procession of tanks, armoured cars, lorries transporting troops, field guns and motorised cavalry, all streaming down from Lyons to the Italian frontier; and behind and in front of us was a similarly uninterrupted file of north-bound, empty lorries obviously coming back to fetch more troops. All this was an encouraging sight; all the more so as such a large display of mechanised forces seemed clearly to indicate offensive action against Italy; so perhaps after all that *bobard* we had heard in Toulon had only been an anticipation of events to come.

After Lyons we were clear of the traffic and spent the night in a small place in the valley of the Loire. The next day was Sunday, September 3rd; we had lunch in Pouilly, in a sunny garden overlooking the river and surrounded by vineyards. It was our last halt before Paris; in a few hours we would reach our journey's end. We had smoked ham and a bottle of *Pouilly fumé*, the wine that makes you happy and wise like no other wine in the world. We looked at the river, and emptied the bottle to the last drop; and then, shortly before Melun we met two cars with people shouting excitedly to us; and when we stopped a mile further on to fill up, the woman at the petrol pump told us that Britain had declared war on Germany.

On the last fifty miles to Paris the road was practically blocked by people running away from the capital in their cars and in taxis. Everybody believed that the Germans would bomb Paris immediately after the declaration of war, or even before; and everybody expected they would use some horrible new invention, and was obsessed by the idea of poison gas. There were only a few cars which fought their way with us against the stream; the disorder of this first exodus from Paris gave a tragic foretaste of that second one which was to take place ten months later and seal the fate of France.

We arrived at my flat in Paris at four o'clock in the afternoon. When I shook hands with our old *concierge*, she gave me a strange look. At first I thought it was only the general excitement, but when I handed her the bottle of *Pouilly* we had brought her, she took me to a corner of her *loge*, so that G. should not hear :

'I am not allowed to tell you,' she said, 'but you had better leave at once. The police were here at 2 a.m. this morning; they have taken away Dr. Freeman handcuffed and they wanted to arrest you too.'

VIII

Dr. Freeman occupied the flat next door to mine to the left. He was a doctor of medicine, and suffering from tuberculosis in an advanced stage. He had been staying for the last three months in a sanatorium in Switzerland, had rushed back to Paris to enrol as a volunteer in the French Army, and had been arrested on the very night of his arrival. He was a political refugee and his loyalty to France beyond doubt; but he was of German origin and so, after all, there might have been some explanation for his arrest.

As to myself, there was none. I am of Hungarian nationality, and Hungary was a neutral state; my parting with Communism one and a half years ago had given rise to certain comments in Left circles; and if the French secret police knew that I had been a Communist previous to 1938, they must equally well know that I was one no longer, and that I had even been repeatedly attacked by Communist papers as a 'supporter of Imperialism'.

I was convinced that the whole matter was a mistake and that the best thing to do was to go straight to the police and ask them what they wanted of me. So we got back into the car and drove to the police station of my district. Before I went in, I told G. that if they really had a warrant against me they might possibly keep me for a while, or even send me to prison for a few days, until the matter was cleared up. G. was slightly bewildered, and we took somewhat sentimental leave of each other; then I walked into the lions' den.

Inside, there was a *commissaire* who knew me, thanks to Theodore's frequent misbehaviour on the public road, which had already cost me a few hundred francs. I greeted him with a *bon jour* which I tried to make sound as casual as possible. '*Bon jour,*' he said. 'The French declaration of war has just come through. I am very busy. What can I do for you?'

I could not give away my old *concierge*—since the days of Fouché all the *concierges* of Paris are supposed to collaborate with the police and use a professional discretion. If I told them that she had warned me, she might get into serious trouble. So I said to the *commissaire* that I had just arrived from the Côte d'Azur and thought that, being a foreigner, I had better report to the police. And with that I handed over my identity card—in case he should have forgotten my name. He examined the card with a professional glance and said, rather annoyed: 'I really don't see what you want. What do you think would happen if all foreigners came running here?'

When G. saw me coming out of the station, hardly five minutes after I had gone in, she was rather disappointed; she said she had been looking forward so much to see me being marched off by an armed escort. (Later, when her wish was fulfilled, she did not enjoy it.)

I spent the night in my flat and nothing happened. Next day we went to the *Préfecture de Police*—the Paris Scotland Yard; if the local police station did not know, at headquarters they would know about this mysterious affair. I had a welcome pretext, for my identity card would expire in a few days and had in any case to be renewed. And for that purpose, I supposed they had to look up my *dossier*. Once more we said a feeling farewell, and once more I came back twenty minutes later, feeling vaguely guilty towards G., and with my identity card renewed, stamps and all.

The *drôle de guerre* had begun; the days went on and

nothing happened to me. Perhaps our good *concierge* had been dreaming? But she was not the kind of person to dream. And Dr. Freeman had disappeared without a trace. It was only a fortnight later that we learned that he was in the Santé prison, kept in solitary confinement and prevented from consulting a solicitor or communicating with the outside world. This sounded bad enough. And there were other things of a similar kind: inexplicable arrests of apparently harmless people, who were dragged at night from their beds, handcuffed, beaten up, and clapped into a prison cell, without being interrogated and without being allowed legal support. They were not Germans—all Germans, refugees or not, had already been interned during the first days of the war.

We had planned to go on to London at once. The day after our arrival I went to the British passport office to help a friend to get his *visa*. I saw Captain C., the Assistant P.C.O., whom I knew. He said it might take quite a long time. 'What a pity,' I said, 'I am leaving tomorrow and I thought he could come on the same boat.' 'I am afraid,' said Captain C., 'you can't leave tomorrow either.' 'Why?' I asked, very disagreeably surprised. During the last few years I had lived half the year in Paris and half in London, and my permanent twelve-month visa to the U.K. had been renewed quite recently.

'Because,' said Captain C., 'all visas to the U.K. were cancelled yesterday at midnight. We have to make on your behalf an application for a new visa to the Home Secretary. I am sorry, but as from yesterday we have definite instructions not to grant any visas to foreigners without special authorisation from London.' 'And how long will it be till the authorisation comes through?' The A.P.C.O. gave a rather discouraging shrug; he could not commit himself to a definite date, but gave me to understand that I might have to wait for anything between three and six weeks. Then he made out my application to the Home Office. As 'reason for the intended journey' I gave 'to join His Majesty's Forces'.

There was nothing to do but to wait. I could have, of course, volunteered for the French Army—but the only unit open to aliens was the Foreign Legion, and I thoroughly disliked the idea of it. I had lived in France, although with long interruptions, for almost ten years, and was quite willing to risk my skin for it, but on condition that I was granted the same duties and privileges as the ordinary French soldier. The tide of xenophobia swept over France with morbid rapidity, and the idea made me sick to remain, even in uniform, a *sâle métèque*, which signifies, in a scholarly translation, dirty foreigner. So I preferred to wait until my permit from the Home Office arrived, and meanwhile expected every night to hear the police ringing at the door of my flat.

It was an uncanny feeling, and I wrote to friends in London asking them to speed up my application. Then I rang Jubert, a well-known and brilliant young barrister, and arranged lunch with him. We met on the day when the troops of the Red Army marched into Poland to liberate the Polish proletariat, calling a rape a betrothal. Jubert was in uniform; he too had once been a Soviet sympathiser—who among the intellectual *élite* of his generation had not?— and was in a black mood. When he heard my story, he looked worried and said it seemed a rather serious matter. He knew of a few similar cases—arbitrary arrests of people whose loyalty could not be doubted, but who, for one reason or another, were unpopular in certain high quarters. Some of the victims were personal friends of his, but in not a single case had he been able to help. He had even been given to understand that he had better keep out of it, if he wanted to avoid serious trouble for himself. The country was living under the *loi des suspects*,[1] which gave the police practically

[1] The *loi des suspects* was a French forerunner of the British Regulation 18B, but without the precise guarantees preventing abuse contained in the latter.

D

uncontrolled power over the individual. 'The times of Fouché have come back to France; may God preserve us from a return of the times of the guillotine.'

Half an hour ago, before I had told Jubert my story, I had feared he would accuse me of persecution mania; now I almost believed it was he who had it. He kept on talking in a low, worried tone, quite different from the nonchalant and noisily brilliant manner he had had before; most successful French lawyers behave as if constantly in the footlights. And while he talked, he kept on glancing at the neighbouring tables to make sure that nobody was listening—a habit long familiar in public places east of the Rhine and the Alps, and which now was spreading with disquieting rapidity in Paris restaurants and cafés.

'But if they think they have something against me,' I asked him, 'why haven't they arrested me since my arrival?'

'Whom do you mean by "they"?' said Jubert. 'Do you mean the *Sûreté Nationale* or do you mean the *Deuxième Bureau*, or do you mean the *Préfecture* of Paris? They each have their own record of you and their own black list, which are not lying about at local police stations or identity-card desks. They proceed by periodic round-ups. You cannot go and have yourself arrested at your own leisure—that is a simply anarchist conception. You have to wait until they come for you.'

A fortnight before I had looked at the matter rather from the humorous side, and believed that the best protection against the police was consciousness of one's own innocence. Now I began to feel like that hero of Courteline's, who said that if he were accused of having stolen the Eiffel Tower he would not try to disculpate himself, but run away at once.

Next day Jubert rang L., an M.P., and L. rang D., a high official in the Ministry of the Interior, who promised that he would look the matter up. A few days later D. rang L. back, and L. rang Jubert, and Jubert rang me. To get a

matter arranged in France was always a question of finding
the connecting links of a chain with a given beginning and
end. The disadvantage of the system was that the reliability
of the chain stood in inverse ratio to its length.

But this time the chain did not work at all. D., the high
official, having looked into the files, had blandly refused to
discuss the matter with L., although they were on very good
terms. L. had expressed his regrets to Jubert. Jubert looked
even more worried. This time we had met in his office.

'There is a sort of silent pogrom going on against the
people of the Left,' he said. 'It is chiefly directed against the
Communists—but that is only one side of the matter, and in
fact things are much more involved. There is a definitely
pro-Bonnet gang in the *Sûreté Nationale*. They try to put
things on people who belonged to the "anti-*Munichois*"
camp. Then there is Spain. We are naturally keen to keep
Spain out of the war, and this serves our would-be Fascists
in the *Sûreté* and the *Deuxième Bureau* as a pretext to
persecute the former supporters of the Loyalists. There is
even a rumour that Pétain has given a verbal promise to
Lequerica, Franco's Foreign Minister, to the effect that all
foreigners in France who had fought in the International
Brigades or had taken a public anti-Franco attitude would
be interned for the duration of the war. I don't think they
believe you still to be a Communist, but they naturally know
that you were condemned to death by Franco,[1] and if the
Deuxième Bureau has got a copy of the Spanish black list,
which doubtless it has, you are certainly among the first
names on it. Things look rather black for you, *cher ami*.'

I asked Jubert what he would do in my place.

'Try to get to England as soon as possible. But I wonder,'
he added, 'whether they would give you an exit permit.'

[1] While correspondent of an English Liberal paper in the Spanish civil
war, the author was imprisoned by General Franco's troops for having
denounced in the British Press German and Italian intervention on
the Nationalist side. See *Dialogue With Death*.

There was no more to be said, and I took leave of Jubert. When I was at the door, he called me back and asked me, if I rang him again, to do it from a call-box, as he expected my telephone to be tapped. Then he said, somewhat doubtfully:

'There is, of course, one thing you could try: money. Some of those German film yids have got themselves released from internment by bribing officials in the *Sûreté*. The tariff is from 20,000 francs upwards.'

I told him that I would not do it—firstly because I had not got 20,000 francs, secondly because I thought it was too risky.

'Right,' he said. 'I always knew you were an honourable man.' And all of a sudden he added, in his best manner of addressing the jury in a sensational trial:

'May God protect you on your way—and all of us in this unfortunate country.'

On the way home I mused over the expression 'those German film yids', which had particularly struck me in Jubert's mouth. Certainly, I too hated that detestable set in the cafés and bars around the Champs Élysées, which was chiefly responsible for the widespread animosity against the German exiles, but I could not see that an Aryan member of the film racket was much more attractive. It was a sad symptom that this young spokesman of the Left, member of numerous *comités* against racial persecution, should be affected by the general contagion.

A week later Jubert left for the Maginot Line. I wonder what has become of him—but this is a remark which applies to most people in this story.

Without the war, he would in due time have become a *député*; by and by he would have changed his sports roadster for a black limousine, his radical friends for more sedate members of society, and his seat on the left benches of the Palais Bourbon, first for one in the centre, and then on the extreme right. With the war, if he is still alive, he will probably reach the same goal by a shorter cut.

One of the things which were wrong with Left politics in France was that they seemed to be a sort of passing stage of youth, like making debts and having mistresses. The typical career of the French politician, from Clemenceau to Laval, reads like a book, from left to right; but has one ever heard of a single example of the reverse?

IX

For thirty nights I slept with a small suitcase beside my bed, ready to go to prison at any moment. Sometimes I dreamed that I had heard the shrill ringing of my door-bell, but when I woke it was only the air-raid siren and I slept on, reassured. The arrests being usually carried out at night, I set my alarm-clock for seven in the morning; its ring was my signal for 'danger past'. True to the old rule, that the more you are prepared for an event, the more it takes you by surprise, they actually came for me, on the morning of October 2nd, long after my 'all clear' had sounded, at half past eight.

During that first month of the war, while still at liberty, I could watch Paris turn grey. Not the people—the town. It was as if some morbid disease had attacked its very roots in the alluvial clay of the Seine Valley. The pavement in the streets had lost its magic. 'In Mecca,' Abu Suleiman once said, 'the pious man should not walk on his soles, but on his head.' In Paris everybody walked on their soles, and usually the heels, even of the women, were worn-down and askew, but one felt the vivifying current mount up to one's head. Now the current was gone. This town has always been thought of by her lovers as a person alive—not metaphorically, but as a psychological reality. Now they felt the beloved grow cold and stony in their arms; they watched life fade out of her, inverted Pygmalions; and they walked in despair through her suddenly hostile avenues, as on tombstones.

Across the mists of the Channel, London, the broad-shouldered big brother, said : I can take it. But she couldn't. The people of Paris could fight on barricades built of paving-stones, mattresses, and bird-cages, as in the heroic days of 1848, as in the days of the Commune, and in the days of Sacco and Vanzetti. Had not even the Marne, with the crazy improvisation of driving in taxis to the battlefield, been but a sort of improvised barricade fight ? No, the people of Paris could not 'take it'. If the heroic craziness got hold of them, they could live on grilled rats and charge the enemy with their bare nails and bite the nose off his face. *If*. But where was the heroic craziness ?

On September 6th, on the third day of the war, Gallus, the famous editorialist, wrote on the front page of *L'Intransi-geant* :

'Whoever pretends that we lead this war in defence of Democracy, Liberty, or any other "ideology", is a dangerous liar. I am sick of hearing this sort of stupid babble. France fights to defend her skin, and only to defend her skin. All else is rubbish.'

After *Paris-Soir, L'Intransigeant* had the largest circulation of all French evening papers. It was the favourite paper of the *petit employé*, of typists and office workers; hundreds of thousands read it in the Underground on their way home from the office. The censorship, which cut out everything of any political colour, including passages of the speeches of British statesmen and quotations from the *Manchester Guardian* and *Daily Herald*, let this and similar poison-stuff pass without a murmur.

After this, what precise idea could the man in the Underground form of the reasons for this war ? Of course, he no longer travelled in the Underground; he had to creep into a crumpled uniform and peel potatoes in the Maginot Line or some *dépôt*, for a pay of 50 centimes, or ¾*d.*, a day, while his job or his shop or his office went to the dogs and his wife had to queue up at the *mairie* and produce document after document to get her allowance of about 80 francs, or 9*s*., a week. If there had been a branch of the Mass Observation movement in France, or of Gallup's Institute of Public Opinion, and if they had established a cross-section of what French people thought of the war, they would have been led to the conclusion that France had morally lost the war long before the actual military collapse.

Let us take three specimen examples of French people who, I think, were fairly typical for the social strata they represented.

The first one is Henry de Vautrange, a salesman of motor-cars, aged thirty-two. He had been a patient of Dr. Freeman's and had tried to sell me a Citroën. His father was a *fonctionnaire* at the Ministry of Finance, retired after thirty-five years of service, with a coloured ribbon in his buttonhole and a starvation pension. He himself had sold cars since the age of twenty-seven, without being able to afford one of his own. The reason for this was that the high salaries of the workers ate up the nation's income. France was in decay, thanks to the *Front Populaire* and the *côterie* of corrupt politicians, Freemasons, and Jews. International plutocracy, international Socialism, and Communism conspired together against the men of goodwill. The only salvation for France was an authoritarian régime, which would mercilessly clean the stable, like Hitler had done in Germany. Hitler might be a bit pompous and *boche*, but undeniably he had achieved miracles with his own people. France needed a Hitler. That is why the *Front Populaire* tried to drag the French people into war against him.

But the Left were not only warmongers; they had at the same time disarmed France. They had voted against military credits. Their stay-in strikes in 1936 had led the country to the brink of anarchy and disorganised war production. Pierre Cot had sold hundreds of French fighter-planes to the Reds in Spain. They encouraged the worker's inborn laziness and greed. Forty-hour week, paid holidays, and a Ministry of Leisure! That was what it had been really called: a Ministry of Leisure. But only for the workers, of course. As to others—if he, Henry, would keep to the forty-hour week, he could starve tomorrow. Now, on the other hand, look what Hitler had done in his country. No *députés,* no parties, no corruption. There everybody had to work and everybody was in the place where he belonged: those who had the brains commanded, and the others obeyed. And if any of the Red gentlemen did not like it—well, please yourself, there is the next concentration camp. This was de Vautrange's opinion three months before the outbreak of war. He was an honest man and I do not doubt that as an officer he did his duty, at least at the beginning. But obviously he did it without conviction or enthusiasm. His morale was bound to break down with the first defeat. The de Vautranges were usually reserve officers and in the war formed the bulk of the lower ranks of the officers' corps, from *aspirant* to captain. They had no contact with their men and no ideal in common with them.

There were several million Vautranges in France—they supported Laval, Bonnet, the P.P.F., the P.S.F.,[1] or the *Action Française.* They read *Gringoire, Candide,* the *Petit Journal, Matin, Jour,* and *Liberté.* Most of them were honest in their convictions; their leaders were not. They were the unconscious reservoir of the Fifth Column; their leaders in the Ministries and on the General Staff were conscious traitors. Scared by the bogy of a social revolution, they regarded Hitler as their saviour, just as the Condéist aristocracy of 1790 had asked for the help of the King of Prussia to crush the National Assembly.

[1] *Parti Populaire Français* and *Parti Social Français*—the semi-Fascist movements of, respectively, Doriot and de La Rocque. The *Action Française* is the Royalist Party.

Example No. 2 was Marcel, the mechanic in my garage in the rue Olivier de Serre. I never knew his surname—he was just Marcel, a tall, slim young man of twenty-eight, intelligent, unusually serious, and a member of the S.F.I.O., the Socialist Party. He was an excellent mechanic and earned good wages—18 francs, or 2s., an hour. He treated customers rather haughtily, to the despair of his patron, fat little M. Darrouis; but he had read in the *Populaire* about my adventures in Spain, and although he always addressed me correctly as 'monsieur' and not as 'comrade', he considered me as one. We used sometimes to tinker on the car together and he never permitted himself a joke, although poor Theodore was a permanent provocation for a mechanic's sense of humour. Only once did he remark when the starter, which he was trying to open, literally fell to pieces in his hands : 'If you would write for those filthy boulevard papers, monsieur, you could soon buy a Chevrolet' (which was quite untrue : in France the prostitutes of the pen were just as badly rewarded as their colleagues on the street corners).

Shortly before I was arrested, Marcel was sent to a munition factory; he was unfit for military service, owing to a shorter left leg. (His slight limp somehow contributed to the impression of earnestness and dignity which he made.) Two months later, I received a letter from him, in the disciplinary camp for suspects in Le Vernet where I had been taken. The letter was written with a sovereign contempt for the censorship—it was rather astonishing that it had got through. I remember its contents very vividly.

It began by explaining that he had read about my being detained, and that he wanted to express to me his sympathy and indignation. For years the *Populaire* had denounced Hitler's concentration camps as a blot on European civilisation, and the first thing France had done in this war against Hitler was to imitate his example. And who were in the concentration camps? The Fascists, perhaps? No, Spanish militiamen, Italian and German refugees, those who had been the first to risk their lives against Fascism. And so on. For readers of the *Daily Herald* or the *New Statesman* this is familiar stuff; in France no newspaper had been allowed to indulge in this kind of criticism. This was the first remarkable thing about Marcel's letter.

Then it spoke shortly of his own situation. He worked now for twelve hours a day, from seven in the morning to nine in the evening, with two breaks of one hour each for lunch and dinner, Sundays included. He wondered how long he would be able to stand the strain. With all this he earned only about half of what he had earned in the garage.

He wouldn't grumble about these hardships, if he knew whether this war were really in the interests of the working class. But this was a question he was unable to decide. It was worrying him very much; and this was actually the reason why he was writing to me.

The Communists at the works said that it was a purely imperialist war, that Daladier and Chamberlain were just as much enemies of the people as Hitler, and that the duty of the proletariat was to fight against its enemies at home, instead of serving as gun-fodder for their purposes. Put into practice, that would mean to surrender France to Hitler and the French working class to the Gestapo. But if you said so to a member of the C.P., you were a lackey of the bourgeoisie and a traitor. Half a year ago they had said exactly the contrary; they had issued fiery proclamations, urging the entire French nation, workers and bosses, to unite for the fight against the Nazi, and if you said anything critical about it, you were a Gestapo agent and a traitor. It was impossible to argue with Communists, they had a different party line every six months, and they were so fanaticised that they genuinely forgot what the last one had been; and if you reminded them, you were a Trotskyist *provocateur* and a traitor.

Yet, in spite of that, the Communists in the factory had a

growing support. He, Marcel, always got angry if he talked to them, but he couldn't deny that he also admired them for the manner in which they carried on with their propaganda, regardless of incessant persecution by the police. They might be wrong, but the treatment they suffered made them the heroes of the working class.

When the Communists called the war against Hitler a purely imperialist war, they were certainly wrong. But if the others called it a war for democracy, it sounded equally a lie. For years the Socialist Party had urged a firm stand against the totalitarians. Had their advice been accepted in time, the war could probably have been avoided. Instead, the Left had been jeered at, and accused of warmongering. The ruling class had held that Nazism was an internal affair of Germany which did not concern the French. They did not want to admit that any form of Fascism must automatically lead to war. Because in their hearts they were half-Fascist themselves, they rejoiced when Hitler crushed the Socialist movement in Germany, and did not want to see that the solidarity of the European working class was a better guarantee of France's security than the Maginot Line.

Perhaps it was wrong to carp at the past now that the war had begun. But it was the bourgeois Press which had started it. Marcel wondered whether I was allowed to read newspapers. If so, I would soon find out that apparently the reason for every evil had been the forty-hour week and the yearly fortnight's leave which the *Front Populaire* had introduced. The ruling class had fed Hitler with credits and raw material for his armaments against France; believing that he would save them from world revolution, they had allowed him to become the bully of Europe; and now, when they found that his air force was superior to ours, everything was the fault of the few reforms towards a more human life which the French working class had achieved after decades of struggle. Well, the forty-hour week had gone, and the

1936 wages had gone, and if the war for liberty were a question of sacrifices, the French working class had paid more than its share; but so far the rulers had failed to explain to them what their share of the victory was to be. Hitler, with his usual demagogy, had promised the German workers the realisation of all their Socialist aims; in France nobody had bothered even to hint at what the social order would be after the war. And if you listened to those who dreamt of reducing Germany to her state after the Napoleonic conquests and of making eighty million Germans do a century of hard labour to pay reparations, one couldn't help wondering what fate these champions of Liberty would reserve for their own working class when victory was achieved.

Everything about the manner in which this war was conducted made Marcel feel unhappy. There was the reign of the police, the concentration camps, and the censorship. But the worst was that every time the boulevard Press or one of the political leaders tried to prove that France was fighting a war for democracy, it sounded as if an old, pot-bellied comedian tried to act the part of Brutus.

The letter ran over six tightly written pages. I have reproduced its contents in my own words, but this was the essence of it. In conclusion, it said:

'I, and many of my comrades, know what we are fighting against. We are fighting against Fascism, which annihilates the workers' trade unions and their political power, embodied in the Socialist Party; which deprives the workers of their right to express their will by means of refusing to work if they don't agree to the conditions, and makes them slaves of the State. Yes, we know what we are fighting against. But what are the aims we are fighting for? For the preservation of a world which produces enough to meet the needs of all and is yet full of poverty; which burns its stocks of coffee and corn, while millions starve? We fight against Fascism, but we do not fight for the democracy of Stavisky, Bonnet, and the Two Hundred Families. If democracy is to be a programme, it must be filled by a new social order. This we do not see. The only apparent reason why we fight is to avoid defeat. But can one fight without a banner to fight for?'

I tried to answer Marcel; I tried to tell him: Yes, repeatedly in history men have had to fight a merely defensive battle, to preserve a state of affairs which was bad against a menace which was worse. But I do not know whether my letter reached him; and I doubt whether it would have convinced him and his comrades.

Marcel was intellectually above the level of the French working class; but what he had said in his letter expressed the feeling of the overwhelming majority. Their discontent was mainly instinctive and emotional; and, as they were hardly able to formulate its reasons and to keep it within exactly defined limits, it became all the more aggressive in its character, and more defeatist in its result.

As example No. 3 let us take Mme. Suchet, the patronne of the dairy in the rue de Vaugirard, where I used to buy my *crème frâiche* and my cheese. Mme. Suchet belonged neither to the Left nor to the Right; she was, so to speak, passionately non-political. Her opinions can best be résuméd in the form of a dialogue—which, in fact, is a composite of the numerous morning talks we had during the first month of the war:

'Good morning, Madame Suchet. I would like a piece of Camembert, fairly ripe and rather smelly, but not actually running.'

'Good morning, monsieur. I can let you have half a pound, but you will have to pay ten sous over the price prescribed by the Government. If you denounce me, I go to prison; if I keep to the Government prices, I can close down my shop. Drat this war.'

'Thank you, madame. I hope Monsieur Suchet sends you good news from the Maginot Line.'

'He has got boils on his backside, thanks to the filthy food they give them, and asks me to buy him some special kind of medicine. They have not even the proper medicine for boils in the Army.'

'That, of course, is very sad. I will also have a quarter of butter, if you don't mind. You know, in Germany they have not even got butter.'

'That's what the newspapers tell us. But I know what I know. A week ago the brother-in-law of Madame Denise came home on sick leave. He is posted on the Luxembourg frontier. He told her how they had entered a blockhouse which had been occupied by a German advance post. They found a lot of things the Germans had left behind. Aluminium tins of salt butter, half a pound for each soldier, and fresh pork sausages and first-class preserves of goulashed beef and *choucroute*—not the rotten corned beef which our men get. That's facts, monsieur. And here they want us to believe that the Germans are starving.'

'Perhaps they feed their soldiers all right, but as to the civilian population . . .'

'Oh *là là*, monsieur, don't you believe what they tell you. You are too young to remember, but I have seen the last war and lost two brothers, one at Ypres and one at Verdun. And now it is my husband's turn. If I could have a word with those who started this war, I would know what to tell them.'

'Then you had better have a word with Hitler, Madame Suchet.'

'Oh, Hitler is a swine all right. But if the Boches want a Hitler, was it our business to interfere?'

'But, Madame Suchet, he has attacked Poland, and Poland is our ally.'

'I don't know about politics, my dear monsieur, but I

know this: everybody should mind his own business. If France were attacked, I am sure nobody would help us, and the Poles certainly wouldn't care a hoot. So why should we care about them? We didn't care about the Czechs, anyhow.'

'But don't you see, Madame Suchet, that next time it would have been our turn?'

'Perhaps, monsieur, perhaps—so they tell us. But then, I ask you, what is the Maginot Line for? This Hitler has got a loud mouth, but at bottom he is a coward, and he is clever, too. So far he has only gone for small fish and left us alone. He knows that he can't get through the Maginot Line; nobody can. So why raise the devil before he is here?'

'All right, Madame Suchet. I won't argue with you. But you should really understand that we had to prevent Hitler carrying out his plans.'

'What plans?'

'Well, obviously his plan was first to smash the Poles and then to throw his whole weight against us.'

'And how do we prevent it?'

'Well, by helping the Poles.'

'Helping the Poles? Who helps the Poles?'

'Well, we do. And you just objected to our doing it.'

'But who helps the Poles? The Germans are in Warsaw and my husband sits in the Maginot Line and gets boils.'

'Well, would you prefer him to be launched into an attack against the Siegfried Line, which would probably cost us half a million men? You see, the difference between this war and the last is that our General Staff has become very economical of the lives of French soldiers.'

'So our General Staff must have known beforehand that we couldn't help the Poles, anyway. Why, then, did they declare war?'

'Perhaps they over-estimated the Polish Army's power of resistance.'

'Well, who should have known if not the General Staff? If they made such a mistake, they should be shot and the war called off. Now that the Poles are done for, anyhow, what is the use of going on with it?'

It was really impossible to argue with Mme. Suchet. The reason it was impossible was that logically all her arguments were right. Wrong were only the premisses on which her logic was based.

These premisses were conditioned by the experiences of the last years and by the newspapers she read. She believed she stood outside all parties and read independent, objective papers: *Petit Parisien, Excelsior, Paris Soir,* and *L'Intransigeant.* Her mind unconsciously reflected their opinions, and year by year it became more warped. Slowly but surely the forces which were in control of those reactionary papers had killed in her any loftier conception of humanity's aims, had made her outlook on world affairs become narrow, cynical and egotistic; and had prepared her to regard the coming war, not as a crusade for the liberty and happiness of Europe, but as a war for Danzig.

But Mme. Suchet—and the millions of M. and Mme. Suchets all over France—had a logical mind. That is why it was so difficult to convince them. They had perceived that, as a war for Danzig, this war was an absurdity.

Their minds had kept all their formal lucidity—but inside, so to speak, a spring was broken. It had been gradually bent and distorted in the years which followed Versailles, and it finally broke, without their noticing it, in the days of Munich.

It was too late now. Nobody could repair the damage, for it had gone deeper than arguments can penetrate, into the subconscious layers which determined Mme. Suchet's balance of values, and her emotional outlook on words like 'happiness', 'honour', 'sacrifice', and 'death'.

PURGATORY

I WAS sitting in the bathtub when they rang at my door on October 2nd, 1939. The char had not yet arrived; I thought it was the postman and called out that he should wait a minute. They yelled back: 'Hurry up. This is the police.' But the idea that they would come for me at night was so fixed in my mind that I thought it was some harmless black-out business or driving offence. I girded my loins with a towel and went barefoot to the entrance door, thinking how the char would grumble at the traces of my wet feet on the parquet floor. When I had unlocked the door, it sprang open and I was flung back by the impact of the two sturdy men leaning against it. 'Have you a gun on you?' they asked. But, considering my attire, the question seemed rather pointless and they pushed their way to the sitting-room. After a quick glance round, they discovered that this was not a proletarian dwelling and, obedient to their conditioned reflexes of French policemen, their tone became more civil at once.

'I am afraid you have to come with us to the police station,' said the less sturdy of the two. He had bristling hair, pimples on his face, and his name was, as I learned a few minutes later, M. Pétetin, Fernand. 'Never mind, it is only for a verification of identity or something.' 'May I dress in the bathroom?' 'Certainly,' said M. Pétetin, settling down in an armchair and glancing at a bottle of corn brandy on the cupboard. 'I reckon that you have no firearms and no subversive literature in your flat, so we may as well save ourselves the trouble of a search.' 'As you like,' I said. 'Make yourselves at home. This is a corn brandy which I always get at Madame Denise's shop in the rue de Vaugirard. It is cheap and guaranteed fifty degrees. But there are only a few bottles left.'

'I rarely drink so early in the morning,' said Pétetin while I filled his glass and his companion's, and one for myself. '*A votre santé, monsieur.*'

While I finished dressing in the bathroom, G., who lived in the flat above mine, turned up in a dressing-gown, as if she had smelled the danger. 'Who is this?' asked Pétetin, becoming professional again. 'Miss G., a British subject. Her father is in the diplomatic service.' '*How do you do,*' said Pétetin in English, flushing with pride. 'My name is Monsieur Pétetin, Fernand. I am sorry I have to take this gentleman away, but he will certainly be back again soon. You had better take a blanket,' he added to me. 'The formalities may take a few days.'

G. had gone white in the face. She eyed M. Pétetin with such visible disgust that I quickly gave her a corn brandy too. I myself emptied my third; taken on an empty stomach, it was a considerable help towards maintaining a manly composure. Then we marched down the stairs. While passing the *concierge*'s *loge*, I saw her frightened face peering through the curtains; yet the fact that I was not handcuffed may have cheered her up. Out in the street I proposed to take a taxi, and while we were waiting for one, G. came running downstairs after us with some provisions of sausage and cheese, which she had collected in the kitchen. She was still in her dressing-gown and looked even whiter in the face. 'You see how nice the French police are,' I told her in English. 'All this talk about brutality was just rubbish.' As no taxi passed, M. Pétetin, who feared a scene, insisted on our leaving on foot. When we turned the corner of the rue de

Vaugirard, G. still stood in the doorway with wide-open eyes, waving her hand.

On the way to the police station, M. Pétetin started a political conversation. 'I wonder,' he said, 'how this war will end. You as a journalist must certainly know more than we do.' I said that I was no prophet, while silently regretting that I had not taken a fourth corn brandy, for since I had seen G. waving from the doorway in her dressing-gown, my morale had become very low. 'The great problem, of course, is Russia,' explained M. Pétetin. 'If the Russians are going to help the Germans, we are done for.' I said something about America's help being more important than Russia's, and that the latter's potentialities should not be over-estimated. 'Oh, come, come. You must certainly have your opinion about Russia which you don't want to tell us,' said M. Pétetin, whimsical and coquettish. 'You must not think that we want to pump you; we are talking quite privately, as my friend and I are very keen to form an opinion of what it is all about.'

I wondered at his clumsiness; and whether we would ever learn to see certain professional types, romanticised by litera-ture (detectives, prostitutes, reporters, actors), as ordinary and commonplace as they are. Finally, to give M. Pétetin a treat, I told him that I had lived for a year in Russia. This cheered him up visibly; he must have been worrying at having omitted to search the flat. But I wonder whether his report with this important discovery brought him any praise from his superiors, who knew all about my professional travels from the *curriculum vitæ* in their files, written by myself.

It was nine o'clock when we arrived at the police station, and I had to sit for four hours on a wooden bench in the guard-room, where a dozen police constables were playing belotte. On the bench beside me sat two Italian navvies—one arrested for drunkenness in the streets, the other fetched from his room that morning, like myself. About noon I was allowed to send for a bottle of wine and the three of us held a picnic on our bench. Then Pétetin came to the guard-room and winked at me to follow him to an office. He gave me an envelope with G.'s name and address on it, and a sheet of paper. 'Write her whatever you like,' he told me with a conspiratorial look. 'At two I shall be off duty and will take it round to her myself. I will seal the letter in your presence, without reading it. Perhaps there is something important you have forgotten to tell her.'

For a second I was tempted to write, 'Transport the dyna-mite from the cellar to Uncle Bertie's house,' in order to give M. Pétetin another treat, but, remembering that people in the *Deuxième Bureau* have a deplorable lack of humour, I only wrote a few vague words of greeting. M. Pétetin looked away discreetly while I put the letter in the envelope. Needless to say, G. never received it.

About 1 p.m. a *panier à salade*—a salad basket, i.e. a French Black Maria of a conspicuously green colour—took the three of us to the Préfecture. We were unloaded in the courtyard and herded into the so-called Salle Lépine.

The Salle Lépine is a large room with a cinema screen, destined for scientific and educational lectures to the police force. It has rows of seats for an audience of about three hundred; now half of the seats were occupied by aliens, arrested like myself the same morning. On the platform, facing the audience and with their backs to the screen, sat a row of *flics*, rifles between knees. It all looked rather funny, a mixture of a Sunday school and a Revolutionary Tribunal in the days of 1789. I sat down in the fourth row, next to a Spanish-looking youth, who was nursing his cheek with a handkerchief, as if he had a toothache. Everybody was chat-tering more or less aloud and moving from one seat to an-other to talk to friends; from time to time one of the *flics* shouted out: 'Don't make so much noise. This is not a cinema.'

I offered my neighbour an aspirin. He swallowed it and
spat some blood into his handkerchief, disclosing the stump
of a newly broken front tooth in his upper jaw. 'Bad dentist?' I asked him in rudimentary Spanish. 'No, *señor*. Bad
policia.' He pointed with an outstretched hand to the expres-
sionless policemen on the platform, then closed his fist and
moved it slowly against his own jaw, indicating a terrific
punch; then shut his eyes and slid halfway down from his
chair. After this pantomime he pulled a Spanish pamphlet
from his pocket and lost interest in me. I knew if I told him
my name he would give me the Spanish embrace and probably kiss me on both cheeks; so I didn't. But a few minutes
later old Poddach turned up, pushing his way from the last
row of the auditorium. The seat to my right was empty and
he sank down with a dramatic sigh. 'Oh, Arthuro, to find
you here! They say we will all be clapped into the Santé. I
can't face it—solitary confinement and rats. I have asthma,
and I gave up all political activity before the war. You must
know it; everybody knows it.'

Poor old Poddach had been a salesman of lady's underwear in Brno, Bohemia. The year before Hitler marched
into Prague, he had married a girl twenty years younger
than himself, employed in a shoe factory and an ardent
Socialist. In the night that President Hacha went to Berlin, she gave birth to a dead child, and next morning she
died, while the German troops marched past their ground-
floor window and while he tried to make her believe it was
a hallucination. 'It is only the *sokols*,' he repeated to her,
wiping her wet forehead with his handkerchief, until she
lost consciousness; then he packed his suitcase. Without
waiting for the funeral, he made his way to the Hungarian
frontier, and eventually reached France, after a short
stay in an Italian prison. In Paris he sold pamphlets, Party
mags, and cheap stationery at Socialist meetings; that had
been his 'political activity'.

I told Poddach that a cell in the Santé, rats included, was still preferable to a Nazi concentration camp. And eventually, after some weeks or months, the authorities in their wisdom would dig us out again.

But old Poddach wouldn't be comforted. He had been slapped by a young policeman at the police station at Belleville that morning after his arrest, because he hadn't understood what the constable said to him, knowing hardly any French. I told him that beating-up was a routine matter only at police stations, not in prisons, but he wouldn't believe me. He produced a fit of asthmatic coughing, hoping to impress the *flics* on the platform, and when this did not succeed, shuffled on to another acquaintance whom he had spied in the rows in front of us. The Spaniard looked up from his pamphlet.

'*Judio*,' he said disapprovingly, spitting into his handkerchief. 'Socialist refugees good—Jewish refugees bad. All people hate Jewish refugees—so all people hate Socialist refugees.'

'But the old comrade is a Jew and a Socialist at the same time.'

'Then good,' decided my neighbour, and went on reading his pamphlet.

About five in the afternoon another Black Maria arrived, and about twenty newcomers were escorted into the hall. One of them, a young woman, I knew by sight; she was a Pole and a secretary of some *comité* against Fascism and Racial Hatred, or the like. She came up to my seat to talk to me. She had been searched at the police station in a very humiliating way and was depressed, indignant, and frightened. She asked me to help her when I got out. Old Poddach had asked me the same thing. They were convinced that, thanks to my 'connections', I would be released in a few days.

I had arrived at the Salle Lépine at 1 p.m.; at nine in the

evening we still sat there on our chairs, waiting, and facing the *flics* on the platform, who were as bored as we were. The stale weight of anxiety and boredom had gradually stifled all conversation. Some were asleep on their seats. Some of the *flics*, too. They snored, rifles between their knees.

But shortly after nine a wave of excitement went through the audience. First we heard the arrival of several police cars, then a band of plain-clothes detectives irrupted into the room, followed by an escort of *Gardes Mobiles* with fixed bayonets. The latter planted themselves in a row on the platform, like a firing squad. Some frightened women actually thought they were going to shoot and began to cry out. The leader of the plain-clothes men, a little dandy with brilliantined hair, commanded silence. He winked at his colleagues—the dramatic *mise-en-scène* had evidently been a private joke of his and he was satisfied with the effect obtained. Then he began to read out a list. Each man or woman whose name he called out had to march out into the courtyard—dark by now—between two rows of Mobile Guards. By the noises outside, we guessed that they were being loaded into the Black Marias which had just arrived. Whoever did not move quickly enough between the two rows—most of them had suitcases and blankets to carry— received a punch in the back from the plainclothes men. Some of the women and older men stumbled. I remembered—I think all of us remembered—the well-known stories of running the gauntlet in Dachau; here nobody was killed, and the worst that could happen to one was to lose a tooth or two. The Nazi had taught us to comfort ourselves with comparisons.

The Spaniard next to me was one of the last on the list. When he heard his name called, he shoved the pamphlet into his pocket, greeted me with a *salud* and sauntered out. One of the detectives growled at him to go quicker, but the youth gave him a look which made the man drop the idea of hitting him. Then he vanished into the outer darkness.

A few minutes later, with a sigh of relief, we heard the police cars buzz out of the courtyard. About half of the gathering had been taken away, evidently to prison; but as our remaining half had not been called, perhaps they were going to release us? Personally, I still hoped that they would question me, and once the mistake became evident, let me go with some polite apologies.

But nothing happened for the next three hours. The detectives and the Mobile Guards had gone; and audience and *flics* were dozing again, face to face.

At midnight a new shift of policemen came in, and the old ones, drunk with sleepiness, tottered out. A little later we were all herded out into the yard, and down a narrow staircase into a cellar.

It was a large cellar and almost the entire space was filled with coal. It lay man-high against the opposite wall and came down in a slope towards the entrance, leaving a space about ten feet wide, littered with coal-dust and rubbish. 'Now go to sleep,' said the *flics*, who remained outside the door, after pushing us into the cellar. We were about eighty, men and women.

We remained in that cellar until the morning. Some of us had newspapers which they spread over the coal and lay down on. There were three narrow wooden benches, about 12 inches wide. On these the women rested for about an hour in turn. The others tried to clear a square foot or so of the floor, and sat down. The air was thick with our exhalations and with coal-dust. Old Poddach had an asthmatic fit, this time a real one, which lasted with interruptions until the morning. Some of the women were on the verge of hysterics, but restrained themselves with remarkable self-control. We were so worn-out that we would have slept on the hard, knobbly coal, sitting or standing, but our guards went on shouting all night—some of them played cards and some of them drank wine, and some of them did both, getting steadily drunk.

At about eight in the morning we were led in small groups to the conveniences and back. There was no opportunity to wash, not even one's hands. We had arrived twenty-four hours ago as normally dressed people; by now we looked like tramps. At 8.30 there was a roll-call and we were all led back through the courtyard to the Salle Lépine. We were told to sit down on the seats which we had left the evening before. A new shift of *flics* arrived and took their places on the platform.

It was nine in the morning, and we sat there for fifteen hours, until midnight. Then we were taken back to the coal-cellar.

During the day we had been allowed to have sandwiches brought in, at four francs apiece; there were some who couldn't afford more than two sandwiches, and from some their money had been taken away. About noon more new-comers were brought in, but only a few; the great round-up seemed to be practically over. Towards 9 p.m. we had the same performance as yesterday : detectives, Mobile Guards, list of names, running the gauntlet. But this time nobody was impressed by the brilliantined gent's melodramatics. We only hoped to be on the list and to go to a normal prison cell—out of this cursed hall with its dirty-white screen and the row of *flics* on the platform, facing us with their stupid and malevolent expression, hour by hour, until a collective hatred had developed between them and us, stale as the deadly boredom by which it was generated.

Again about half of the audience were loaded into police cars and taken away; only about thirty of us were left to spend our second night in the coal-cellar—and to come back next morning, a procession of ghosts, black with coal-dust and filth, body itching, eyes inflamed, dazed by sleeplessness and nausea, to the empty rows of chairs in that spectral cinema hall. The *flics*, freshly washed, in their crisp uniforms, looked down at us in contemptuous disgust. They were reading the morning papers, and just that morning all the papers had printed an official communiqué explaining that the crowd of aliens which had been rounded up in the last two days by 'our viligant police' represented the most dangerous elements of the Paris underworld—the real scum of the earth.

I looked round at our assembly. There was Poddach, who after these two nights in the coal-cellar had become a very old man; and the woman of the Committee against Fascism and Racial Hatred; and the others. I did not know any of the others personally, but many of the faces which had passed through this clearing-place of the round-up had been familiar to me. I had seen them before, at anti-Fascist meetings at the Mutualité or in the cheap restaurants of Montmartre and the Quartier, where the refugees used to meet; and I had talked to them during these two days and two nights. The minority were Jewish refugees from all parts of Europe—some of them pleasant and some not, little people who had lived their little lives until the roof over their heads crashed down on them. They had done no wrong to deserve their misery and no good to claim it a merit; and they had no convictions to comfort themselves. They wore their martyrdom like a robe too large for them.

But the majority, like Poddach and the Polish woman and myself, had been through prisons and concentration camps in Germany, Italy, Eastern Europe, or Spain. We had been defeated partly by our own fault, partly because the Powers who should have been our natural allies had abandoned and betrayed us. A few years ago we had been called victims of Fascist barbarism, pioneers in the fight for civilisation, defenders of liberty, and what not; the Press and statesmen of the West had made rather a fuss about us,

probably to drown the voice of their bad consciences. Now
we had become the scum of the earth.

But why? Why this general and puzzling outburst of
hatred against those who had been the first to suffer from
the common enemy, and the majority of whom had offered
to continue the fight by volunteering for the French forces
on the first day of the war? It took us a long time to understand this phenomenon with all its implications in the
political and emotional sphere; and when we understood it,
it laid bare one of the main psychological factors which
finally led to the suicide of France.

II

At last, on the evening of the third day, the Salle Lépine
was cleared of the remnants of the Great Round-up.

When my name was called out and my turn had come to
march through the double row of Mobile Guards, I tried
another protest—the fourth or fifth since my arrest—re-
questing that my case should be investigated before I was
taken to another destination. I addressed the Brilliantine-
man—we had christened him Sonny Boy—showing him my
membership card of the Foriegn Press Association. 'Make
this bird get a move on,' was all he said. I got a punch in the
back and stumbled into the courtyard. A year later I heard
that Sonny Boy had been amongst the first to resume his job
when the Swastika was hoisted over Paris.

We were hustled into two police vans, one for the men,
one for the women, and driven out of the *Préfecture*. After
the Pont du Châtelet the women's van forked to the right,
ours to the left. There was a dark young fellow with us, a
violinist from Jugoslavia; his wife or mistress had been arrested with him; they had sat all day in the Salle Lépine and
all night in the coal-cellar, holding hands. When the car

with the women vanished down the boulevard Sébastopol, he began to cry. Later we learned that the women had been taken to a particularly ill-reputed prison, the 'Petite-Roquette'.

We drove along the dusky Quais, past the Louvre and the Tuileries. We were travelling in a sort of open van, painted black, with ten rows of benches on it. On the first and last bench, as well as on the corner seats of each row, sat our guards, with pompous faces and fixed bayonets, enclosing us in a hedge of steel and stupidity. The people in the streets stopped where we passed. They had all read in the papers the notice about the round-up of the scum of Paris—and there it went. After three nights in that coal-cellar, we certainly looked a sight which justified their expectations. They seemed to dislocate their necks staring after us. I turned up the collar of my coat.

I was sitting next to one of the policemen on the corner seats. He was a fat fellow, and he sat, knees wide apart, although we were squeezed tightly against one another; his elbows dug into my ribs and his uniform reeked. By this time, after facing them for three days on the platform of the Salle Lépine, I had developed a personal hatred for policemen. In all these years I had mainly seen them from behind Theodore's steering wheel, directing the traffic with their proverbially graceful and nonchalant airs; without their white sticks and their familiar grumbling, Paris wouldn't have been the same. Presently, scanning my neighbour's face of vacant brutality, I at last seemed to understand why the working class would always regard Left Wing intellectuals with distrust. You may recite Marx and Lenin by heart—as long as you haven't smelled a policeman's perspiration two inches from your nose, you don't know what it is all about.

True, once I had already been taken handcuffed through the streets of a town—two years ago in Malaga; but that had been in the chaos of a civil war and did not count. And true also that I had come in contact with the proletariat, at meetings and Party committees, and known the dizzy emotion of fraternity; but that had been a voluntary act and hence my claim to be one with them mere self-deception. This time, I told myself, you can't go home after the meeting to your flat and feel elated. For once your tongue has tasted the real feelings of the persecuted and dispossessed, and here they are: shame, impotence, and hatred.

We rattled over the Place de la Concorde, all cars giving way at the shriek of our police-siren, like small game scattered by the trumpeting of an elephant. At every bridge we came to, we expected to cross over to the left bank; but as we now turned up the Cours de la Reine, it became evident that we were not going where we had thought. Police cars in their wisdom might choose devious ways, but they cannot look for the Santé in Passy. Our mood brightened with every hundred yards. Presently we passed the new Trocadero, and there across the river stood the Eiffel Tower, looking more than ever like a giraffe in a *pissoir*. Then a rumour spread through the car, of unknown parentage as rumours are: we were bound for the great tennis stadium near Auteuil, named after the late French champion, Roland Garros. This meant internment and not imprisonment.

Thirty chosen specimens of scum began to grin and dig each other in the ribs with pleasure. When we actually saw the barbed-wire fence round the place which was to be our concentration camp, we were as happy as if we had been taken to a fun fair.

III

In the Roland Garros Stadium I spent a week which, in comparison with our experiences before and afterwards, could almost be called idyllic.

The Stadium had been converted into a provisional camp for the detention of 'undesirable aliens'. There were about 500 of us, and we were housed in queer sorts of grottos, under the great stand of the central tennis court. The stand consisted of ascending steps; our abode was the empty space under the steps, which before had partly been used for dressing-room purposes. There were three separate 'grottos', containing 150 to 200 men each; they were called 'First Division', 'Second Division', and 'German Division'.

I was in the Second Division. Our grotto, or den, had no windows; our roof was the underside of one of the grand-stands, ascending over us in a slope of 45 degrees; our bed was the concrete floor with a thin layer of straw on it. The straw was damp, and the roof leaked at the joints of the steps; only half of us had our own blankets and the camp did not provide any; and we lay so closely packed together that many preferred the 'sardine system' : head between the two neighbours' feet, in order to avoid mixing the breath. Nevertheless, morale in our den was excellent and we even had a lot of fun.

During daytime we were allowed to stand outside on the steps leading down from the grotto entrance. There we stood practically all day, breathing the fresh air, smoking, and chatting—a tribe of present-day troglodytes at the mouth of their concrete cave. The Stadium was really a kind of park, with fields and alley-ways, and if on a special fatigue we were even allowed to walk through them. Such fatigues were the *corvée de bois*—collecting dead branches for the kitchen fire; the *corvé ede l'eau*—hauling the buckets of drinking water from the entrance gate to the den; and the *corvée de cuisine*—peeling potatoes, which included a five-minutes walk through the park to the kitchen and back. There were always five times as many volunteers for the *corvées* as were needed. Naturally, we were escorted at every step outside our quarters, but our guards were soldiers, not policemen. And this made all the difference.

It even seems an overstatement to call them 'soldiers'. They were partly *recupérés*—men unfit for military service in peacetime, now mobilised for auxiliary duties, and partly men of the oldest classes, around forty-eight, including several grandfathers. Among the *recupérés* were men with squints and glass eyes, with gout, arthritis, and diabetes, and two who had been gassed in the last war. When they fell in, they reminded one more of the inmates of the asylum in Roquebillière than of a battalion of soldiers. They were indignant and furious at being called up, openly loathed the war and the younger officers who 'thought they could play tin soldiers with veterans and invalids', and particularly loathed their job as our jailors. Whenever they could, they shirked duty and climbed over the barbed wire of the camp to have a *coup* at the *bistro*, or even to spend the night with their families. For the battalion consisted almost entirely of workers from Paris and the suburbs. Whence it follows that they were all Red—Red as the workers of Reynault, Citroën, and Gnome-et-Rhone used to be, and that they looked upon us from a viewpoint diametrically opposed to that of the *flics*—namely, as victims of the same police oppression against which they had struggled all their lives. Their friendly attitude compensated to a certain extent for the appalling material conditions in our den. What a change of climate after the Salle Lépine and the journey in that pillory van!

The first night I spent in the Stadium was strange. I couldn't sleep amidst the general snoring and stink, and about midnight went out to have a breath of fresh air on the steps, although we had been told that after 9 p.m. nobody was allowed to leave the den.

The night was moonless, but there were plenty of stars. I only saw the four steps below me, a few trees of the alley which led round the stand, and the silhouette of the sentry,

F

leaning with his back against a tree and smoking, at a distance of ten yards.

I behaved as if I hadn't seen him, sat down on the steps, and lit a cigarette.

'What the devil do you think you are doing here?' asked the sentry without animosity.

I explained that I wanted a smoke and some fresh air, and that I supposed it didn't do any harm to anyone if I sat there for a few minutes. 'If I try to run away, you have only to aim at the end of my cigarette,' I added.

'Aim hell,' he said. 'Sit there as long as you like, but if a patrol passes, stand up and piss as an alibi. It must be pretty stuffy inside.'

I confirmed this. Then I said it must be rather boring to stand there all night.

This he confirmed. For a while he was silent, smoking and rubbing his back against the tree. Then he asked:

'From what country are you?'

'Hungary.'

'That's neutral—eh?'

'So far, yes.'

'Political refugee?'

'No. I have been a resident in France for almost ten years.'

He seemed disappointed. After a while he asked:

'What is your profession?'

'I used to write for newspapers. Now I write books.'

'For which newspapers? *Populaire* or *Humanité*, perhaps?' he asked hopefully. But before I could answer, he suddenly shouldered his gun and cried out an annoyed, '*Qui vive?*'

It was the patrol. I stood up hurriedly and complied with his instructions. The leader of the patrol flashed his electric torch on me, and they passed on. I sat down again.

'Did you write for *Humanité*?' the sentry repeated.

'No, for an English newspaper. But some of my articles

were reprinted both in *Humanité* and *Populaire.*'

'Really? What were they about?'

'Spain.'

'Man, why didn't you say so at once?' he cried out, delighted. *'Quel idiot!* Do I look like a *Croix de Feu?*'[1]

'How should I know in the dark what you look like?'

'Quel idiot! I have worked for fifteen years as a fitter at Citroën's. Have you ever heard of a *Croix de Feu* at Citroën? All our company is the same way. If it depended on us, you could all go home tonight, and get tight and make love to your sweethearts, and we would do the same. There comes another bird.'

The door of the grotto had been cautiously opened and out crept Yankel, sniffing into the dark air with his long tapir nose. The way he moved and the way he had knotted his red scarf around his collarless neck apparently won him the sentry's approval. 'Sit down on the steps and shut your mouth,' he informed him. Yankel settled down and produced a cigarette stump from behind his ear. He was nineteen, but he had already lived through two pogroms and served two sentences for distributing certain leaflets in Cracow. Before his arrest, he had worked with a tailor in Belleville. Within two minutes the sentry had wormed all this out of him. But for each question he asked, Yankel asked two questions back. Another two minutes later they each knew that the other belonged to 'The Party', without saying so expressly. They discussed Yankel's wages—about £1 a week —and the devices his patron used to dodge the social insurance laws, and the sentry's 50 centimes pay, and conditions in the French Army. The sentry was forty-five, married, with two children, the oldest son in the Army; he had lived all his life in Paris. Yankel was nineteen, a Jew, and he had travelled through seven countries of Europe. He shared his room with his mother, and the only thing that worried him

[1] Organisation of war veterans with pro-Fascist leanings.

was that he did not know on what the old woman was going to live now.

'And what about your girl?' asked the sentry.

But it transpired that Yankel had no girl—what with eight hundred francs a month, and living in one room with his mother, and all the meetings in the evenings.

'But there are the brothels,' said the sentry, astonished. 'I used to know one or two in Belleville, although it is not my *quartier*.'

'Brothels disgust me,' explained Yankel. The sentry did not answer. After a while he said :

'But you can't tell me that you are a virgin at nineteen?'

'Why not?' said Yankel aggressively; one could guess that he had become as red as his scarf.

'*Putain de bon dieu!*' exclaimed the sentry, slapping his knees. 'That's the best thing I have ever heard. *Ça, c'est formidable!*'

He went on for a while with '*putain de putain*' and '*tout de même c'est formidable*'. Then he seemed to notice that Yankel was sulking, and concluded in a fatherly, admonishing tone :

'*Faut aller au borceau, mon petit*. It's bad for your health if you don't.'

Yankel did not answer. He blew his ever-dripping nose in an enormous checked handkerchief. The divergency of national traditions seemed to endanger international understanding. For a while there was silence. It was good to sit there, on the steps, in the cool night, with only the dark trees outlined against the darker background. The sentry paced a few steps up and down, doubtless thinking what queer fish these foreigners were after all, even if comrades. I remembered that Communist refugees from other European countries had never been admitted to the French Party, but were organised in separate sections. The strongest had been the German C.P.'s branch in France, and they had lived in permanent friction with the French C.P.

Finally, the sentry made an effort to overcome the dead-lock, and after a few minutes they were both loathing in unison this *'guerre des riches'* and praising Russia's wisdom for having kept out of it. When I ventured a remark to the contrary, the sentry accused me of being a Trotskyist. He was as indignant about my heresy as he had been with Yankel for refusing to go to a brothel. Fortunately, two other inhabitants of the den turned up, one of them old Poddach, the other an Italian from Trieste called Mario. I had not yet spoken to Mario, but he had caught my eye, wandering to and fro through the den with an absent-minded smile on his face, from time to time twisted by a nervous twitch.

'Merde alors, this is going to become a meeting,' said the sentry. Poddach produced a heartbreaking cough and suffo-cation attack. When he paused, Mario said:

'I mainly came out to tell you that inside one can hear every word you say. There are all sorts of people in our crowd and certainly some informers amongst them.'

'Je m'en fous,' said the sentry. 'I say what I like. If the Commandant didn't prefer to be deaf to the talk that goes on, he would have to court-martial the whole company.'

'That is your affair,' said Mario. 'But for the comrades here it is different. You had better come back,' he said to the three of us, and Yankel, Poddach, and I followed him some-what regretfully, but without argument. In the electric light inside I saw that Mario's hair was half grey, although he did not seem more than thirty. The straw was damp and Poddach had installed himself next to me, keeping me awake with his damnable coughing and moaning, which sounded like a death-rattle.

IV

Not all the soldiers were as talkative as that sentry on our first night, but almost without exception they were kind to us. When the nights were cold or rainy, they simply left their post and came in to warm up in the cosy stuffiness of our grotto; then one of us, usually Yankel, kept a look-out to warn them if the patrol came. Most of them addressed us in the second person singular with '*tu*' and to some of them we said '*tu*' ourselves; a rather unusual style of address between prisoners and jailors.

I said 'prisoners' and not 'internees'; in fact, our legal status was difficult to define. We were officially classed as *étrangers undésirables*—unwanted aliens—and thus belonged to a category different to that of the ordinary German and Austrian internees. The latter had been interned during the first days of the war. They had been concentrated in the great Stadium of Colombes on the outskirts of Paris, and after a week or so sent on to various camps in the provinces. The Government had promised the nomination of an advisory committee which would examine their cases and sort out the Nazis from the anti-Nazi refugees; it was promised that the latter would be released.

But as to us, we had been arrested individually. Most of us were nationals of neutral or allied countries—Russians, Czechs, Poles, Italians, Hungarians, etc. The Germans in our 'German Division' had been picked out from the ordinary internment camps and transferred to us as special suspects. The original intention was to send us all to prison; but the prisons were overcrowded, so the Roland Garros Stadium had been converted into a prison-substitute.

In the next few days most of the foreigners in the Santé were sent to our camp. The majority of them had been arrested in the night of September 2nd—the same night as

Dr. Freeman had been taken away and the police had called for me for the first time. They had been kept in solitary confinement for a month; many were in a state of nervous depression, some had grown beards, and all were full of gruesome stories about the incredible number of rats and bugs in the Santé. I congratulated myself on not having returned to Paris twenty-four hours earlier. Without G.'s insane trip to Geneva or Theodore's frequent breakdowns on the road, I would have spent that first month of the war with the rats and bugs.

Among the newcomers from the Santé were Kersten, the author, Paul Froehlich, the sociologist, Friedrich Wolf, author of *Professor Mamlock*, the famous anti-Nazi film, which was just being shown in London, and most of the collaborators of Willy Muenzenberg, virtual leader of the German Exile. I expected that Dr. Freeman would turn up too, but he did not; I learned that he had been sent to a prison hospital because of his T.B., and that he was in a dangerous condition.

The hundred and fifty men crowded together on the straw of our den represented twenty-three nations, including a Chinaman, a Negro from Senegal, and a family of six from Georgia—father, three brothers, cousin and uncle, going by the name of Eligulashwily. It was a real Tower of Babel—

> *Dans ce tour de Babel*
> *Des indésirables—*

(which, in French, happens almost to rhyme), was the beginning of a poem that I wrote to G.

Almost half of my division were Russians, and they were divided into two camps—the White-Whites and the Red-Whites, which were not on speaking terms with each other. The White-Whites were *émigrés* who had remained hostile to Bolshevism. The Red-Whites were also *émigrés*, but in twenty years of exile they had become converted to the view that the revolution could not be undone and that it had to be accepted as a *fait accompli*; hence they had applied to the Soviet Embassy for visas to return to their native country. But the Red-Whites were again divided into two groups: half were still anti-Communists but Russian patriots and desired to make peace with their Government, whatever it was, and to collaborate loyally; the other half had actually asked for admission into the Communist Party.

The third category, which would have to be called the Red-Reds—namely, genuine Russian Communists living in France with Soviet passports—was not represented. It was said that the Soviet Ambassador had taken a very firm line with the Quai d'Orsay to protect his nationals. In other words: if a Russian tried to get a Soviet passport, he was arrested; if he actually had one, he was not.

And yet in this apparent cock-eyedness there was the same administrative logic which made conditions in the camps for German Nazis more comfortable than conditions in the camps for German anti-Nazis. The former were protected by the International Red Cross and the fear of retaliation on French prisoners of war in Germany; whereas those who had chosen their side according to their conviction, and not according to the colour of their passports, were unprotected and could be treated accordingly.

Most of the White-White Russians were former Tsarist officers and N.C.O.s who had fought under Koltchak or Denikin in the civil war, and who still went on conspiring in more or less secret societies with a more or less fishy background. The sensational trial which followed on the kidnapping of General Millner had revealed an amazing scene of plots, intrigues, spies, and double-agents, which reminded one of Chesterton's *The Man Who Was Thursday*.

Our White-Whites were a mixed crowd, including a well-known surgeon, owner of a château near Versailles; an opera singer with an enormous belly and a Chaliapin bass; a homosexual architect with a beard; two night-club porters, and a lawyer who sold Jewish refugees visas for a certain Central American republic, which on arrival turned out not to be valid. As rain and moisture were constantly dripping through our roof, the White-Whites had built themselves with blankets, trench-coats, and sheets a sort of tent in the middle of our grotto; there they camped all day, sleeping, singing, and heating tins of sturgeon in tomato sauce on an illegal spirit-stove.

The Red-Whites were less numerous and less well-to-do. They included several students, members of the Friends of Russia Society, a Montparnasse painter well known in the Dôme because of an enormous purple growth on his forehead, a few Embankment sleepers, and poor Pitoun, a little publicity artist with whom I used to play chess and who bored us with tales of his complicated misfortunes until one day he surprised everybody by dying of appendicitis.

The White-Whites maintained that they had been arrested on the strength of a list which O.G.P.U. agents in France had played into the hands of the Sûreté; whereas the Red-Whites alleged that they had been denounced as Bolsheviks and agents of the O.G.P.U. by the White-Whites. There was probably some truth in both stories, as it had been a long-cherished habit of the Russian émigrés in France to denounce their adversaries to the French Secret Police, who for their part had their informers and agents-provocateurs in every faction. Yet, in spite of all this, it happened once or twice that White-Whites and Red-Whites sang together during the long evenings, and when Christmas approached they actually formed a mixed choir which gave several first-class recitals of Russian songs.

The White-Whites were the only 'right-wingers' in our

division; the rest consisted of a small minority of non-political refugees and a majority of anti-Fascists from all over Europe, including adherents of the Croat Peasant Party, Spanish Syndicalists, Czech Liberals, Italian Socialists, Hungarian and Polish Communists, German Independent Socialists, and one Trotskyist. All of them bore the physical or mental marks of torture and persecution in the countries from which they had escaped, and for a more enlightened administration these marks should have been regarded as the stamp of their *bona fides* and loyalty.

V

This is also true for the majority of the Communists—that is, for the rank and file.

Yankel was a good example of their reactions. The Hitler-Stalin pact had been a bolt from the blue for him. For somebody outside the Party it had been conceivable for the last few years that Russia might come to terms with Germany; for a member of the C.P. the mere thought of this was blasphemy. If, on August 22nd, 1939, you had told Yankel—or any member of the French, English, or German C.P.—that within twenty-four hours a Soviet-Nazi pact would be signed and the Swastika hoisted in Moscow, he would have either laughed at you or hit you in the face.

During the fortnight between the signing of the pact and the actual outbreak of war, they still tried to convince themselves that the pact was really a supreme stratagem of Stalin's to preserve peace—that is, to postpone the final settlement of accounts with Nazism to a more opportune time. But when the war actually broke out and Russia's betrayal of the anti-Fascist cause could no longer be denied, Yankel and his comrades lived for weeks in a sort of daze. Everybody heaped insults on them, shrieked at them, spat on them—but the simple truth about the Communist rank and file was that they *did not understand what had happened.*

They were utterly helpless, tottering from the blow they had received, looking in despair for an explanation. The Party papers had been suppressed, and the whispered slogans which trickled through from 'above' made neither head nor tail. It was equally hard for a slow-thinking French Reynault worker of forty-five and for a little Polish Jew of nineteen to realise that the messianic belief to which they had each in his way devoted what was purest in him, was a fake; that they had been taken in like fools, borne beating and imprisonment for nothing; lost the prospect of advancement in the factory for nothing; suffered, dreamt, quarrelled, argued for years and years—all for nothing.

There were several million of them—the toughest, most active and most violently anti-Nazi part of the French working class. They were, by their Party tradition and Party education, the best fitted to give the example of comradeship and reckless sacrifice in the struggle. They had lived for years in the anti-Fascist *mystique*; and now, at the beginning of the great crusade for which they had been preparing all this time, they were left without leaders. It was an historic opportunity for the French nation to regain control of their *enfants terribles*. They had but to revive the three words, *Liberté, Egalité, Fraternité*, from their heraldic petrifaction, to explode the dynamite latent in the word *patriote* when spoken with the accents of St. Just and Danton.

It was murderous stupidity on the part of the French Government to start a police pogrom against the Communist rank and file, instead of seizing this unique opportunity to win them over. And it was suicidal selfishness on the part of the French ruling class to prevent the war against Fascism from becoming an anti-Fascist war.

The effect of this policy soon became visible. The outward pressure saved Yankel and his friends from the painful task of digging into their consciences and of repudiating a faith as strong as any religious belief. The *loi des suspects*, the farcical trial of the Communist Deputies, and the unprecedented wave of political persecution that swept over France cured the Communist rank and file of their heretical doubts. Caught between the devil and the deep sea, they opted for the deep sea. They closed their eyes, as they had been trained to do, and took a headlong plunge back into the familiar depths of blind, unquestioning, absolute faith.

Then a second event came along which helped them to reaffirm their shaken beliefs. The Red Army marched into Poland; half of that country was annexed, with only a minimum of bloodshed, by the Soviet State. Of course it was more a conquest by force than a genuine revolution; but had not Lenin himself adopted a similar policy in 1921, when he ordered the troops of the Revolution to march against Warsaw? Now Stalin had expanded the radius of world revolution without declaring war; he had cheated Hitler of half his prey; and once the Nazis were bled white, the Soviet Army would march into Germany and throw them out.

In their hearts Marcel and his Socialist friends were not much happier than Yankel and the sentry. The difference in their reaction was merely one of intensity—a question of political temperament. The Socialists had been trained to compromise and collaborate with the ruling class; it was easier for them to accept the war without a banner, and to fight for the only apparent reason, to avoid defeat. But their attitude was from the very beginning one of disgusted resignation; and later on the disgust prevailed.

If a nation is a body, the working class are its muscles and sinews. By cutting them, the body became paralysed—a helpless prey to be stamped on by the boots of the conqueror.

VI

On the notice-boards of the Stadium the posters still announced the results of the last match, Cochet-Borotra; others indicated that the mixed doubles were to take place on court No. 3 just behind our stand. These mixed doubles were an occasion for obvious and ever-repeated jokes. Meanwhile our guards, the soldiers, blasphemously indulged in playing soccer on the tennis courts.

The Stadium was not fitted with any conveniences for the housing of about six hundred prisoners, but even haphazard improvisation soon develops its own routine. We had some water-taps in the open air for washing; a covered cloakroom as a refectory, where we ate our meals in turn; court No. 3 for our two hours of exercise, and for the rest of the day the four authorised steps at the entrance of the den to stand and chatter. The food was surprisingly good : black coffee and bread in the morning, a substantial dish of meat and potatoes for lunch, and a thick soup in the evening. The reason for this was that our quartermaster, contrary to the traditions of French prisons and concentration camps, was not allowed to steal. The commandant of the camp, Comte de N., saw to that. He was a professional soldier and a charming man; and on top of that he had the rare gift of the old soldier of judging his man after a few words. In a day or two he had formed his opinion of our crowd and did all he could for us. To a friend of mine he once remarked that he knew the majority of us were arrested quite wantonly.

We were not allowed visits, but twice a week our next-of-kin and friends could bring parcels of food and clothing to the entrance gate. Sometimes we could catch a glimpse of them at a distance of four hundred yards, but all we could see was the top of a hat emerging from above the hedge of the enclosure and a pathetically waving hand. The sight of such amputated sections of relations was rather bad for morale.

On the third day of our stay in the Stadium, the arrival of Fuhrmann, a German Liberal journalist, created some hilarity. Fuhrmann, a man of forty and quite a well-known figure in the Weimar Republic, had been put in a concentration camp by the Gestapo and had escaped a few years before to Austria. When the Nazis marched into Austria, he escaped to Eger. When Eger was attached to Germany after Munich, he escaped to Prague. When the Nazis occupied Prague, he escaped to Italy. When the war broke out and Italian non-belligerency began, he escaped to France by means of a fishing boat, which took him by night from San Remo to some lonely spot on the French shore near Nice. He had arrived in Paris forty-eight hours before by train, and gone straight from the railway station to see P., a German refugee and fellow journalist, whose address he knew. He found Mrs. P. at home, who nearly fainted when he walked in. Then she told him that P. was in a concentration camp, that all German refugees had been interned, and that he must get himself interned at once, else he would get into a frightful mess with the police and be put in jail. The best thing he could do was to drive at once to the Stadium at Colombes, the clearing camp for German internees. She was so panicky that poor Fuhrmann also got the wind up and told the taxidriver, who had been waiting downstairs with his luggage, to take him at once to Colombes.

In Colombes he found the Stadium empty—the Germans had all been sent on to various camps in the provinces. But he found an official in the camp to whom he explained his case, and the official scratched his head and grew quite sympathetic. 'Well,' said Fuhrmann, 'I suppose the only thing for me is to report to the police, and ask them what to do.'

'If you go to the police they will clap you into jail immediately,' said the official. 'You are an exceptional case, and they dislike exceptional cases.'

'But what else can I do?' asked Fuhrmann, who was getting more and more alarmed. 'I can't even go to an hotel. When I fill in the form they will denounce me at once.'

After some more scratching, the official produced an idea.

'Tell your taxi'—the meter had meanwhile reached about 60 francs—'to take you to the Roland Garros Stadium. It is a camp for *indésirables*, but still better than prison. Once you are in a camp, you become a routine case and don't risk too much.'

Fuhrmann expressed his heartfelt thanks and drove to Roland Garros. It was a nice long journey; the meter approached the 100-francs mark and Fuhrmann had exactly 120 francs in his possession. When they reached the camp it was dark and the driver had missed the main entry. Fuhrmann deposited his luggage near the hedge, paid the driver and sent him away. He thought that alone and with all his luggage he stood a better chance of being allowed to stay. He waited patiently at the gateway, and after a few minutes a sentry turned up. 'What do you want here?'

'I want to be interned,' said Fuhrmann timidly.

'This,' said the sentry, 'is no place for drunks to hang about and make funny remarks.' Then he noticed the luggage, and that Fuhrmann meant it seriously. He called out to the other sentry:

'*Hé, dis-donc*, there is a lunatic here who wants to be let in.'

Sentry No. 2 appeared and flashed his torch on Fuhrmann's face. When they were both satisfied that he was neither drunk nor mad, they held a colloquy and tried to dissuade him from his intention. 'It's a rotten place,' they told him, '*a sale bordel de dieu*, and next week you will all be sent to an even worse place, somewhere in the Pyrenees. Haven't you got a friend who could hide you?'

But Fuhrmann remained firm, so they had to take him to the bureau and report to the officer in charge. The officer in charge reported to the Comte de N. The Comte de N. asked Fuhrmann a few questions, then offered him a cigarette. 'I am, of course, not allowed to take you in charge without orders from the *Préfecture*,' he said, 'but I will speak to them.' And he rang the *Préfecture*.

The *Préfecture*, of course, insisted on Fuhrmann's being handed over to them. The Commandant asked that he should at least be allowed to spend the night in the camp, as it would, anyhow, be too late to question him. The *Préfecture* refused; they asked the Commandant to send him over at once under escort. The Commandant said that he could spare none of his men, but that he would send Fuhrmann in a taxi—and what was the use of escorting a man whose only wish was to get himself interned? But the *Préfecture* refused; they would send a Black Maria for him.

This was at 10 p.m.; the Black Maria arrived at 3 a.m. Until then Fuhrmann slept in a chair in the office—he hadn't slept since San Remo. On his arrival at the *Préfecture* he was locked into the coal-cellar. There he had to stay until 10 a.m.; then, without having been asked a single question, he was put back in the same car and taken back to the camp; this time to be officially interned.

He arrived with a radiant face, entered the den of the German division with the words '*Es ist erreicht*'—a favourite expression of the ex-Kaiser—and lay down on the damp straw to sleep for twelve hours on end.

'First Divison', 'Second Divison', and 'German Division' lived in separate dens, but during exercise we were together. Yet there was also a 'French Division', which was kept strictly separate from us. In the three divisions of aliens 90 per cent of the men were detained for political reasons; the

French Division consisted entirely of *durs*—habitual criminals.

They lived in a former cloak-room similar to ours, but outside their door there was a double fence of barbed wire; and they were guarded, not by our friendly soldiers, but by specially chosen Mobile Guards. They were never allowed to leave their quarters and stand on the steps of the tribune; they could not go out on a *corvée* and not even to the refectory—the food was brought to them in tins and they had to swallow it without spoons, knives or forks. There were seventy of them, and they were kept day and night in their dark pen, which had no electric light, very much like wild animals in a pit.

Compared with the French Division, our life was pleasant. One of the reasons for this was that they did not come under the authority of our Commandant, but directly under the Penal Administration. Their treatment gave one an idea of what Devil's Island might be like. The second reason was that they seemed indeed a particularly tough lot. During the ten days which we spent in the stadium, two riots occurred in the French Division, both at night. The first was an attempt at mutiny; some of the men had managed in the dark to cut through the first barbed-wire fence, had jumped over the second, and attacked the Mobile Guards on duty with knives and bricks. The result was that the Guards charged into the den with bayonets, and that one Guard and four of the prisoners had to be carried away in an ambulance. The second incident was a disgusting story of rape on a homosexual prostitute; six or seven of the band had participated in it and the end of it was that an ambulance had again to be called.

We learned all this from our friends, the soldiers. They told us that the crowd of the French Division consisted of old lags with either at least three sentences or altogether ten years of hard labour on their record. They had not been

G

arrested on any actual charge, but the police had picked them out of the Paris underworld as individuals considered dangerous in wartime. The soldiers also told us that the Commandant had protested against their presence in his camp.

VII

Towards the end of our stay in the Stadium, a new notice about us appeared in the French papers. It said, in the matter-of-fact tone of official communiqués, that the amount of robbery and other crimes had suddenly dropped during the last few days, in consequence of the internment in the Roland Garros Stadium of the foreign rabble which for years had infested the capital. In the very first week of their internment these dangerous elements had attempted a mutiny which had to be quelled by a bayonet charge, resulting in several casualties.

This notice was reprinted in the same wording by all newspapers, including the Liberal *L'Œuvre* and the Socialist *Populaire*; it had been issued by the Ministry of Information. The Ministry of Information knew, of course, that the criminal section in the camp consisted exclusively of Frenchmen, and that these, not the aliens, were responsible for the mutiny referred to. But they also knew that if there were any spontaneous popular feeling left in the apathetic masses of France, it was the feeling of hatred for foreigners.

During the first months of the war it was the deliberate policy of the Ministry of Information to feed the people on gruesome stories of the crimes committed by foreigners (this was long before the parachutist scare started) and to represent the Government as engaged in a heroic fight against the dragon called *sale métèque*. They had not much other news to feed them on, and here, at least, they could be sure of popular support. It must be borne in mind that there were about three and a half million aliens living in France, almost 10 per cent of the total population. They were a much better scapegoat than Germany's barely half a million Jews. From the point of view of mass psychology, it is fascinating to see that to all intents and purposes, French xenophobia was but a national variation or *Ersatz* of German anti-Semitism.

In both cases one must distinguish clearly between the popular origin of the mass psychosis, with its deep, mainly unconscious roots, and its conscious exploitation for political purposes. Hatred of foreigners, as such, seems to be the oldest collective feeling of mankind since tribal days, and anti-Semitism only one of its specific forms. The Old Testament laws, racial and economic, against the Stranger in Israel could have served as a model for the Nuremberg Code; the Greek word 'barbarian' simply means 'foreigner', and for the Frenchman, more conservative in his habits than the Greek, the foreigner has never ceased to be a barbarian —whether he be an Italian navvy, a Polish miner, or a German refugee.

When the French Government discovered this welcome diversion and outlet for the general discontent, they merely followed an ancient recipe of political quackery; the sacrifice of scapegoats is an old-established institution. Up-to-date rulers, however, want something more spectacular than a goat; they need at least a dragon. Hitler had invented the first composite super-dragon called the Judeo-Liberal-Stalin-Rothschild-World-Conspiracy. Stalin followed with the Trotsky-Nazi-Menshevik-Imperialist-Well-poisoning-Crop-wrecking-Fire-spitting-Monster-Dragon. One of the advantages of the modern dragon over the antiquated scapegoat was that it received one deadly blow after another, but never completely died, and when slightly tickled in the solar plexus at once regained its menacing ferocity, thus allowing the modern St. George to continue the fight over an unlimited number of rounds. Another of its advantages was that the dragon could be re-baptised and consisted, so to speak, of interchangeable parts. Thus, in Hitler's dragon, the vital organ called 'Bolshevism' was replaced by 'Capitalism', and in Stalin's dragon 'Fascism' by 'Pluto-Democracy', without in the least weakening its effect.

The French dragon, of course, was less ambitious and of a poorish aspect. They painted it red, but this somehow missed the point, as the enemy unfortunately happened to be brown. So they had to stuff it with all sorts of old rags and trash, Prussian boots and Hun caricatures and *Sauer-kraut* and Nietzsche; but its only impressive feature was provided by the *métèques*. It was not a very splendid dragon, yet good enough to stage a fight in a Punch and Judy show, and to receive some thudding whacks amidst general applause.

Who looked close enough to find out what a poor, tired beast this dragon was, with its mangy skin and long, melancholy nose, reminding one oddly of Yankel's—and that it looked more like a half-drowned cat than a stately dragon?

VIII

On the day when we were to leave the Stadium and Paris for an unknown destination, I obtained permission from the Commandant to talk to G. for two minutes. I bribed three of our guards, independently of one another, to take a taxi and bring her to the camp—for, in spite of all their feelings of sympathy and 'solidarity', they were not too reliable. Actually only one of the three turned up at G.'s flat, but he brought her to the camp all right. She waited at the outside entrance and the Commandant personally escorted me to her, as the matter was against all regulations. The two minutes became five, and when they were over I knew that

the Home Office had refused my application for a visa—as
a consequence of my arrest, I presumed—and that G. had
decided not to return to England, but to wait until I was
released. To my surprise, I found that the effect on me of
the second bit of news outweighed the first.

We didn't learn where we were going until we were in the
train. Then, for the first time, we heard the name of Le
Vernet, in the department of Ariège, about thirty miles from
the Pyrenean frontier. It was supposed to have been one of
the camps for Spanish militiamen, evacuated six months
ago because of its unsatisfactory hygienic conditions, and
serving now as a sort of disciplinary camp for unruly
Spaniards and internees in general, sent to Le Vernet from
other camps as a measure of punishment.

This sounded bad, but in the excitement of the railway
journey we did not bother too much about it. There were
about five hundred of us; we made the journey under heavy
escort, but in ordinary third-class carriages. They were attached to the Toulouse Express, which leaves the Gare
d'Austerlitz at about 10 p.m. During the civil war I had
several times travelled by the same train to catch the 5 a.m.
plane from Toulouse to Barcelona, Alicante, and Madrid.

In Toulouse our wagons were attached to a slow train
and at about eleven next morning the train stopped in an
apparently deserted stretch of country with the white chain
of the Pyrenees as a grandiose but far-away background,
and with nothing in the foreground but a tiny little station
house bearing the inscription LE VERNET. We got out; the
train left; our escort began to form the five hundred of us
into a long queue.

It was apparently a very difficult task, for they went on
shouting at us and pushing us about for more than half an
hour. Then we began to move along the road which ran
parallel to the railway track. Meanwhile it had begun to

rain—the sort of steady, melancholy October rain which goes on for hours and days and confers on a bare landscape an aspect of utter hopelessness. We moved very slowly, laden as we were with luggage and blankets. After a few minutes the blankets were soaked with water and we had frequently to stop, as the older men—there were amongst us many over sixty and a few over seventy—would drop their luggage and stand still, panting, after every hundred yards.

Halfway to the camp we were caught up and passed by a troop of men coming down the road at a quick, military pace.

There were about thirty of them. They carried spades over their shoulders, and were escorted by Mobile Guards with leather crops in their hands. The heads of the men were shaven, but their faces were stubbly. They were clad in rags; some marched through the mud in slippers, some with their toes sticking out of their shoes, some wore rubber galoshes over their naked feet. Obviously they were being marched back from work to the camp. We stared at their naked skulls, overcome by a despairing horror. They looked back at us, with a superficial glimmer of curiosity on their apathetic faces. Some of them tried to speak to us as they marched past, but were quickly silenced by their whip-waving escorts. They vanished round a bend in the road to the rhythm of their guards' hoarse '*Un-deux. Un-deux.*'

A few hundred yards further on we reached the barbed-wire enclosure of the camp.

In those days the European continent had already reached a stage where a man could be told without irony that he should be thankful to be shot and not strangled, decapitated, or beaten to death.[1]

[1] *P.S. 1968.* In 1941, when this was written, the gas chambers had not yet started to work.

A fairly high percentage of the continent's population had become quite accustomed to the thought that they were outcasts. They could be divided into two main categories: people doomed by the biological accident of their race and people doomed for their metaphysical creed or rational conviction regarding the best way to organise human welfare. The latter category included the progressive *élite* of the intelligentsia, the middle classes, and the working classes in Central, Southern and Eastern Europe.

Nevertheless, the psychological pressure of persecution and defeat had developed in them a complex of guilt. Men of exemplary courage and daring, after having been labelled 'refugees' and beaten out of three or four countries, went about as if carrying an invisible leper's bell. Eminent scholars and dignitaries shed tears of happiness when taken to a 'democratic' jail after their escape. Girls with strong views on feminine emancipation accepted, as a square deal, to marry a passport or to prostitute themselves for a *permis de séjour*. Combative idealism turned into a squashy inferiority complex, and martyrdom into neurosis.

The standard of comparison in the treatment of human beings having crashed to unheard-of depths, every complaint sounded frivolous and out of place. The scale of sufferings and humiliations was distorted, the measure of what a man can bear was lost. In Liberal-Centigrade, Vernet was the zero-point of infamy; measured in Dachau-Fahrenheit it was still 32 degrees above zero. In Vernet beating-up was a daily occurrence; in Dachau it was prolonged until death ensued. In Vernet people were killed for lack of medical attention; in Dachau they were killed on purpose. In Vernet half of the prisoners had to sleep without blankets in 20 degrees of frost; in Dachau they were put in irons and exposed to the frost.

This sort of comparison, for all the tragic irony it contained, had a concrete meaning for most of us. Each of us carried a weight in his memory to put in the Past scale of the balance and lift the Present scale. Yankel carried the weight of his two pogroms and the prison in Lubliana, where people were made to talk by introducing rubber tubes into their nostrils and pouring water through them; Mario had the weight of his nine years of prison in Italy, including torture by electric shocks during the preliminary investigation; Tamàs, the Hungarian poet, had his three years of hard labour in Szeged—to quote only my three immediate neighbours in Hutment No. 34 in Le Vernet. The fourth one, myself, had his hundred days under sentence of death in Seville.

We were two thousand in the camp of Vernet. The average time each of us had previously spent in jail or internment was an estimated eighteen months. If our past sentences were added into a single file of time, it would reach back to 1000 B.C.

Most of us had our periodical nightmares, dreams of falling once more into the hands of our persecutors, regularly recurring repetitions of the rubber tubes, the electric shocks, the death-patio in Seville. Those amongst us who had no personal experience of jail or torture replaced it by the fear of it. They had a more acute, obsessive fear of the O.V.R.A. and the Gestapo than those who had actually passed through their hands. It was an almost mystical horror. If somebody screamed at night in our barrack, we knew he had dreamt of the Gestapo. And, regaining consciousness, he recognised with relief the smell of the rotting straw of Vernet.

An unconscious cowardice has made me write the above paragraphs in the past tense. They should be written in the present.[1] For Vernet still exists; of its 2,000 prisoners only about fifty have been released; Yankel and Mario and Poddach and all the others are still there; and the camp is now under the control of the Gestapo.

[1] March, 1941.

IX

The camp of Le Vernet covers about fifty acres of ground.

The first impression on approaching it was of a mess of barbed wire and more barbed wire. It ran all round the camp in a threefold fence and across it in various directions, with trenches running parallel.

The ground was arid; stony and dusty when dry, ankle-deep in mud when it rained, knobbly with frozen clods when it was cold.

The camp was divided into three sections : A, B, and C. Each section was separated from the others by barbed wire and trenches. Section A was for aliens with a criminal record. Section B for those with a political record. Section C for those without any definite charge on their record, but who were 'suspects' either in the political or criminal line. I was in C; and so were most of the people who came with me from Paris.

The hutments were built of wooden planks, covered with a sort of water-proofed paper. Each hutment housed two hundred men. It was 30 yards long and 5 yards wide. Its furnishings consisted of two lower and two upper platforms of planks, each two yards wide, running along the two long walls and leaving a narrow passage in the middle. The space between the lower and upper platforms was one yard, so that those on the lower planks could never stand erect. On each row slept fifty men, feet towards the passage. The rows were divided into ten compartments by the wooden poles supporting the roof. Each compartment contained five men and was 105 inches wide; thus each man disposed of a space 21 inches wide to sleep on. This meant that all five had to sleep on their sides, facing the same way, and if one turned over, all had to turn over.

The boards were covered with a thin layer of straw, and

the straw was the sole movable furniture in the hutment. It was, in fact, a barn. There were no windows, only rectangular slabs cut out of the wall-planks, which served as shutters. There was no stove during the winter of 1939, no lighting, and there were no blankets. The camp had no refectory for meals, not a single table or stool in the hutments; it didn't provide dishes, spoons, or forks to eat with, nor soap to wash with. A fraction of its population could afford to buy these things; the others were reduced to a Stone Age level.

The food consisted mainly of the daily ration of 11 oz. of bread. In addition, there was a cup of unsugared black coffee in the morning and a pint of soup at midday and in the evening—a pale liquid, containing no fat and only a few grains of chick-peas, lentils or vermicelli. The number of grains varied between 30 and 50. There were also 3 oz. of boiled beef with the midday soup, but so smelly that only the hungriest would eat it.

Work lasted in winter from 8 to 11 a.m. and from 1 to 4 p.m.; the working hours were limited by the daylight and by the physical debility of the undernourished men. The rate of sickness was always over 25 per cent. in all the barracks, although malingering was heavily punished.

The work consisted chiefly of road-building and the various labours necessary for the maintenance of the vast camp. It was unpaid, and the camp did not provide working clothes. As the majority of the prisoners possessed only what they stood up in—they had long ago sold the last spare shirt or undergarment for a packet of cigarettes—they worked in rags and soleless shoes, in twenty degrees of frost, and slept without blankets in their barns when even the spittle on the earth was frozen.

Four times a day there were roll-calls, which lasted from half an hour to an hour each. For the most of this time we had to stand immobile in the frost. The slightest offence was reprimanded by a stroke of the fist or the leather crop of the Mobile Guards. More serious offences were punished by a minimum of eight days' imprisonment, the first day without food or drink, and the next three days bread and water only.

These, roughly, were—and doubtless still are—the material conditions in the camp of Le Vernet. It has to be remembered, however, that it was notoriously the worst in France. But it must also be mentioned that as regards food, accommodation and hygiene, Vernet was even below the level of Nazi concentration camps. We had some thirty men in Section C who had previously been interned in various German camps, including the worst reputed, Dachau, Oranienburg, and Wolfsbüttel, and they were experts on these matters. I myself could confirm that the food in Franco's prison had been far more substantial and nourishing, although in the *carcel* of Seville we had no work to do, and in spite of the fact that it was in the middle of the Civil War.

x

There were twenty barracks in Section C, but only three were occupied. It would have cost the administration not a penny more to distribute us over the empty barracks and thus allow us each a space of, say, a yard wide for the privacy of sleep. They refused; we had to live in our *Lebensraum* of twenty-one inches. It would have cost them nothing but the price of a few planks of wood to transform one of the seventeen empty barracks into a refectory by our work; they refused. We had to eat our meals standing or sitting on the frozen earth.

The barracks in Section C were numbered 32 to 51. They stood in two rows in an enclosure. Nos. 32 to 34 (and later on 35 and 36) were the inhabited ones. I lived in No. 34, in the second compartment to the left on the upper row. The other four inhabitants were Mario, the Italian, Tamàs, the Hungarian poet, Pitoun, the Russian publicity artist, and Klein, a Rumanian shoe model designer. Yankel slept next to Tamàs, in compartment No. 3.

The day of our arrival we had to camp outside the enclosure while one by one we were searched, luggage and person, had our names filled into various books and files, were labelled A, B and C, and finally led into the barracks. Mario, Tamàs, Klein, Pitoun and I had stuck together during the journey, so that we should become neighbours in our new abode. We were among the last to be let in, after six hours' waiting in the rain. The barrack was pitch dark, and so was the vast camp around it—dark, uncanny and oppressive. We lay down on the straw, shivering in our wet clothes, and sharing three blankets between the five of us.

The next day we did not yet have to work and were told instead to queue up in front of an empty barrack to have our heads cropped. On our arrival, when we had seen the first wretched inmates of Le Vernet on the road, it had been mainly their naked skulls which had made such a horrifying impression on us; they reeked of the convict. Prison experts all over the world know the extraordinary psychological effect of imposing the convict skull on a man—which is why political prisoners in more enlightened countries are exempt from it.

When the order came through, Mario, Albert and I held a consultation and decided to start a protest action. Albert, an exiled German author, was housed in the neighbouring barrack, No. 33, together with most of the people from the former 'German Brigade' of the Roland Garros Stadium (except those who had been taken to Section B). We agreed that, if we did not show backbone from the very beginning, we would be done for and treated like dirt.

We prepared two lists, one for Barrack 33 and one for 34

(32 had been complete before our arrival), and began, with a certain caution, to collect signatures for our protest. We were soon disappointed. Everybody in my barrack seemed to have a different idea of how the protest should be worded. Some found it too polite, others too provocative; some suggested it should be a petition, not a protest, others that we should threaten to go on a hunger strike at once. A German barrister warned us that we were under martial law and thus liable to be tried for incitement to mutiny—which was quite true. Old Poddach implored us between fits of coughing 'not to make us all even more unhappy than we are'. The Red-Whites and the White-Whites (most of the Russians were in my barrack) all spoke at once, gesticulating and quoting history, Lenin, and the Gospels. It was a complete madhouse, and meanwhile the first men with cropped hair returned from the barber, looking like galley-slaves.

Mario pulled my sleeve and drew me outside the barrack. I looked disgustedly at the crumpled list in my hand. 'Let's drop the whole thing,' he said. 'It is no good trying with this crowd.' I tried to defend the crowd, putting all the blame on the accursed Russians. Mario smiled. *'Cosa sinistra,'* he said, 'Leftist tradition. Fill this barrack with Fascists of any country and you would see them sign in a jiffy.'

I wanted to go on, nevertheless, but I could never argue against that particular quiet smile of Mario's; it made me feel futile and childish, although he was younger than I. I knew it had taken nine years of imprisonment to form that smile—three years of fermenting in solitary confinement and six further years to become ripe and mellow, while he shared twelve square yards of space with comrades. He had been nineteen when the cell-door had closed behind him—and twenty-eight when it opened again, two years ago. This kind of experience either crushes a man or produces something rare and perfect; Mario belonged to the latter category.

Then Albert turned up with his list. The German Communists in Barrack 32 had declared that they were all prepared to sign it—some of the others too, but the Communists in bulk. '*Cosa sinistra*,' I said to Mario with a grin. For there was a particular, sour humour about this—all three of us had once been Communists, had left the Party in resentment and disgust, and were loathed as renegades. Anyhow, we could not present the camp authorities with a Communist petition—either everybody signed, or the whole thing would appear in an ominous political colour. And the Communists knew that, of course—they had learned their dialectics well. Yet whatever their motives were, we had once more to realise with bitterness that they were the only people with, so to speak, collective guts. It was the tragedy of the European Left, reflected in our miniature society.

Cosa sinistra—a truly sinister state of affairs. Finally we concocted a list with only a few signatures selected from the intelligentsia of our barracks—there were two ex-members of the Reichstag on it, two authors, two doctors of medicine, several doctors of philosophy, lawyers, and two members of the Légion d'Honneur—and Albert wrote a flowery letter in his best Comédie Française style, full of *honneur* and *dignité*. This we handed to Adjutant Pernod, who was in charge of our section. An hour later he came back, his face even redder than usual—he was a heavy drinker of apéritifs, hence his nickname—threatening everybody whom he should see tomorrow with a single hair on his head with eight days of imprisonment. So in the afternoon we all queued up and got our convict skulls. That was the end of our only attempt at collective action.

The next morning we were grouped into working squads. I was sent with about thirty others to dig up and level the uneven waste behind our double row of barracks.

It was a stretch of ground about 300 yards long and 150 yards wide, inside the barbed-wire enclosure of Section C. We used it as our exercise ground—a privilege which distinguished us, simple 'suspects', from the 'Criminals' in A and the 'Politicals' in B; they had no space for exercise other than the narrow path between their hutments.

The order was to dig up the stony ground thoroughly, remove the larger stones, fill up the holes and cavities, and make it 'all nice and smooth'. We worked with picks and spades under the supervision of two Mobile Guards. They did not hurry us—they hung about with a bored expression, slapping the calves of their boots with their little whips, and during the first hour I thought that the work was rather easy. I had earned my living by manual labour at one time, and although that was thirteen years ago, I still vaguely knew how to handle a spade. The sun was pouring down on us full blast; we were in the middle of October, yet we worked stripped to the waist. After an hour or so I felt tired, and after an hour and a half the pick had doubled its weight and I felt my pulse throbbing at the sides of my neck. At about that time the first incident occurred. One of the Guards approached Varga, a young Rumanian of rather frail appearance, and told him to dig deeper into the ground. Varga was already very flushed and his eyes had the goggling look of physical strain. He said, panting, and in a somewhat wrangling tone, that he was a student and not accustomed to manual labour. In the next instant the Guard's large fist crashed down under Varga's ear, who stumbled and fell. Two of us helped him up, and he went on digging with his spade without a word. The Guard walked slowly back to his colleague, looking as bored as ever.

I worked alternatively with pick and spade. About ten o'clock I felt my eyes starting out of my face and every heartbeat resounding in my chest like in a hollow drum. At intervals of ten minutes I allowed myself one minute's rest, leaning against the spade. The Guards did not object to this, but in their bored faces they had eyes of professional keenness, which saw at once if a man did not keep up with his neighbours or merely pretended to work.

At 11 a.m. work was over, but there was no possibility of rest. First we had to carry our working implements to the toolshed, about half a mile away at the other end of the camp, and hang about the place until somebody turned up with the key. Then back, *un-deux, un-deux*, escorted by the same Guards to our barracks. Then fall in for the roll-call, which lasted half an hour. It was twelve when we queued up for the soup, but the soup did not arrive until 12.30. It was distributed in the open air and gulped down standing, out of rusty tins which we had dug out from the camp rubbish heap. I was amongst the fortunate ones who had brought aluminium eating bowls and cutlery, and shared mine with Mario. After the soup we were more hungry than before. We had just the time to rinse our tins in cold water under the taps—there was a row of taps next to each barrack in the open air—then we had to fall in again for the third roll-call of the day, march back to the tool-shed, put spades and picks on our shoulders and, *un-deux, un-deux*, march back to work.

Those hours of work in the afternoon were torture. I kept glancing at the hands of my wrist-watch, which seemed unable ever to accomplish three complete revolutions. My bones ached, my heart thumped, my pulses throbbed, and I listened with dumb bewilderment to the odd 'han', 'han', which every stroke of the pick pressed out of my lungs. There was a dense fog in my brain, impenetrable to any coherent thought, except the dull obsession of counting the minutes —an aching state of semi-consciousness and numb idiocy.

As far as I could see, most of the others were in a similar state. In the morning they had still talked to each other; now nobody spoke a word; they worked like panting automata. Two of our squad were taken to prison on the first afternoon for unsatisfactory work.

Yet it would be unfair to say that the Guards drove or

goaded us. They simply hung about with their keen eyes and bored looks, and kept up the routine speed of work by their mere presence, with a minimum of threats and brutality. Up till that day, when I had heard of forced labour in German concentration camps and elsewhere, I had imagined something in the nature of illustrations in *Uncle Tom's Cabin*—sadistic slave-drivers hurrying about with long horse-whips whistling in their hands. The reality was, as in most forms of lasting suffering, quite undramatic. During the day there had only been one case of physical ill-treatment, and the speed of work was not over that of professional routine. But for people unskilled in heavy manual labour and underfed to the degree of acute and chronic hunger, the routine became plain torture. An undramatic, everyday torture which transformed our crowd within a few weeks into grey-faced, hollow-eyed, apathetic wrecks. When winter came, the lack of adequate clothing and the lack of fat in the nourishment made one after the other break down. There was not a single man in our squad who had not to be taken to the hospital for a few days. They came out still unsteady on their feet, for space in the hospital was scarce, to be sent back to forced labour. And that is what they are doing still, drudging with spade and pick, hammer and saw, unpaid, underfed, hopeless. Not time, only space separates us from them as they stand on the arid downs north of the Pyrenees, swinging picks in their blue, frozen hands, little clouds of steam in front of their naked heads, apathetic ghosts of the great defeat.

After three days of work I had a sort of collapse and had to put myself on the list for the medical visit. I had suffered from some cardiac trouble for the last three years, perhaps a heritage of hunger strikes in the Seville prison, nothing serious, but now enough to make me feel miserable with palpitations and giddiness.

H

We knew already that there were two doctors in the camp, the 'good one' and the 'bad one'; the 'good one' was a young *sous-lieutenant*, the 'bad one' a lieutenant and member of the Croix de Feu. The trouble was that one never knew beforehand which of the two would be on duty. The day before, the lieutenant had sent two men to prison for malingering. One of them was a fifty-year-old Turkish Jew with chronic conjunctivitis. He had been attached to a squad of cleaners and had to sweep the barrack with a broom four times a day—rather easy work, but the thick dust made his inflamed, watery eyes become worse and worse. He had asked the doctor for an eye lotion and for a few days of exemption from work. Without even a pretence of examining him, the lieutenant had dictated the prescription to his orderly: *'Visite non-motivé—quinze jours de prison.'* The old Jew was stunned and began to cry. Whereupon the lieutenant pronounced the stereotyped sentence:

'We are at war—French soldiers in the Maginot Line suffer worse hardships than you, and wouldn't pester their superiors with trifles.'

There was no answer to that. The next patient was a young German Socialist, suffering from a floating kidney, but with a tough and healthy appearance. He also got his fifteen days of jail, and afterwards returned to work. Three months later we buried him in the cemetery of Le Vernet, with the ceremonial assistance of the Camp authorities. He was twenty-four years old; I have forgotten his name.

The day when I was called to the doctor's room the *sous-lieutenant* was on duty. He took my blood-pressure and examined me fairly thoroughly. Then he asked: 'You are an author?' 'Yes.' 'Writing for English and American papers?' 'Yes.' *'Tiens,'* he said and, turning to his orderly:

'Exempt from all work and also from marching.'

When I was outside my heart beat a tattoo and all the way back to Section C I was whistling the *Carmagnole* to the rhythm of the Guard's *un-deux*. On arriving at Barrack 34, I found Mario and Tamàs, who had just returned from work with their squads. They were lying on their backs on the straw, their faces grey with exhaustion. All my happiness fell to ashes. But when I had told them, rather reluctantly, the result of the visit, Tamàs gathered himself up and congratulated me with his usual solemnity, while Mario jumped to his feet and embraced me with as radiant a face as if the news had concerned himself. He had grasped at once the contradiction in my feelings and said, lying back again in the straw : 'It is very lucky for all five of us. You will keep the straw tidy, and clean our blankets, and bribe the cooks for hot water for tea. *En somme*, we shall exploit you and prevent you falling back into the parasitical ranks of the bourgeoisie.'

Thus we began to organise our lives. Klein, the Rumanian shoe model designer, became permanently attached to the kitchen, and through him and through an elaborate system of bribing the cooks, I managed to get our tins filled with hot water twice a day and to prepare tea before the others came back from work. The next step was that Klein, Tamàs, and I had thermos bottles sent to us from home, so that I could supply the labouring members of our group with hot tea while they were actually at work. The Guards did not object to this, as long as the work was not interrupted and the tea gulped down at once. Besides, they had begun to know us individually, and both Tamàs and Mario were respected by them.

Food parcels began to arrive from home—irregularly at first, then punctually, one parcel a week. After a few weeks canteens were established in the camp—one in each section —where one could buy cigarettes, cheese, condensed milk, bread, chocolate, and bacon for prices about 50 per cent higher than the usual ones. The canteen and the food parcels quickly led to the establishment of a miniature class society in our huts, with very queer consequences.

XI

The camp was run with that mixture of ignominy, corruption, and *laisser-faire* so typical of the French administration.

The three sections were strictly isolated from each other by means of barbed wire and trenches, and by the infliction of severe punishments for shouting over the fence or sending messages. But inside the enclosure of our Section C we could move freely, visit our friends in other barracks, or walk on the large stretch of waste behind them, until 8 p.m. From 8 p.m. to 6 a.m. we were confined to the barracks, but, as the latrines were outside, one could always use this pretext for a smoke or a breath of fresh air, if the nights were mild. The camp was heavily guarded, but the sentries were posted outside the barbed-wire enclosure, and the premises of our section were only visited during the night by an occasional patrol.

We were guarded, not by soldiers as in the Stadium, but by the *Garde Mobile*, that is to say gendarmes—both in human material and tradition notoriously the most reactionary and brutal force in France. The dictator plenipotentiary of Section C was Adjudant Pernod. His staff consisted of two sergeant-majors, 'Fernandel' and 'the Corsican'. Fernandel owed his nickname to his resemblance to the well-known French actor; he had the same long horse-face and protruding horse-teeth, and the same imbecile grin, changing without transition to sudden accesses of fury. The Corsican was long and lean, with the yellowish complexion and the resentful melancholy of a man suffering from chronic stomach trouble. His wife, as we learned later, was in bad health; she had recently had a miscarriage, and was now again expectant, and complained continually in her letters. She lived somewhere in northern France, and his next leave was not due for three months. Every time the Corsican received another reproachful letter from his wife, his face grew yellower, right to the white of his eyes, which slowly moved in their sockets, looking our ranks up and down for a victim. When he found it—a man who did not stand correctly to attention or whispered to his neighbour during the roll-call —he pounced forward to use his crop; and while he hit, he bit his lower lip with his teeth.

Adjudant Pernod, Fernandel, and the Corsican made their regular appearances four times a day, at the four roll-calls before and after work. They were accompanied by about thirty Guards. At the 8 a.m. and the 1 p.m. roll-calls Fernandel and the Corsican detailed off the working squads and the Guards who were to escort them. At the 11 a.m. and the 4 p.m. roll-calls they distributed letters. Apart from these four daily ceremonies, they left us alone and did not care what we did out of working hours. They hardly ever came inside a hut—the smell of the rotting straw and of the two hundred men tightly packed into those dark, long, tunnel-like barns did not attract them.

Thus the details of the everyday routine of life were regulated not so much by the camp authorities as by the *chef de barraque*. Each hutment had to elect a *chef de barraque*, who to a certain extent was responsible to Fernandel and the Corsican for order and discipline. The *chef de barraque* had three *chefs de groupe* to assist him. No. 33, the German barrack, had elected Albert, who, as a former Commissar with the International Brigades in Spain, had the required authority, and, as a former pupil of a Jesuit seminary, the necessary diplomatic smoothness for this post. The Communists in 33 could perhaps have prevented his election, but for dialectical reasons they preferred not to have one of their own people exposed.

In our barrack the Russians, who were in the majority, had after much wrangling come to an agreement in the person of Kuryatchuk, a giant over six feet tall and somewhat slow-witted, but endowed with a sort of authoritative sleepiness like an elephant. Politically he was on the extreme White wing of the Red-Whites and thus is some way situated just in the axis of the centrifugal forces. The good thing about Kuryatchuk was that you could not argue with him—he just looked down at you silently with his little elephant eyes and gave no answer, being unable to think of one; and the solemn silence ensuing ended the argument. Unfortunately, Kuryatchuk's régime was brought to an end after a few weeks by the above-mentioned development of a class society in our barrack, the first consequence of which was a phenomenon best described as the Irruption of the Criminals.

I have said that Section C was composed of 'suspects', both in the political and criminal sense. The 'criminals' were mainly concentrated in our hut. Most of them were not criminal at all, but interned on the strength of a so-called 'blot' on their police file. Klein, for instance, was a refugee from Rumania. He had lived in France for seven years, but had been unable to obtain a *permis de travail*—the working permit necessary for aliens. He had the choice between starving or working illegally, and naturally chose the latter, as did thousands of foreigners. The French authorities knew all about it, of course, and more or less closed their eyes. According to a long-cherished tradition, they preferred to tolerate semi-officially an illegal state of affairs, rather than to admit officially that a man who is allowed to live in France must also be allowed to earn his living. Three years ago Klein had been denounced by some personal enemy for 'working illegally'. There followed the usual sequence of events: expulsion order; physical impossibility to comply

with it (he had, of course, no passport and nowhere to go);
six months' imprisonment in the Santé. According to the
paradoxical French routine, the expulsion order was cancelled on his release—otherwise the French administration
would have been obliged to keep him in prison until the end
of his days—and he was allowed to go on working just as
illegally as hitherto. But the blot on his *dossier* remained, and
at the outbreak of war he was interned as an undesirable
alien, 'suspect on account of a former conviction'.

It was a typical case, and most of the 'criminals' in Section
C had a story more or less on the same lines. But there were
about twenty real *types du milieu* in our barrack, and, in
spite of their numerical inferiority, they succeeded in bringing about a sort of social fermentation which soon poisoned
the atmosphere.

It all began with the food parcels and the canteen. The
nourishment provided by the camp was just sufficient to
keep a man alive in a state of permanent, aching, stomach-
burning hunger, with constant day-dreams of food. Yet in
the same hut some of the prisoners fed on tinned meats,
sausage, bacon, cheese, butter, chocolate, and fruit. The contrast between rich and poor reached the pungency of a social
satire. The dark tunnel of our barrack became an exag-
gerated model of human society, a kind of distorting mirror.

Some dilettantish attempts to introduce practical Communism were nipped in the bud : principally because, out
of the two hundred in our hut, only about ten belonged to
the moneyed (or, more correctly, the 'parcelled') class—
that is, received food from outside regularly. Besides, the
number of the parcels was limited to one a week, and their
weight to ten pounds. As to the canteen, those who possessed
some cash were only allowed to spend about 10s. a month.
Thus, in a general share-out, one man's share would have
amounted to an average of 6 oz. of food per week, or practically nothing. Besides, only three or four of the regular

parcel-receivers were willing to submit to such an extra-ordinary sacrifice. The collective sense, as it generally is, was mainly a privilege of the have-nots.

The attempt at 'socialism'[1] having failed, 'capitalist' cor-ruption and decay took its inevitable course. In the begin-ning, for a few cigarettes or a bit of sausage, one could bribe the cooks to give one hot water for tea, or hire people to wash one's shirts and polish one's boots; later on, when the *milieu* had established its rule over the barrack, one could by bribery obtain practically anything : exemption from work, larger living-space, alcoholic drinks, and protection from de-nunciation to the authorities.

The *milieu* in our barrack had its recognised leader in the person of Cyrano, a scarfaced young Spaniard with a high-pitched voice oddly contrasting with his sturdy build. He pretended to be a political refugee and former member of the F.A.I., the Anarchist Federation, and had for the past two years exercised the profession of *maquereau*, or pimp, in the rue du Faubourg Montmartre. We knew this from his friend Ornato, a dark, elegant Italian who had been a cocaine pedlar in the same district, and went about day and night in a conspicuous, bright, and fluffy teddy-bear coat. They had as a permanent hanger-on George, a little Armenian of seventeen, who had made a living in Paris by alternately stealing bicycles and prostituting himself. His beat com-prised the public conveniences between the Place Pigalle and Place Blanche, and the permanent amusements fair at the Palais Berlitz.

Cyrano and Ornato had proclaimed themselves *chefs de groupe* when Kuryatchuk was elected barrack chief. How exactly they had managed this nobody remembered clearly afterwards—they went about with some lists amidst the general excitement of the first day, when all the interest was

[1] 'Socialist' and 'capitalist' in quotes, as property in our community included no means of production, only goods for consumption.

centred on the election of the barrack chief and on the barber question; and next day they were firmly established in their posts. To be *chef de groupe* had considerable advantages : exemption from work, power to settle minor disputes concerning the distribution of vacant places whose tenants were in hospital, and custody of the lists of those temporarily exempted from work by the doctor. As at least one-quarter of the hut was always ill with influenza and dysentery, and as only a fraction of them could be accommodated in hospital, it became mainly a question of a bribe to Cyrano or Ornato whether one had to join a working squad or was allowed to lie all day on the straw. Adjudant Pernod and his staff never bothered about the lists; they found it simpler to rely upon the *chef de baraque* and the *chefs de groupe*, as long as they had the required number of men for work.

But to buy Cyrano's favour—Ornato only played a subsidiary role—was expensive and required a certain diplomacy. One couldn't simply put a tin of sardines into his hands and ask to be let off work for a day. A certain ritual had to be observed, an indirect, roundabout language used, an atmosphere of confidence and intimacy created. Only a few had the means and the technique to obtain Cyrano's favour. Besides, he was touchy and proud. I had a row with him in the very first days, and he made life difficult for me, although he could not force me to work. Later, when Mario was on the verge of collapse and refused to report for sick parade I had to come to terms with Cyrano in order to buy Mario a couple of days' rest. The only occasion that I seriously quarrelled with Mario was when he found out about it. I never tried it again. Mario had one *idée fixe* : to avoid any occasion of being humiliated by those who had power over us. This obsession, result of nine years of prison life, determined his conduct in the camp and almost suicidal behaviour : to go on working with a temperature of 103.5; to refuse to write petitions for his release in the flowery

French style required in such documents, and even to refuse a written declaration of his loyalty to the Allied cause—he had volunteered for the French Army from the first day of the war—for fear that it might be interpreted as an enforced and not a voluntary political act.

It was the ever-recurring and fatal constellation : the Cyranos and Ornatos and their patrons and protégés got on swimmingly in our rubbish heap of a camp, while the Marios and Tamàses played the eternal role of Don Quixote.

Yet one obstacle to Cyrano's ascendancy still remained : Kuryatchuk the elephant. He was still *chef de baraque*, and from time to time even his slow-moving brain discovered an irregularity on the lists and put a stop to one of Cyrano's rackets. Cyrano tried everything to kick him out of the way, but Kuryatchuk just looked down at him with his sleepy eyes and occasionally gave a roar through his proboscis that made the barrack quiver.

One day, in the second month of our stay in Le Vernet, during the midday break, a troop of gendarmes suddenly raided our hutment, pushed everybody out, locked the doors and allowed nobody to approach. We stood around in a crowd, stunned. Then Adjudant Pernod, Fernandel, and the Corsican arrived in a solemn group, followed by Cyrano and Kuryatchuk. The rumour soon went round that they were searching the barrack for stolen goods; actually complaints of thefts had been multiplying during the last fortnight. Ornato remained outside; he moved from group to group in his bright teddy-bear coat and made one or two confidential hints that the search might lead to 'very unexpected results'. After half an hour or so the five emerged into the daylight, the officials looking very official, Cyrano with a triumphant wink, and Kuryatchuk carrying a large bundle in his hands and looking more stupid than ever. He lumbered along behind the staff and disappeared with them in the direction of the office. But Cyrano joined the crowd and, after letting himself be pressed for a while, he informed us confidentially that the stolen goods—some two or three shirts and a few pairs of socks—had been found in the barrack chief's bag.

We suspected at once that the elephant was innocent and that Cyrano had played a dirty trick on him; and even Pernod and his staff guessed that something of the sort must have happened. The investigation was carried out secretly, but we learned that three compatriots of Kuryatchuk, amongst them the opera singer, had testified to having played cards the previous evening on Kuryatchuk's suitcase, which had been emptied for this purpose and found to contain nothing but a dirty pair of pants, strewn with tea-leaves and tobacco. He was acquitted, but nevertheless resigned from his post; he seemed to have taken the suspicion to heart, and henceforth led a shadowy and melancholy existence on his heap of straw in a corner, out of the limelight of public interest.

Against Cyrano nothing could be proved; yet his hopes of becoming Kuryatchuk's successor were cut short by Adjudant Pernod, who, abolishing the election system with a majestic and somewhat unsteady gesture, appointed a Swiss named Storfer, an odd character and a newcomer amongst us, to the post of *chef de baraque*.

Storfer had arrived at the camp only a fortnight before; he was about forty, under middle height and burly, with the twisted, stunted, and cunning face of a peasant from the mountains. He wore khaki trousers and a green hat with a feather which he never took off, not even when asleep. He went about alone, hardly talking to anybody, except to George, the Armenian nancy-boy. The first we learned about him was that he was liable to epileptic fits, as he had one the night after his arrival. The second, that he had spent twelve years in the Foreign Legion, and afterwards worked in a circus. The third, that he was an informer who reported everything that happened in our barrack to the Corsican.

Storfer's nomination inaugurated a new era. He had us all in his power by the simple expedient of denouncing anybody he disliked to the gendarmes. His first victim was Cyrano himself, who was in Storfer's way. Cyrano made a remark about the ceremony of 'saluting the flag'—every morning twenty men were marched to the camp entrance and had to stand to attention while the tricolor was hoisted on the flag-pole; they had to get up half an hour earlier than the others, and Cyrano had said something to the effect that this was a bloody nuisance. The remark was made in Storfer's presence. An hour later three Guards came for Cyrano and marched him off. He was kept in jail for three weeks, terribly beaten up and transferred to Section B for having 'insulted the French flag'. We never saw him again.

Having got rid of Cyrano, Storfer methodically developed bribery into a system. We all more or less became his tributaries, according to our means. He 'took' money in any amount, from ten sous to a hundred francs, and bestowed favours accordingly. Cyrano's régime had been old-fashioned, nineteenth-century banditism; Storfer introduced the modern form of racket into our society, with its typical feature of collaboration between the gang and the authorities. For Pernod and his staff, of course, knew what went on, but the advantage of having their own informer as barrack chief outweighed their moral scruples if they had any; their only interest was not to be bothered with anything, and Storfer saw to that.

The new régime brought forth a marked development in the process of class differentiation. The privileges of the parcelled class were no longer confined to food and cigarettes, but gradually extended to housing conditions and the general style of living.

The first member of the plutocracy to have an entire five-man compartment to himself, and a valet to attend to him,

was Mr. Goodman, agent of a well-known American arma-
ment firm in France. He was of Balkan origin, had worked
for the French *Deuxième Bureau*, and was detained under
suspicion of being a double agent, which I believe he actually
was. There were always vacancies in the barrack, and Goodman, by paying a considerable weekly sum to Storfer, secured exclusive possession of the corner compartment on the
upper platform opposite to ours. Parta, his valet, was a little
Hungarian salesman who slaved for Goodman as maid-of-
all-work in exchange for a share of Goodman's gorgeous
meals of tinned foods and an occasional American cigarette
or a glass of brandy, smuggled to Goodman by the gendarmes
through the intermediary of Storfer.

Parta had transformed Goodman's compartment into a
kind of cosy attic. There was no straw on the floor; Goodman slept on a pneumatic mattress and Parta on a palliasse.
They had a table—the planks of an old crate nailed together
—and stools, and shelves serving as a larder. In the evening
they burnt smuggled candles. They had separated their compartment from the adjoining one with brown paper pinned
on to the wooden framework, and from the outer corridor
by hanging blankets over a wire. From time to time Goodman gave parties to other members of the plutocracy.

Opposite to Goodman, in the upper corner compartment
next to ours, lived Storfer with his two satellites: George,
the little Armenian bicycle thief who had become Storfer's
girl friend, and Emil, another Swiss and former *légionnaire*,
also homosexual. They too had a table and candles to burn.

So had we. A table, five stools, a larder-shelf and even a
bookshelf, all in a space of six by nine feet. The straw was
stuffed into five palliasses which we had been sent from
home, all neatly piled on top of each other during the daytime. We couldn't afford candles, but we had two lamps
made of old tins filled with oil and a wick steadied by a wire
hook. We represented the lower ranks of the plutocracy, as

between the five of us only two received parcels, which we shared. They usually arrived on Thursday and we had a rigid rationing system to make them last the whole week; every bar of chocolate and every biscuit was counted and divided into five times seven rations, and the skin of the sausages was marked with a scale like a thermometer. The same system of refined economy was applied to space. We had to share six square yards between the five of us, and to sit round the table was only possible if we arranged our limbs in one particular way, like a jig-saw puzzle.

The life we led was a proof of man's capacity for adaptation. I think that even the condemned souls in purgatory after a time develop of sort of homely routine. That is, by the way, why most prison memoirs are unreadable. The difficulty of conveying to the reader in his armchair an idea of the nightmare world from which he has emerged makes the author depict the prisoner's state of mind as an uninterrupted continuity of despair. He fears to appear frivolous or to spoil his effect by admitting that even in the depths of misery cheerfulness keeps breaking in.

On the other hand, the above-mentioned *douceurs de la vie*, such as tables, stools, palliasses, and light, were confined to a small fraction of the hut—about twenty out of two hundred, and to five compartments out of a total of fifty. They were the five next to the door at the southern end of the barrack. There was Storfer's compartment and ours on the left-hand upper platform and the Eligulashwily clan below us; there was Goodman's compartment and the 'Carluccio group' facing us on the right-hand upper platform and some of the well-to-do White Russians under them. These first six yards of the barrack looked like a cross-section through some miniature Japanese doll-house, very primitive but still quite habitable; the remaining twenty-four yards were simply a stable, dirty and oppressing, the air unbreathable, for men smell worse than horses.

It was a revolting contrast and apparently irremediable. All the privileges the plutocracy enjoyed were illicit; the tables and stools were made of planks stolen from the Military Administration, candles and oil lamps were officially prohibited. Their use by a few was tolerated, but it could not be generalised. By all their traditional standards, Fernandel and the Corsican found it natural that Mr. Goodman, who was dressed like a gentleman, or Mr. K., whose name had been 'printed in the papers', should enjoy privileges which Yankel and other have-nots were denied. One of the reasons for the bankruptcy of the European Left was their failure to realise how deep were the mental roots of class distinctions. The only measure of levelling in which we succeeded was to provide all the inmates of our barrack with blankets and to introduce a weekly collection to improve the soup.

In No. 33, the German barrack, conditions were better and the class distinctions less sharp. It was a more homogeneous and more disciplined crowd.

Finally, there was Barrack 32, or the Leper Barrack. Its inmates had been there long before us; it was they whom we had seen on the road to the camp, as a horrifying revelation of the depths of abjectness and misery to which man can be reduced.

If the pauper section of our barrack was a purgatory, Hut 32 was the real inferno. It was in complete darkness and the smell was appalling. None of its inhabitants possessed a change of shirt or socks, and many of them had actually sold their last shirt for a packet of cigarettes, and went about naked under a thin and ragged jacket. The barrack was infested with vermin and disease. Outside working hours, its inmates did odd jobs for others, washing their linen for the price of a few slices of bread, mending shoes, cleaning boots. They received no letters and wrote none. They lingered about the camp, picking up cigarette ends out of the mud and from the concrete floors of the latrines, where most were to be found. Even the most wretched in the other hutments looked upon these with horror and dismay.

These hundred and fifty men of the Leper Barrack were remnants of the International Brigades—once the pride of the European revolutionary movement, the vanguard of the Left. They had been the material for the first experiment since the Crusades to form an army of volunteers which would fight for a cosmopolitan creed. A strange historical constellation had focused Spain into the symbolical position of the Holy Land and endowed the struggle for Madrid with the emotional content of the battles for the Holy Sepulchre. Not unlike the hordes of Godfrey of Bouillon and Peter the Hermit, the Crusaders of the anti-Fascist *mystique* were in the majority men of good faith, with a mentality which combined enlightenment and sectarianism, brotherliness and intolerance, charity and ruthlessness, self-sacrifice and mercenary greed. Like their mediæval predecessors, they included men who had given up everything to join the movement and men who had joined it because they had nothing to lose; and in many cases both these motives and many others were involved and the men themselves were unable to say which had propelled them. One half of the world worshipped them as heroes and saints, the other half loathed them as lunatics and adventurers. Actually they were all of these; but above all they were the militant vanguard of their creed. And, as in the case of their predecessors, their creed was cynically exploited by those who pulled the wires behind the scenes. The heroic horde was but an unconscious tool of power politics, and when it had played its role was sacrificed in an immense holocaust, the memory of which would linger on and make all lofty aspirations a stink in the nostrils of the common man.

The International Brigades were a creation of the Comintern and were controlled by the Comintern. Their rank and file consisted mainly of Communists and sympathisers, their officers and political commissars were exclusively members of the Party, directly responsible to the Party apparatus. The Third International had started the Crusade in the days when Spain became the battlefield of Europe and Stalin still backed the democratic horse. When he changed sides, he made a thorough job of it; he dropped Spain (as a betrothal gift to Fascism, long before anyone foresaw the marriage), he dropped the Comintern, he dropped the European working class. The survivors of the International Brigades—more than two-thirds had been killed on the battlefield—were thrown into French concentration camps; not one of them was allowed to enter the Fatherland of the Proletariat, the country which had acclaimed them in hysterical hero-worship, which had boasted of having abolished unemployment and of having work for all. The gates of Russia were closed, the ears of the Party were deaf and the tills of the Workers' Aid Fund were empty; but then it had always been said the Party was not a philanthropic institution.

So that was the end of the crusade—the Leper Barrack in Le Vernet. Half of the human ruins who lived in it came from Germany and Austria, like Willy Schulz, a fair, blue-eyed, frail, and fanatical little fellow, who was spitting out his lungs in instalments on the straw of No. 32 (men of the Leper Barrack were hardly ever taken to the hospital); and their *curriculum vitæ* was more or less on the same lines as his:

1930–3 :   living on the dole;

1933–5 :   concentration camp in Germany;

1935–6 :   unemployment in Paris, but no dole;

1936–9 :   volunteer in Spain, twice wounded, the second time in the lung;

1939–? :   concentration camp in France.

I

That makes ten years of outcast life, and Willy was twenty-nine. For some it was only five or six years, for others eleven or twelve. Some of the younger ones had never known what work was like; some of the older ones still remembered vaguely the golden times when they were allowed to slave in a factory, workshop, or mine. Some had a wife and children in Germany of whom they had not heard for years; others had left a girl in Paris when they went to Spain, but that too was almost four years ago now. In the beginning there were letters; later they became rare; gradually all ties with the outside world became thin and frayed, and finally they tore. Communism? Democracy? Fascism? A cigarette end in the gutter was a reality, while political ideas had gradually lost all meaning; but few admitted this. The sectarian hatred between Stalinists, Trotskyists, and Reformists still existed; fractional conspiracies and denunciations still went on—and whispered memories or political controversies which had been settled by a bullet in the back on the battle-fields of Spain. Some of these were legends, many of them were true; and the dark silhouette of the Tchekist, the 'Aparatchik', or G.P.U. agent had replaced the once bright and lively symbols of the struggle for a happier world.

A happier world! What derision for the inhabitants of the Leper Barrack. The essence of politics is hope and hope had gone; but parties throw shadows and the shadows had stayed on. And the shadows went on fighting each other after the defeat.

Ten years of constant defeat had reduced them to what they were; and their fate merely exemplified what had happened to all of us, the European Left. They had done nothing but put into practice what we had preached and believed; they had been admired and worshipped, and thrown on the rubbish-heap like a sackful of rotten potatoes.

XII

The weeks passed by, in the strange prison rhythm of monotony and excitement. Looking back on the succession of events and incidents, they appear to me oddly out of proportion. In the chain which they form in my memory, there are links of different size and weight : there is the small and inconspicuous one of the day when Russia declared war on Finland, and the large and shining one when I won the second prize in the chess tournament of Section C; and the heavy and rusty group of the week when I received no letters from G. It is not a very long chain, extending over not more than a hundred days; but I have a queer feeling that it hangs irremovably suspended inside my skull, somewhere between the two ear-drums, and whenever I hear the word 'France', it begins to swing and to make me sick with its vibrations.

Following the incoherent sequence of the chain, the first event I remember after the barber action was the destruction of the *Admiral Graf Spee*. At last something had happened in the phoney war, and the *Dépêche de Toulouse* magnified it almost to the proportions of a Trafalgar. Yet its vivifying effect was noticeable in the camp; victories, big or small, are vitamins for the morale.

Next week the vitamins were followed by a dose of poison. It came from a series of photographs featuring the life of German prisoners of war in a French camp. We saw them having a meal in a tidy refectory, and there were tables and chairs and dishes and knives and forks. And we saw them in their dormitory, and they had real beds and mattresses and blankets. The pictures told an eloquent story : if you were a Nazi, you were treated decently; but if you were an anti-Nazi, you were treated as mud. After my release I heard that a certain German refugee in Hut 33 had written a letter to the French authorities, with the laconic statement that he had changed his political views, become loyal to Hitler and an enemy of France, and requested to be treated as a civilian prisoner of war. He was actually transferred to a Nazi camp. It should go to the credit of his comrades that nobody followed his example.

The next thing I remember was the first dysentery epidemic. Almost half of Section C caught it; fortunately it was a benign form of the disease and we had only one death.

The name of the man who died was, I think, Max Heymann. He had been over sixty, a refugee from Germany, a quiet and unobtrusive old Jew. He had slept next to old Poddach in Barrack 33. Fifteen men were allowed to follow him to the cemetery, and Dessauer, a former rabbi, said the prayers.

Then came the November rains, with their soft and sad drumming on the barrack roof going on day after day. The mud in parts of the camp was ankle-deep, and most of the men had no coats, and the dysentery epidemic was followed by an influenza epidemic.

In between these events the Russians attacked Finland and the Communists used their dialectics to prove that this was a revolutionary war, whereas the war against Nazism was an imperialist war. The most exasperating thing about our Communists was that they made it so difficult for one to hate them; they had none of the traditional vices, did not steal and did not squeal and were neither corrupt nor selfish, but bursting with virtues. In fact, their only fault was that years of systematic doping with Stalinist dialectics had affected their grey matter with a sort of colour-blindness both in their logical and ethical outlook. It was their only fault, but disastrous in its effect.

Yet this only applies to the proletarian rank and file. There were some of the leading functionaries of the German C.P. in Barrack 33, and for them the opposite was true; they made it difficult for one not to hate them. With perhaps one exception all of these men had been accomplices, passive or active, of the shooting of scores of their comrades in Russia and Spain; they had actively supported a policy which in its practical results served the Nazis' aims, and had drawn a monthly salary for it. And yet not even they (again with one exception) could be accused of corruption in the traditional meaning of the word. They were corrupt in a subtler sense, by inserting between self-interest and political action the mental cogwheels of self-deception. This psychological device allowed them to eat their cake and have it—to commit the basest infamies and yet enjoy the luxury of a clean conscience. They had developed the technique of lying to themselves to such a degree of perfection that the term 'in good faith' no longer had any meaning; when self-deception becomes a routine, it ceases to be an excuse.

They were morally guilty and logically wrong, but they were in a strong position, because the arguments used against them were generally even wronger. In fighting the Communists, one is always embarrassed by one's allies.

I remember the day when I learnt from a letter that the Communists in the U.S.A. had embarked on a propaganda campaign against the blockade of Germany and against American help for the Allies. When I had finished the letter I ran into F., a member of the Central Committee of the German C.P. He was cleaning the latrine in front of Barrack 33, a man of fifty, a former lumberjack, with a hard and clear-cut face like some portrait by Dürer. We used to avoid each other, but with that letter in my hand I could not restrain myself. 'Read that,' I told him.

F. took the letter and adjusted his spectacles—they were steel-rimmed spectacles, the educated proletarian's implement, as opposed to the bourgeois' horn-rimmed ornaments. He stood very erect while he read it, the latrine broom in his hands. 'And what about it?' he asked when he had finished.

'Do you agree with this?'

'Of course I do. This war is no concern of the international working class.'

We had the usual argument. Everything he said sounded utterly convincing. One could almost see the well-oiled cog-wheels turn in his brain, grind the words out of their meaning, turn them round and round, until it became self-evident that real anti-Fascism meant support for the Fascists. At the end he said :

'If you were in a responsible position would you release us?'

'Yes. Most of the people from 32, and the rank and file in general. As for you, D., G., S., etc., I would keep you behind barbed wire for the duration, under more decent conditions, of course.'

'Because you are a renegade skunk and afraid of us.'

'Because you play into the Nazis' hands and must be prevented from it.'

'Then why don't you report what I have said to your friends the gendarmes?'

'I am not an informer.'

'Why not? It would only be the logical inference from your convictions.'

'Because I have ceased to believe that the end justifies the means—and that is why I have left the Party.'

'Petty-bourgeois liberalism,' said F. with finality, and went on sweeping the latrine with his slow, thorough, dignified movements. I never argued with him again. He had all the advantages of his passionate error against my shabby truth.

A few days later a friend reported to me a conversation which he had overheard between F. and a newly arrived young Party member.

'Is that K. the writer?' the newcomer had asked, pointing at me.

'Yes.'

'Is he a member?'

'No.'

'But an anti-Fascist?'

'Even that is doubtful,' F. had replied. 'Be careful if you talk to him.'

December came and the first spell of frost, with an icy gale blowing down from the Pyrenees. It kept the thermometer 4 or 5 degrees below zero, Fahrenheit, for days on end. And there was still not a single stove in Section C, and out of the total population of the Leper Barrack still only fifteen had blankets. They could not even cover themselves with straw, as the layer was barely one inch thick; their teeth chattered and they shivered all night. During the day they still had to work in their rags, without overcoats and with their toes sticking out of their shoes.

In the middle of the cold spell a new epidemic broke out, a sort of diarrhœa which forced the men to go to the latrine five or six times a night; and the latrines were in the open air. Some of the old man simply could not do it. The consequences were as might be expected.

There were several doctors in Section C, and two of them, a German and an Armenian, did their best to help. They looked after the sick in the barracks and they had been authorised to receive medicaments from friends in Paris, which they distributed gratis. It was a real blessing for all of us, as the medical stores of the camp consisted mainly of aspirin, belladonna, and castor oil.

One day in December, during the Age of Diarrhœa, the younger or 'good' camp doctor sent a message to Section C: he thanked Dr. Weiden and Dr. E., the Armenian, for their 'valuable support to the camp authorities' and expressed the desire to make their personal acquaintance. Would they be good enough to come next day during the consultation hour to the infirmary?

The message was delivered verbatim by Dessauer, the ex-rabbi. Dessauer had lost his right arm during the First World War, and, being unfit to work, had been appointed to keep the hospital book and accompany the sick to the medical visit. Weiden and E. were naturally pleased. Next morning they joined the detachment of sick going to the infirmary. There they found, instead of the young doctor, the Croix de Feu lieutenant on duty. Dessauer's function was to call in the patients from the waiting-room according to his list, and to read out the nature of their complaint. When the turn of the two doctors came—both were men over fifty—Dessauer read out their names and academic degrees.

'What complaint?' asked the lieutenant.

Dessauer explained that *Monsieur le sous-lieutenant* had asked the two doctors to report. The lieutenant looked up with his red-veined drinker's eyes. Everybody knew that he hated his younger colleague, who was a reserve officer and, on top of that, a Jew, and that he hated Dessauer for the same reason. He thrust his head forward and roared at him:

'I asked you the motive of their visit.'

Dessauer's only defence against humiliation was his dry humour. He answered in his calm service tone:

'Motive: *visite de politesse.*'

The end of it was that the lieutenant ordered the two doctors to be sent to prison for fifteen days. Reason: *visite non-motivée.*

The entire camp was in effervescence, even the gendarmes. Both doctors were very popular, especially Weiden, and some of the guards, suffering from boils or rheumatism, used to consult them instead of the military doctors. They had always refused any offer of payment or personal privileges, and this had profoundly impressed the French gendarmes. But the camp Commandant, for reasons of discipline, was backing up the lieutenant, and Weiden and Dr. E. were taken to prison.

The young French doctor felt his personal honour involved. He protested to the Commandant, and the affair became a matter of prestige between the lieutenant, a regular officer and member of the Croix de Feu, and the *sous-lieutenant,* who was only a reservist and a Jew. In view of the spirit of the French Army, there could be no doubt about the outcome, but the pretext employed by the camp Commandant to made an arbitrary act appear legal was truly remarkable. He confirmed the prison sentence on the two doctors, but changed the reason from the obviously absurd '*Visite non-motivée*' to 'distribution of prohibited drugs amongst the internees'. The 'prohibited drugs' were tablets of veramon which by mistake had not been marked on the list of medicaments which Weiden had received from Paris.

The *sous-lieutenant* took the only course open to him and asked to be transferred to the front. A few days later his request was granted. We never heard of him again.

If he was killed it happened because he believed, not in Socialism, revolution, or any great ideal, but in the simplest form of decency. In his age and country the qualifications required to become a martyr were reduced to a modest minimum. If he survived he will fall under the racial laws of old Pétain.

When Weiden came out of prison he was a broken man. This was partly due to something having gone wrong with his denture so that he could not wear it any more, and his lips and jaws were sunken as if the framework underneath had been removed. But the main damage was to his morale : the consciousness of the injustice suffered had eaten into his mind and destroyed within a fortnight his former jovial cheerfulness. Dr. E. soon got over the shock, but Weiden never recovered. His medicaments were confiscated; he was strictly forbidden to give any medical advice; and this enforced idleness amidst so much physical suffering finished him off. He crept about the camp, muttering to himself, unshaven, neglected and filthy. Before the tragedy he had looked forty-five; now he looked seventy and was hardly distinguishable from the Russian embankment sleepers in our barrack. It was an uncanny sight, this slow annihilation of the human substance in a man, going on before our eyes.

Only on one occasion did I see old Weiden happy again. On Christmas Eve three gendarmes came with a conspiratorial air to Barrack 33. One of them had a festering cut on his finger and asked Weiden to bandage it; the others had come to keep a lookout. They had brought all the necessary things from the medical stores and even candles to make a light. Old Weiden solemnly performed the simple operation and the three guards marched off, after ceremoniously saluting and shaking hands with him. Had they come to please and flatter him—as a sort of Christmas treat? Too subtle and romantic a thought for French gendarmes. Or on the contrary, to make fun of him? Or simply, because nobody else was available in the infirmary? I never found out.

After the second death in Section C, the camp management became apparently afraid of the responsibility incurred by letting men of sixty and seventy sleep on straw in unheated barracks at a temperature around zero Fahrenheit. They furnished two empty hutments with bedsteads, palliasses and two stoves, and ordered all the men over the age of fifty-five to be transferred to them.

These old-man barracks were situated outside the enclosure of Section C, and the exodus of the old men was a pitiful sight. They marched in single file, each accompanied

by a younger comrade to carry his luggage; they were
anxious and depressed, having to leave their friends behind, and those dreadful icy hutments which had nevertheless become a sort of home; and they were frightened, as
every prisoner is frightened, by a sudden change of conditions. It was a kind of funeral march, and half-way down,
just outside the barbed-wire of Section C, one of them
broke down. It was *Kammersaenger* Schiller.

Kammersaenger Schiller had sung leading tenor parts on
the stages of German provincial opera-houses; and, like
many actors, he had Closing-Time Neurosis: the obsessive
fear of becoming old. He dyed his hair, and his wife in Paris
kept sending him cream-coloured silk pyjamas, Russian eau-
de-Cologne, and a special discreet nail varnish. We all
thought he was in his early forties; and now it turned out
that he was over fifty-five and sent to the old-man barrack.

It was a sickening sight—*Kammersaenger* Schiller clinging to the barbed-wire fence of Section C, tears streaming
down his clean-shaven face, and begging the gendarmes to
let him go back. He was not really old, he could endure all
hardships, he did not belong in the old-man barrack, and he
would not go—no, he would not. The guards stood around,
looking at *Kammersaenger* Schiller open-mouthed. Finally
he joined the procession: 'I am only yielding to force,' he
cried helplessly, although nobody had touched him.

From that day he began to decay. He stopped dyeing his
hair and keeping up his appearance; in the old-man barrack
he became an old man.

The third breakdown was Mr. Goodman, the suspected
double agent. Strange things were happening to him. It
began with an attempt to hang himself, which was presumably staged, for it was Parta, his valet, who found him;
but staged with an uncanny realism—for he found him
actually hanging on a cord from a beam over the latrine.
From that day, Mr. Goodman became, so to speak, invisible,

although he went on living in our barrack. Except for the four daily roll-calls, he never left his corner compartment, which was protected from curious eyes by an arrangement of blankets and rags. During the roll-calls we saw that he was growing a black beard, that he wore a strange sort of Basque beret with the lining turned outwards, and that his face was frozen in an idiotic grin. A week later he began to shout in the middle of the night that he wanted a bicycle with three wheels. He had to be taken to the hospital and there probably he still is. Whether he had really gone mad or was only malingering, I do not know; if he was malingering, it was a remarkable performance.

But another man actually did go mad—the unfortunate Turkish Jew who had been sent to prison for asking the doctor for an eye lotion. He lived in the old-man barrack and one night in January he suddenly got up and attacked his neighbour with a pocket-knife. Afterwards he calmed down and was taken to jail. Next morning they found him dead— he had hanged himself with his tie on a hook.

These were extreme cases—but most of us suffered a certain transformation of mentality. Tamàs developed symptoms of melancholia, spinning himself into a cocoon of morose silence; Pitoun, a nervous talkativeness, all the more tiresome as he spoke very slowly and with a strong Russian accent; Klein became insupportably querulous and irritable. I myself tried in vain to defend myself against a queer neurotic obsession in connection with G. : whenever a letter was late, I had the *idée fixe* that something must have happened to her, and when it turned out that she was all right, I flew into a choking fury with her for causing me so much anxiety; and, as I could not blame her for what was not her fault, I looked for pretexts in her letters and even in the composition of the food parcels she sent; and I spent two days composing letters which I knew must hurt and insult her, and then another two days on a letter of apology. The odd thing was that I was perfectly capable of giving a sober analysis of my own neurotic state, but that did not in the least prevent it from becoming worse every week. On two occasions, when I had expected a letter and my name was not called at the distribution of the mail, I lost my voice for almost half an hour, the first time without noticing it. I spoke to Mario and did not understand why he looked so bewildered until I realised that my lips were moving, but no sound came out. I was more angry with myself than frightened, and after a while it passed.

Detention, drudgery, the unspeakable physical conditions, and the continuous chain of humiliations did this slow work on our minds. Perhaps the worst of it was the complete lack of privacy. To live for months on end in 22 inches of space, in the buzzing beehive of the barrack without an hour of solitude, without ever being able to come up for air, affected even robuster proletarian nerves. I had a feeling that the contents of my brain had melted to a sort of amorphous jam which did not allow the formation of any consistent thought. The mills of misery ground slowly but surely.

There were, however, exceptions. For some in our camp, beggars, tramps, and *clochards*, the barrack meant material safety and comfort: the safety of a roof, an inch of straw, a cup of coffee, and two tins of soup a day. One day, when there was a rumour of an armistice, I heard an old Russian embankment-sleeper ask in an anxious tone: 'If they make peace, do you think they will allow us to stay here?'

And there were others who seemed to flourish on this dungheap. Cyrano gave the impression of a perfectly happy man until Storfer brought about his downfall, and Storfer himself visibly had the time of his life; he grew fat and dignified, and even his elileptic fits became less frequent.

Incidentally, we had learnt in the meantime that after leaving the Foreign Legion, Storfer had been a tiger-tamer's assistant in the famous Circus Amar. His function had been to stand behind his master with an unloaded revolver and pull anxious faces, to make the act look more dangerous; and he had performed his task, especially the face-pulling, with so much success that he eventually became second clown in the Amar team who had to run round the ring in the intervals between two numbers, turning somersaults and kicking each other in the pants.

XIII

Christmas came, and all the pitiful fuss to prepare for the traditional prisoners' *Ersatz* rejoicements. The barracks were decorated with green branches over the door, and with the inscription: 1940! VIVE LA FRANCE! LIBERTÉ, ÉGALITÉ, FRATERNITÉ. When all was over the branches were used as latrine brushes and the Liberté, Égalité, and Fraternité scratched out. The camp Commandant, whom we saw on this occasion for the first and last time, delivered a speech and gave us permission to make a collection in the barrack for the purchase of a barrel of red wine, half a litre per head. The food was not improved; chick-pea soup and nothing was the menu on Christmas Eve, chick-pea soup and nothing on New Year's Eve.

The festivities consisted of an amateur variety show in an empty barrack. It was on this occasion that the Commandant's speech was delivered. I do not remember what the speech was about, but it was in the best French oratorical tradition, very melodious and elevating. Albert also said a few melodious words on behalf of the prisoners, and then the programme began; there was a Russian choir which sang Russian folksongs and a Hungarian choir which sang Hungarian folksongs; an acrobat from Barrack 32, a Jugoslav

choir which sang Jugoslav folksongs, a clown solo of Storfer's, a Polish choir which sang Polish folksongs, a Czech
choir which sang Czech folksongs, and then we all sang the
Marseillaise and were marched back to our barracks, to
the accompaniment of our escorts' no less rhythmocal *un-
deux, un-deux*.

The next day a feud broke out between Storfer and Albert; both were barrack chiefs, but Pernod had appointed
Albert Director of the performance which was to be repeated on New Year's Eve, and Albert wanted to cut out
Storfer's clowning act, which was indeed sickening; on the
other hand, Storfer thought that on the strength of his past
as an artist and tiger-tamer, the honour of being Director
should fall to him. The result was that Storfer denounced
Albert for having said derisive things of the French Army
while queueing up at the canteen; but Albert proved that
he had never been to the canteen, as he received all the
foodstuffs he wanted from his wife, and remained Director.

Section A and Section B also had their performances, and
we learnt that B, the 'politicals', had put up an excellent
satirical revue about conditions in the camp. This illustrates
the difference between the collective atmosphere of political
prisoners and that of our mixed crowd. It goes to the credit
of Pernod and his staff that they watched the performance
of B to the end, holding their bellies with laughter and slapping their thighs. Their attitude was a perfect illustration of
the traditional French respect for *l'esprit*—and of the
futility of it: for naturally the conditions of life of *Homo
Verniensis* remained the same as before.

The conditions became even worse. After Christmas Pernod was transferred elsewhere and replaced by Lieutenant
Cosne. Lieutenant Cosne wore a corset, spoke in a high
falsetto, and was the deplorable incarnation of an inferiority
complex walking on two knock-kneed legs with a riding-
crop in its hand. The first time I saw the riding-crop in action

was on the face of old Poddach, the day of Lieutenant Cosne's arrival; and from then onwards at least once a day.

Poddach's crime had been that he had shaded his eyes with his hand while talking to a sergeant. The next day, Yurvitch, a Jugoslav violin virtuoso—the dark young man who had held hands with his wife in the Salle Lépine, and had cried when they were separated—reported to Cosne's office. He requested to be exempted from heavy work until the festering blisters on his hands had healed, as he feared they they would become unfit for his profession.

'Show your hands. Put them on the table,' said Lieutenant Cosne.

Yurvitch put his hands on the table—long nervous hands with the knuckles all swollen and the skin cracked, and then Lieutenant Cosne's whip lashed down on them and lashed a second time in his face. 'This will teach you to shirk work while our soldiers are fighting in the Maginot Line.'

The next victim was Klein. Klein was rushing to the kitchen with a boiling kettle in his hand and did not see Lieutenant Cosne pass. Cosne had the *idée fixe* that we avoided saluting him on purpose. 'Teach this man how to behave,' he said to the Corsican. Klein received his lesson in correct behaviour squirming on the ground, with the kettle pouring hot water over his feet.

A few days later Barna, a Czech writer over fifty in Section B, fell from the upper platform in his barrack and broke his arm. He had to be taken by train to the hospital in the nearest town, Pamier, to be X-rayed and put into plaster. Lieutenant Cosne ordered the escort to handcuff him for the journey; and so it happened: the man with the broken arm had to travel in handcuffs. The week after the accident Barna's son, a boy of fifteen, came from Paris to visit him. Permission was refused, and the boy had to travel the five hundred miles back to Paris without having seen his father.

The worst things happened in the camp prison. At night the gendarmes got drunk and, as there was no other entertainment available in Le Vernet, they went to the camp prison, opened the cells and beat up the prisoners. This entertainment was traditionally called '*passer à tabac*'. Cyrano, for instance, had the bad luck to be the only inmate of the prison for a few days; and as the cell was so small that only one man could amuse himself at a time, the sergeants took their turn and beat Cyrano for about two hours. Next morning he had to be treated in the infirmary.

All the time I was in Vernet new prisoners kept on arriving; after Christmas two more barracks—35 and 36—were by and by filled with men. We looked down on them with the same patrician contempt for the newcomers as travellers in a railway compartment have for the people who get in at a stop in the middle of a journey. '*Un type du 35*' was a term of derision with the men of 33 and 34.

Amongst the newcomers were some rare curiosities. There was old Gouget, a man of Belgian origin, who had for thirty years kept a greengrocer's shop in a mountain village near Grenoble. In a backyard of his little house he had bred pigeons. On a Sunday the Gouget family was just eating roast pigeon with *salade de cresson*, when Mlle. Monnier, an old spinster, passed and saw them through the dining-room window. Mlle. Monnier had read in the papers that carrier pigeons were used for military purposes, and that whoever shot one would be court-martialled for military sabotage. Next morning the village gendarme came to Gouget and put him into jail. The report was duly transferred by the gendarmerie to the military authorities, who dropped the charge as idiotic and returned the act to the district *préfet*; and the district *préfet*, to prove his patriotic zeal, ordered Gouget to be interned because 'although no precise charge could be proved against him, the alien

K

Gouget was to be considered as politically suspect with reference to paragraph X of the *loi des suspects*'.

Then there was Uetzli, a Swiss lad of seventeen, who had run away from his parents' farm near Berne to enlist as a volunteer in the French Army. On his arrival in Paris he walked down from the Gare de l'Est to the Opéra, as he had heard that this was a famous building and he wanted to have a look at it before he became a soldier. So he had his look and then approached a policeman in front of the Café de la Paix, and asked him with his strong German accent where the next military barracks were.

'Why do you want to know that?' asked the policeman.

'To become a soldier,' explained young Uetzli.

'Show me your *carte d'identité*,' said the policeman. Young Uetzli had only a passport, but no French *carte d'identité*. 'Where do you live?' asked the policeman. Young Uetzli explained that he lived nowhere, because he had just arrived from Switzerland. 'So you have just arrived from Switzerland to become a soldier, eh? Come along, I'll show you your barracks.' Five minutes later young Uetzli found himself in a cell at a police station, an hour later at the Salle Lépine in the *Préfecture*, and a week later at Barrack 35 in Le Vernet.

There was also the ex-Buddhist monk from Mongolia who sold postcards of nudes in Montparnasse cafés, and Balogh the Hungarian, who had been commander of a warship on the Danube and a stamp-collector, and who had been invited by King George V to London in 1912 to show his collection. And there was Pacek, the famous agent of the Czech military intelligence, who had learnt the Hungarian language during seven years for a mission in Budapest, and had marched with the German Army to Vienna disguised as a soldier of the Reichswehr, and been twice condemned to death; he alleged that he had been sent to Vernet because of some incautious remarks in the presence of French officers about Daladier's betrayal of the Czechs at Munich, and was released four weeks after myself. There was Dessauer, the ex-rabbi and medical orderly, who wore his wrist watch on the wrist of a prosthesis which replaced his right arm; at night the prosthesis with the watch hung on a nail over his place in Barrack 33, and whoever wanted to know the time took Dessauer's arm and carried it to the oil lamp next to the entrance. And there was Herr Birn, a German business man who had spent the four years of the First World War as a civilian prisoner in England and had learnt all the variants of the Italian opening by heart from the chess book and now, interned for a second time, learnt with the same German thoroughness the variants of the Queen's Gambit; and yet, when it came to playing, lost every game within twenty moves. And there was Negro, the black Alsatian dog, which had followed the Internationals everywhere, from the Battle of Brihuega to the Leper Barrack; and Jacob, the tame jackdaw, whom they had acquired at the camp of Gurs and which had a predilection for stealing Birn's chess men, but only the white ones.

All these odd figures, and many others, were a sort of Byzantine arabesque against the grey background of misery. They reminded me sometimes of the grotesque dancers wearing masks and distorting their limbs, who used to accompany the funeral processions of the Greeks.

XIV

Our chief preoccupation, pastime, and obsession was, of course, the weighing of our chances of release. In fact, there seemed no hope at all. For the Austrians and Germans in 'normal camps' a sort of Advisory Committee had been instituted and a considerable proportion of them were released. But Vernet seemed surrounded by an iron curtain.

We were the outcasts amongst the internees, the untouchables.

Our friends and relations in Paris wrote despairing letters. For weeks on end they had not even been able to discover which authority they should approach on our behalf. The *Préfecture de Police* alleged it was the *Sûreté Nationale,* the *Sûreté* alleged it was the 'Military Authorities'; the Military Authorities, if they succeeded in approaching them, sent them back to the *Préfecture*. The French administration was in those days already in a state of disintegration; a few months later it was to collapse in a cloud of dust.

While I was still in the coal-cellar of the *Préfecture,* David Scott, Paris correspondent of the *News Chronicle,* began to make inquiries about the reasons for my arrest. He approached a responsible official at police headquarters, who looked up my *dossier*. 'Monsieur K. has been interned because he is a German national,' said the official. 'He is not,' said Scott. 'He is a Hungarian.' 'That's what you think,' said the official with a superior smile. 'Have you seen his passport?' Of course, Scott had not seen it—one does not as a rule ask one's acquaintances for their passports. And, even had he asked me for it, I could not have produced it at that moment, as the passport in question, issued by the Hungarian Legation in London, was to be found in the *dossier* on the official's table.

It was plain sabotage and it was the same in all other Government departments. The war had at last provided the bureaucracy with an outlet for their traditional xenophobia; but in our case there was an additional motive involved. The bureaucracy was pro-Bonnet and pro-Munich and, although not consciously pro-Hitler, it had to all intents and purposes a Fascist outlook. They hated the war and they hated all the refugee warmongers, who in their opinion had dragged peaceful France into this ordeal.

The German radio in its French broadcasts efficiently exploited this feeling. 'The French people do not want to fight; they are the unconscious tools of British Imperialists, refugees and Jews,' psalmodised Radio Stuttgart; and in the murky *cabinets* of the French Ministries an inaudible chorus sighed an inaudible 'Amen'.

Echoes of Radio Stuttgart's famous Thursday talks even reached our camp. Newcomers from Paris transmitted to us Goebbels' ironic congratulations on our cordial reception in the Land of Freedom. *Voelkischer Beobachter*, the official Nazi organ, published a list of anti-Nazi authors interned in France, asking them whether they still clung to the blessings of democracy. It was cheap irony, but it cut to the quick; it stung and burnt.

Fainter echoes also reached us of the campaign which the British and American Press had started against the scandal of the French camps. A smuggled cutting from the *New Statesman* or the *Manchester Guardian* was a great event and something like a soothing lullaby from the far, far-away shores where men still lived in a state of relative decency.

To try to prove the innocence of a prisoner in Le Vernet was to run one's head against a wall. Most of us had been arrested on September 1st, 1939; in January, 1940, it was still impossible to say whether our cases would be examined and by whom. In fact there was no responsible body to address. Petitions and protests remained without answer. I have seen copies of the correspondence between Politis, the Greek Minister Plenipotentiary, and the French authorities, on behalf of T., a very well-known Greek journalist and the Minister's personal friend, interned God knows why in Barrack 33. Politis had first approached the Quai d'Orsay on T.'s behalf and was, of course, promised that the case would be investigated at once. After the matter had dragged on for three months, he got fed up and wrote directly to M. Langeron, the *Préfet* of Paris, including a personal guarantee for his friend, cast in the most flattering terms. Langeron re-

plied with a syrupy letter saying that he could not do anything about it, and that the only advice he could give was to
write to the *Préfet* of the Départment of Ariège, where Le
Vernet was situated. The Minister Plenipotentiary of
Greece indeed wrote to that obscure provincial *préfet*—
and received a reply saying that his letter had been for-
warded at once to M. Langeron, the *Préfet* of Paris. When
I left Le Vernet, T. was still there.

If not even a Minister could help, who could? The military authorities had an intelligence officer posted in the
camp who in his civilian capacity was a lecturer in Oriental
languages at the University of Toulouse. Captain Nougerolles was a charming man, but he had no influence whatever on the administration of the camp. He used to call Albert or myself to his office under some official pretext—in
fact, because he was deadly bored by Lieutenant Cosne and
his like, and longed for a friendly chat. After Christmas he
showed me the copy of a letter which he had written a
month ago to the Advisory Committee on Albert's and my
behalf, recommending our immediate release—and the reply of the said Committee, declining to have anything to do
with internees in Le Vernet. 'It is the first time,' said Captain N. with resignation, 'that a suggestion from me has
even been answered by Paris.'

'What do you advise us to do, *mon capitaine*?' I asked.

'Well—just carry on with your *pistons*. There is nothing
else.'

The *piston* is a French national institution; it is, as the
name indicates, the part of the machinery which keeps the
whole thing going. If the hopeful young Frenchman has
passed his exams, he needs a *piston* to get into the Civil Service; if he is a young priest, he needs a *piston* in the diocese
to procure him a parish; if he has passed the cadet school,
he needs a *piston* to procure him a commission; if he is an
author, he needs a *piston* to procure him a literary prize.

In other words, the *piston* is a man of influence, who, for money or out of friendship, does the necessary and traditional things, such as writing letters of recommendation, bribing, flattering, blackmailing, and sitting on the plush sofa in the ante-room of the Minister's *chef de cabinet*, until the goal is achieved and the hopeful young man has got the coveted job as Junior Assistant in the Administration of Taxes and Customs with a salary of 9s. a week.

The intellectuals amongst us all had their *pistons* in Paris, but the great anonymous majority had nobody. And as not even the most powerful *pistons*, including foreign diplomats, the P.E.N. Club, the Foreign Press Association, the League of the Rights of Man, and many others, could break the resistance of the hostile bureaucracy, how could there be any hope for them? The *dossiers* of Le Vernet were never opened—until the Gestapo came and opened them.

In the first days of January, 1940, a sensational bit of news went through the camp : the Italian Consul from Marseilles had arrived at Le Vernet, to get in touch with those amongst the Italian internees who wished to place themselves under the protection of the Fascist Government.

January, 1940, was still the heyday of Italian non-belligerency, and as far as one could still talk of a French foreign policy in Europe, it was appeasement of the Duce. The Italian Consul was the first person from the outside world allowed to enter our taboo camp. There were about three hundred Italian internees in the camp, and out of these fifteen accepted the Fascist Government's protection. The other 95 per cent. preferred the rotting straw and forced labour of Le Vernet.

Each of the fifteen had a personal interview with the Consul, who made minute notes of the conditions in the camp, and promised them that within a fortnight they would be released and allowed to return to their country. He kept his word. By the middle of January, the fifteen men had been released and escorted to the frontier. Most of them were of military age; I presume that they were amongst the few in the Italian Army who felt a genuine enthusiasm when, five months later, they marched against France.

The first person to be released after the bunch of Italian Fascists was I. I am almost ashamed to say so; my excuse is the fact that I was the only person in the camp who, though not a British subject, had some backing in this country. A few days before I left Vernet, the *Voelkischer Beobachter* had published an article on the French concentration camps and had ironically asked whether the English friends who had obtained my release from Franco's jail would do the same thing for me now. They did.

It happened all of a sudden. At 3 p.m. on January 17th I was still emptying the latrine-bins of Section C, without knowing anything; at 7 p.m. on the same day I was sitting alone in a second-class compartment of the train to Paris, sucking a bottle of Courvoisier brandy, eating an enormous piece of garlic sausage, and from time to time touching the door handle and the window pane to convince myself that it was a real door handle and a real window pane.

The last weeks in Vernet had been the worst.

In the first days of January, all men who had been exempted from work by the departed *sous-lieutenant* were ordered to pass a second medical examination. The control was carried out by the lieutenant, who, hardly looking up from his files, crossed out one by one his younger colleague's 'Unfit for work' or 'Unfit for heavy work', and replaced them by 'Fit for every kind of work', written by his own hand in red ink. The next morning I was detached to the *corvée de tinette*, the latrine-emptiers' squad.

Our work consisted in collecting the latrine-bins of Section C and of the gendarmes' quarters outside the camp.

Each squad was composed of twelve men and had to deal with about twenty bins. The contents of these twenty bins were collected in six bins, by means of decanting them into each other. As the handles of some of the bins were broken, they were difficult to manipulate, and it required a special technique to avoid the contents splashing over one's clothes. Each of the six full bins weighed from 60 to 70 lb. and was carried by two men across the camp to a narrow-gauge railway. The bins were loaded on to the trucks, and the trucks were pushed to the bank of the River Ariège, about half a mile outside the camp. The contents were emptied into a large open hole next to the river, the exhalations of which could be smelled at a distance, varying with wind and weather, from a hundred yards to a mile. Then the empty bins were carried down a slope, slippery with ice or mud, to be scrubbed in the river. When the river was frozen we had first to break a hole in the ice. Then the bins were carried back up the slope to the trucks, the trucks pushed back to the camp, the bins carried back to the latrines. The only protection against infections was to wash one's hands in cold water after work; the repeated epidemics of dysentery were an inevitable consequence of this sanitary system.

The operation was repeated twice a day. On the first two occasions I was sick; later I became accustomed to it. Sometimes Jacob, the jackdaw, made the journey to the river with us, perching on top of a latrine-bin and looking at the men who pushed the truck with glittering eyes full of black irony; sometimes Negro, the dog, accompanied us too; sometimes, on the backward journey, we sang the Song of the Latrine Squad, which combined a beautifully sad melody with an utterly unprintable text.

I could possibly have obtained permission to return to navvy work. But the Latrine Squad had only to work one hour in the morning, one in the afternoon, while the navvies, stone-breakers and road builders had to work six. In my present occupation I was quit for two hours of nausea a day. And for this very reason the Latrine Squad was the most coveted form of work in the camp. This filthiest and most degrading labour was a desirable escape from the murderous strain and monotony of the others.

I had been in the Latrine Squad for about a fortnight when, coming back with the empty trucks on January 17th, I was told to report at once to Lieutenant Cosne's office. I thought it was because of the gloves: that morning a gendarme had told me, out of mere chicanery, to take off my gloves while decanting the bins, and I had refused. He had not insisted, but I was convinced that he would report me, and was prepared for the worst. When I came in, Lieutenant Cosne rose and said solemnly:

'I have the pleasure to announce to you that we have just received from the Ministry of the Interior a telegraphic order for your release.' He pressed his left hand against his corset and stretched out the right, after having placed the leather crop on the table. I was so completely taken aback that I actually shook hands with him. I regret it to this very day.

I stumbled out. There stood the Corsican, and his lips moved, but I only stared at him stupidly and he had to repeat twice that Captain Nougerolles wished to see me. When I entered Captain N.'s office, he saw on my face that I knew already, and was very disappointed.

'That man Cosne spoils everything,' he said. And he added, with some melancholy: 'If Albert goes too, I shall die of boredom in this desert.'

At 6 p.m. I stood at the barbed-wire enclosure of Section C. I had said good-bye to all my friends, and the only one left was Mario. There he stood in the dusk, with his cropped convict skull, the nervous twitch which came back at intervals to his face, and his peculiar smile.

Farewell, Mario. He leaned with his back against the wire

of the gate, which in a minute would open for me, but not for him. Good-bye, Mario, comrade and friend. You were nineteen when they put you in jail and twenty-eight when they let you out. You were allowed two years of liberty and you spent those two priceless years, into which your youth was compressed, in working twelve hours a day at the Italian émigré paper's office, and another four hours writing a history of the revolutions of 1848. And when the two years were over and they came for you again, they tore your manuscript to pieces before your eyes and insulted before your eyes the woman with whom you lived and who was pregnant with your child. The child was born while we were still in Paris, but you were not allowed to see it; and it was baptised 'Roland', to commemorate for ever the barbed-wire fence under the sign of which it came into this world.

'Good-bye, Mario,' I said to the dark figure at the fence. 'If I should ever write your life story, I should put as a motto the words : "There was a man in the Land of Uz, whose name was Job, and that man was perfect and upright." '

Mario smiled : ' "After this lived Job an hundred and forty years; and died, being old and full of days." I'll miss you. If I get transferred to the Latrine Squad, I might use the spare time to write an essay on Benedetto Croce's *History of the Nineteenth Century*.'

We embraced, and the Corsican came and opened the gate with his key, and closed it again behind me. How simple it was.

The Corsican accompanied me to the outer enclosure of the camp, and opened the last gate. How very simple it was. Then I stood in the road, alone, my valise in my hand. It was dark, and from time to time a car hurried past, with dim blue headlights, and was swallowed again by the darkness.

I had a last look at the notice-board outside the main entrance gate :

CAMP DU VERNET D'ARIÈGE

When I came to the bend of the road, I could still see through the wire the black barracks of Section C. There they lay in the straw, the Men of Uz of our time, under the burden of their afflictions. But instead of remonstrating with God, Mario was to write an essay on Croce and remonstrate with History. But History will not come back to him and speak out of a whirlwind; Mine eye seeth thee, and bless him with fourteen thousand sheep and a thousand she-asses and ten sons and daughters. And he will not live an hundred and forty years.

XV

A few weeks after me Albert was released and left for Mexico. Pacek was allowed to join the Czech Army; Tschorbatscheff, a Bulgarian whose brother-in-law was a general, and David, a Pole whose father had lots of money, were released, and Tamàs got out in the last hour of the collapse; he too went to Mexico.

But these were exceptions. Perhaps fifty altogether were released; the other two thousand, including Mario, remained in the trap, and the week after the armistice was signed the Gestapo paid its first visit to Le Vernet.

The men responsible for the defeat of France have committed, amongst others, one crime which passed almost unperceived in those chaotic weeks. In American parlance it is called 'putting a man on the spot'.

The French Government has put the two thousand men in Vernet on the spot, together with several tens of thousands of other refugees from political and racial persecution, including those who have served in the ranks of the French Army, the wounded in the hospitals, their women and children. Legally, the crime was consummated when

Philippe Pétain, Marshal of France, accepted paragraph
19 of the Armistice Treaty, providing for the extradition of
political refugees,[1] while his senile lips babbled of an
'honourable soldiers' peace'. But this was only the legal side
of it. Those who prepared the way for Vichy had put these
men in camps, and used them in their propaganda as scapegoats. When English and American public opinion began
to protest, they promised to investigate the cases, but never
did so. For every ignominy they made the prisoners suffer,
they comforted them with the argument that the ignominies
of the Gestapo would be worse; and when the cock had
crowed thrice, they delivered them properly and solemnly
into the Gestapo's hands.

In the days of the French collapse there was plenty of
time to save the prisoners of Vernet from the Germans by
shipping them to North Africa or by simply letting them
escape. They refused. They kept the prisoners in their
barbed-wire trap, to hand them over complete, all accounts
properly made out, all confidential records of their past
(given trustingly to the French authorities) neatly filed.
What a find for Himmler's black-clothed men! Three hundred thousand pounds of democratic flesh, all labelled, alive,
and only slightly damaged.[2]

[1] Theoretically this only applies to German and Austrian nationals;
but who on earth will protect the others, subjects of countries under
direct or indirect Gestapo rule, from meeting with the same
fate?

[2] As this book goes to press, the following two news items were
published by English newspapers:

'The Vichy Government have agreed to hand over to Germany a
number of political and racial refugees who went to France to escape
from the Nazi régime. The Nazis have drawn up lists of the men they
want back.'—*Evening News*, April 10th, 1941.

'Some hundred and fifty people are reported to have been killed
when guards opened fire on mutinous prisoners during the revolt at
the internment camp at Vernet. The camp has been evacuated and the
prisoners transferred to Africa to work on the projected trans-Saharan
Railway.'—*The Star*, April 10th, 1941.

APOCALYPSE

'Where shall the Holy Tabernacle rest?
What land is promised, Lord? I cannot see.
Only the bitter deserts to the north.'

ROBERT NATHAN:
A Winter Tide.

Bᴀᴄᴋ in Paris again, in January 1940.
After the first days of greed and animal pleasure—
food and drink and bath and bed—the paralysing oppres-
siveness of the atmosphere returned. Nothing had changed.
Last autumn France had accomplished a diplomatic formality in proclaiming the state of war, and then quietly gone
to sleep.

Nothing had changed—at least not perceptibly. Mme.
Suchet's husband was still nursing his boils in the Maginot
Line. Mme. Tabouis still explained in *L'Œuvre* that,
according to the latest information in well-informed political
circles in Stockholm, which had reached her through diplomatic channels from Ankara, Hitler had spent a sleepless
night. Laval, Bonnet, Doriot, Luchaire, de Brinon were still
at liberty, and Pétain was still French Ambassador in Madrid, and accepting invitations to dinners at which von
Stohrer, the German Ambassador, was also present. The
best broadcasts in French still came from Radio Stuttgart,
while Radio Paris still provided retired *maîtresses* with old-
age pensions for singing 'Parlez-moi d'amour' and 'Au
temps des cerises'. The French soldier's pay was still $\frac{1}{2}d$. and
his wife's allowance still about 1s. a day, and the theatres,
boîtes, and *restaurants de luxe* were still overcrowded. The
censorship continued to suppress Kerillis's Cassandra-cries
against the traitors in the Ministries, and he still went on
publishing his paper with a blank column over his name in
place of the editorial. The Ministry of Information in the

Hotel Continental was still familiarly called 'The Brothel', the Press was still threshing the straw of Patience, Discipline, and Faith. President Lebrun still opened cattle shows with the looks of an undertaker, four million aliens were still denied gas-masks, Mussolini was still the hope of Democracy, and the *concierge* was still wondering what the war was about.

By the end of 1918, France had lost one and a half million men; up till May, 1940, she had lost less than a thousand. In 1917, the nation nearly bled to death, but survived; in 1940, she was succumbing to a kind of moral anaemia, more deadly than any wound.

The only warlike event during the first three months of 1940 happened north of the Arctic Circle. Practically everybody's sympathies were with the unfortunate Finns, but the manner in which the French Press treated the Finnish War was nauseating. While France gave no help to the Finns except to offer them the scrap iron of her arsenals, and while she watched their death struggle as passively as she had watched the death struggle of the Czechs and Poles, in reading the French Press one got the impression that somehow the successes of the Finns were victories of France. The hysterical Mannerheim cult of the French Press, its delirious cries of triumph at the Russian failures, had the character of what psycho-analysts call 'disguised wish-fulfilment'; the Mannerheim Line stood for the Maginot Line and Russia for Germany—a twofold treat. Altogether, the French attitude to the Finnish War reminded one of the *voyeur* who gets his thrills out of watching other people's manly exploits. And when, on March 13th, the Finns were forced to sign Molotov's *diktat* treaty, some of the French papers were shameless enough to accuse them of cowardice.

After Finland the French Chamber of Deputies asked for Daladier's head. The terrible malaise which lay over France found its expression in the way the Chamber made him go. The majority did not vote against him—they just made him go by abstaining from voting. And when Reynaud took the succession, they received him in the same way: about 200 abstentions and a majority of two voices out of a total of 500. The *abstentionisme* of the Chamber was intended as a subtle parliamentary manœuvre; in fact it was a declaration of irresponsibility, an unconscious expression of their resentment, not so much against Daladier or Reynaud, as against the war in general. Reynaud, that miniature Tartar, who looked as if somewhere a pocket-sized dynamo were hidden inside him, which made him jerk and vibrate with energy, could possibly have saved France had he come a few years earlier. Now it was too late. Three weeks after he presented his Cabinet to a Chamber frozen with hostility, Norway was invaded; and another four weeks later the hour of the French apocalypse had come.

II

On my departure from the concentration camp, I was given a scrap of paper saying that *le nommé* A. K. had been released from the Camp of Vernet for Undesirable Aliens on the order of the Ministry of the Interior and was to present himself at the police station of the XVth Arrondissement on his arrival in Paris. *Le nommé* A. K. would not be under escort.

The day after my arrival I went to the police station, where I was told that I had to go to the *Préfecture* in order to get my *carte d'identité* extended, which had expired during my stay in Vernet. The *carte d'identité*, corresponding to the British Aliens Registration Book, is the most precious possession of foreigners in France. Without it he is outside the law.

Next day, I went to the *Préfecture*. After queueing up for an hour at the window which dealt with these matters, they told me that before my *carte* could be renewed I had to get a *cachet de déconcentration*—a stamp certifying that I had been properly released from a concentration camp. Would I go to room No. 34 on the fourth floor to get the stamp, and then come back.

I went to No. 34 on the fourth floor—and from the moment that I entered that room a chapter in my life began which could have been written by P. G. Wodehouse if it had not been at the same time so nightmarish and nerve-racking. It is an idiotic story, almost incredible and entirely typical of conditions in France in the last three months before the collapse.

The official to whom I spoke in room No. 34 was a rather nice young man. He did not at first look thoroughly at my papers and had already picked up the magic rubber stamp, when his glance fell on the words: Nationality: Hungarian.

'But you are a neutral,' he said in astonishment. 'How on earth could they have sent you to a camp?'

'I come from Le Vernet,' I said.

It must be borne in mind that I was the first 'political suspect' to be released unconditionally from Vernet.

'That is different,' said the man in an entirely changed tone. 'We only have instructions to deal with enemy aliens released from ordinary camps. I have to ask the *chef* for instructions.'

He knocked at the door of the adjoining room, the *cabinet du chef*. I heard an asthmatic '*Entrez*' and he disappeared into the room, leaving the door ajar. I did not hear what he said, but I heard the cracked voice call out indignantly:

'Vernet, you say? *Incroyable!* I'll see to that.'

And then he spoke into a telephone. I only heard fragments of the conversation:

'. . . *Oui, mon pauvre ami*, they have begun to release people from Vernet. Can you beat that?'

. . . . .

'. . . Order of the Ministry of the Interior. Probably through bribery.'

. . . . .

'. . . Quite. I'll see that he is clapped into jail again as soon as possible.'

. . . . .

'Quite. I'll pass him on to the *Éloignement*.'

The *Département de l'Éloignement des Étrangers* dealt with the deportation cases.

. . . . .

'. . . Quite. Alas! *mon cher*, alas! *Au revoir, cher ami.*'

The official came back shrugging his shoulders.

'Listen,' I said to him. 'I have heard what your *chef* said. Let me talk to him and straighten matters out.'

'Impossible.'

I tried to convince him. I showed him my Press card and letters from several 'influential persons'. I had already got into the humiliating habit of carrying them on me. Finally, he knocked once more at the door of the *chef*. Once more, the cracked, bellowing voice, and the young official came back with a flushed face. 'Impossible! You have to go to the *Éloignement.*'

The *Éloignement* was on the fifth floor. As, owing to the war, it was practically impossible to deport a man, the French bureaucracy had invented a new, refined form of torture, called '*le régime des sursis*'. It consisted in refusing a man the authorisation to stay in Frence—*refus de séjour*, equivalent to an expulsion order—and granting him only short-term '*sursis*', i.e. reprieves. Every time the *sursis* expired, he was liable to be put in jail or a concentration camp.

On that day the *Éloignement* gave me a reprieve of twenty-four hours.

When that expired they gave me five days.

After the five days, they gave me forty-eight hours.

After that, they gave me a month.

Then again forty-eight hours. Then a week; then twenty-four hours; and so on for four months, until they arrested me again, when the Germans were within fifty miles of Paris. Each time one had to come to the *Éloignement*, one had to wait in the ante-room for seven to eight hours—from nine in the morning to four or five in the afternoon. It was just a little additional torture. Every time I went there, I wondered whether I would be allowed to leave the building or be sent down to the coal-cellar again. On the first few occasions, G. accompanied me, later she waited for me at my flat, wondering whether I would return or not. The big, blue 'E' ('*Éloignement*'), which was stamped on my papers with every new *sursis*, marked one as a sort of convict on leave. Again I slept every night with my suitcase packed and the clock set at the danger hour. All night the letter E hung invisibly suspended over my bed.

I was not the only one with whom the bureaucracy played this cat-and-mouse game. During those long hours of boredom and deadly anxiety in the ante-room of the *Département E* I could once more watch the parade of the wretched of the earth, the funeral procession of European freedom. I met people whom I had not seen for years : an architect, with whom I used to play chess in the Café Central in Vienna, a doctor whom I had consulted in Prague, and Rubio Hidalgo, with his green spectacles, whom I had last met in 1937 in Valencia, when he was still director of the Press Department of the Spanish Ministry for Foreign Affairs. The scum of the earth. . . .

Most of my time during those last four months in France I spent in desperate efforts to get my situation straightened

out. I was obsessed by the fear of being sent back to Vernet
—not so much because of what it was like, but because I felt
that France was doomed, and that the French concentration
camps would become as many death-traps. By the beginning
of March I received a warning from a Somebody who knew
a Somebody at the police that I would be arrested again at
the next round-up. On March 12th, my flat was raided by
detectives, who turned everything upside down and carried
away half my manuscripts and books, but did not ask me a
single question. And that was the most exasperating, the
really maddening thing about it all: I had been arrested
without any explanation, and let out after four months without any explanation, and all that time had never been
properly questioned, never given a chance of defending myself against an accusation the nature of which I did not
know. It was like struggling for a foothold in a morass which
gave way at every step, until you suffocated in the mud.

When I had received that warning, I obtained a letter of
recommendation from a former Cabinet Minister to M.
Lambert, *adjoint du préfet de la Seine*—the right-hand man
of the almighty Police Chief of Paris. When I was shown into his office on March 7th, he was reading *Le Temps*, which
on that day had published a review of the French translation of my book *Spanish Testament*. M. Lambert was very
affable:

'*Mais c'est ridicule ce qu'on vous embête chez nous!*' he
exclaimed when I had told him my story. 'It must have been
some idiotic mistake of a subaltern to treat a man of your
merit in this way. I'll see to that at once.'

He went to the adjoining room and spoke into the telephone. Then he came back.

'I have spoken to Monsieur Louit, the *chef du département des renseignements généraux*,[1] he said. 'Louit will
be very pleased to see you in twenty minutes. He just wants

[1] Intelligence Department of the Aliens Branch.

to glance at your *dossier*. In half an hour from now all your worries will be over. *Au revoir, cher monsieur*. Delighted to have met you.'

G. was waiting for me in the *bistro* at the corner. I ran down the staircase, jumping three steps at a time and almost breaking my neck, to tell her the marvellous news. We had a Pernod and then I went to see M. Louit.

'Monsieur Louit is busy—he cannot see anybody,' said the usher in M. Louit's ante-room.

'But he is expecting me. Monsieur Lambert has just spoken to him on the telephone.'

The attendant went in, grumbling. He came back after a minute. 'Monsieur Louit is busy. Wait if you like, but you might have to wait very long.'

I waited for an hour and a half. Then a slimy little secretary came out and asked me what I wanted.

I explained to him. He went back into the room. He came out of the room.

'Monsieur Louit is very busy. Cannot see anybody. But he promised to look at your *dossier*.'

So that was that. Five days later my flat was raided and the *Éloignement* gave me again forty-eight hours. I tried several times to see M. Louit; he was always busy. I tried to see M. Lambert once—his secretary told me that he was not in the office, but I heard his voice from the next room. Then I gave it up.

I met Mrs. Vandervelde, the widow of Emil Vandervelde, the Belgian ex-Premier, whom I had known in Brussels. '*Mais c'est grotesque*,' she said, 'the French have all gone mad. Why don't you go and see Léon Blum about it?'

I had never met Blum, but, in spite of his disastrous Spanish policy, I had a great admiration for his personal integrity. I would never have dreamt of pestering him with my private affairs, but now the water was up to my neck, and Mrs. Vandervelde persuaded me that it would be a matter of principle for Blum to intervene in such a revolting case of political persecution. So I went round to Blum's house on the Ile Saint-Louis. There was a bodyguard of young members of the Socialist Party posted at the staircase —the rowdies of the *Action Française* had attempted one or two assaults on him, and the severe censorship which cut out Kerillis's attacks on the Nazi Fifth Column in France had no objection to *Gringoire*'s pogrom campaign against the Socialist leader.

Blum could not receive me—he was in bed and conferring with members of the Party Executive—but when his secretary had explained my case to him, he at once rang up M. Combe, the chief of the Aliens Department in the *Sûreté Nationale*. The door was left ajar, and I heard him speaking on the telephone. He gave a short and concise account of my case, expressed his thanks for what must have been a promise from the other end, and then the secretary came back and told me to take a taxi to the *Sûreté Nationale*. Combe would receive me at once.

I went to the *Sûreté* and sent in my card to M. Combe. After about half an hour a little man with a nutcracker face came out and said:

'President Combe is very busy. So am I. What do you want?'

I told him I was recommended to M. Combe by Léon Blum.

The manikin looked down at his hands. He was cleaning the dirt under the nails of his left hand with the pointed fingernail of his right hand:

'I know that. *Enfin*, what do you want?'

This time I lost my temper. I told him that all I wanted was to come at last face to face with the responsible person who would tell me for what crime I was being persecuted, cross-examine me if necessary, charge me if there was a charge, and discharge me if there was none; that this was the procedure in any civilised country; that to release a man because there was obviously no case for his detention, and then go on persecuting him, was contrary to the law, arbitrary, and infamous; and so on.

All the time I spoke, the manikin kept on cleaning his nails, with his eyes fixed on the operation. When I had finished, he said:

'This is all very regrettable, but it concerns the *Préfecture* and not us. *Au revoir, monsieur.*'

Once I almost believed to have at last found firm ground in the bureaucratic morass. I had obtained an interview with one of the unapproachable M. Louit's assistants, Detective-inspector Benoit, who promised to start a *contre-enquête*—a re-examination of my file—in order to obtain my complete rehabilitation. He took a very sympathetic attitude. In fact, he said, the *contre-enquête* was a mere formality, as there was, of course, nothing serious against me, but it might take three or four weeks until it was definitely settled. So there was 'nothing serious'. But what *was* there against me? —Oh, really nothing. By the way, had I not some friends amongst the German *émigrés*?—Of course I had.—Did I know Lion Feuchtwanger and Heinrich Mann and X. and Y. and Z.?—Of course I did.—Then I certainly knew that some of them were very likely to be stood up against a wall within the next few days?—No, that I did not know; but I had the funny feeling that under my hair my scalp became moist with perspiration.—And that I myself had had a very narrow escape from falling under the same suspicion and sharing the same fate?—No. I hadn't known that either. What suspicion, for heaven's sake?—Never mind, he said amiably. I might consider myself a lucky man to be so unaware of my own dangerous position. But of course, once the *contre-enquête* finished, the danger would be over for me. Anyhow, he would see to that.

Then he became even more amiable and talked about himself. How thoroughly fed-up he was with his job, with the stink of denunciations and counter-denunciations he had to deal with; some time he would retire to a quiet little spot in the country and write his memoirs. It must be interesting to be a writer and be in touch with so many thrilling people. Had I read X.'s latest book? What was my impression of him? No, not of his literary qualities, but what I thought of him as a person, of his political opinions, of what he lived on, etcetera. And Y? And Z?

While we talked, Inspector Benoit was lounging non-chalantly against the edge of the table, smoking cigarettes, smiling and looking straight into my eyes. He led the conversation on so brilliantly, that it took me quite a while until I realised what he was up to. He did not propose to me openly to become an informer, and the shorter and more reluctant my answers were, the more amiable and chatty he became. He reminded one of a jovial doctor trying to make a child swallow a laxative in a chocolate pill, and actually I told him that. He raised both his short arms in vehement protest, but his eloquence had gone and a few minutes later he brought the interview to an abrupt end. On taking leave, I asked him whether the *contre-enquête* could not be speeded up. 'Oh yes, the *contre-enquête*,' he said. 'You had better write me a detailed *curriculum vitæ*.'

I guessed that it was useless, that his hint about a mysterious suspicion and being stood up against a wall was bunk, as well as his promise to obtain my rehabilitation, but I nevertheless wrote the *curriculum vitæ* and brought it to his office the next day. From his surprised face I gathered that he had completely forgotten about it.

When the delay of three weeks was over, I went to see him as agreed. I tried several times, but whenever I sent my card

in he was too busy or had just gone out. I never heard of him
or of the *contre-enquête* again.

Finland was defeated, Denmark and Norway invaded,
and while the night began to descend over France, I was
still busy struggling against my own particular nightmare.
It had a strange resemblance to Kafka's novel, *The Trial*—
that dream-like allegory of a man who, having received a
mysterious summons to attend his 'trial', strives and
struggles in vain to find out where the trial would be held
and what it would be about; wherever he inquires he re-
ceives non-committal, elusive replies, as if everybody had
joined in a secret conspiracy; the closer he seems to get to
his aim, the farther it recedes, like the transparent walls of
a dream. The High Court which Kafka's hero is unable to
find is presumably his own conscience; but what was the
symbolical meaning of all these nut-cracker-faced, nail-
biting, pimpled, slimy figures, spinning their spider webs of
intrigue and sabotage in the bureaux of the French administration?

The answer came three months later, when the Louits
and Benoits, the nut-crackers and pimple-faces, crawled on
their bellies before the victor and crawled back to their mil-
dewy cabinets and bureaux to go on spinning the same web
under a different name; for this time it was called the
National Revolution of France.

In between I finished *Darkness at Noon,* the novel on
which I had been working at Roquebillière. The feeling of
doom, regarding the fate of France and my personal fate,
had by now got such a hold on me that I no longer cared for
anything except for G. and for finishing the book. I knew
that I was working against time. The manuscript was
eventually despatched to my English publishers on May 1st
—just ten days before the invasion started. We celebrated

the event with a few friends and got happily drunk; the work was done, *après nous le déluge*.

The nightmare in which G. and I lived had its grotesque aspects. A few days after the raid on my flat, the doorbell rang again at the critical time, at 7.30 in the morning. Again I was just having my bath; again, when I called out, the answer was : '*Préfecture de Police*.' But it was followed by the unexpected remark : 'Take your time. There is no need to hurry.'

I opened the door and in came our friend M. Pétetin, Fernand, the detective who had arrested me six months before in October, 1939. The pimples on his face were as flourishing as ever, but he stepped into the room in a curiously timid way, as if not sure of himself. After some preliminaries, it turned out that M. Pétetin had seen a book of mine in a shop window—a very nice-looking book indeed, but rather expensive to buy; and that Mme. Pétetin happened to have her birthday tomorrow; so M. Pétetin had thought that perhaps . . . As we were, so to speak, old acquaintances . . .

I told him it would be a pleasure for me. 'How lucky,' I added, 'that your colleagues left me a copy when they took away half my library last week.'

'Did they? Oh, the rascals,' remarked M. Pétetin indignantly. Then he asked me to write a dedication to him into the book. I objected that this might spoil its value as a birthday present, but he said no, Madame would love it. So I wrote : 'To Monsieur Pétetin, Fernand—souvenir of our first meeting on a misty October morning,' and he said it was very nice and *poétique*.

On taking leave, I told him that his coming to see me was a charming idea—but could he explain to me why on earth it had to be so early in the morning?

M. Pétetin's pimples went red like baby radishes :

'You see,' he explained, 'for ordinary people like you it is perhaps an unusual hour—but we have got into the habit of calling at seven o'clock if we want to be sure that the bloke is at home.'

The colleagues of M. Pétetin who had searched my flat had also behaved rather oddly in their selection of 'suspect material'. They took away the second volume of *Crime and Punishment*, possibly in the belief that Dostoievsky was a Bolshevik; Rauschning's *Hitler m'a dit*, an illustrated volume called *Histoire de l'Érotisme en Europe*, Chalmers-Mitchell's *My House in Malaga*, and a bunch of anti-Nazi pamphlets.

That was the grotesque side of it. But they also took away the collection of articles I had published from the age of twenty—the results of fifteen years of journalistic work—and the only typescript copy of an unpublished book on my travels through Soviet Central Asia, and to the Arctic on board the *Graf Zeppelin*. In ordinary times these losses would have driven me mad—now I hardly cared at all. Both G. and I lived in a state of apocalyptic *je m'en foutisme*.

By and by the normal activities of life seemed to come to a standstill around us. First the central heating in the house broke down, then the hot water, then the lift. It was a modern block of flats. Some of the tenants were foreigners and put in concentration camps; most of the others mobilised and neither paid the rent; so the proprietor did not care for repairs. Poor Theodore had been immobilised long ago and stood flat-footed in a corner of the garage, in a pool of oily water on the concrete floor. Next the telephone was cut off, just on the day after the invasion began; I had not paid the bill since my first arrest and now it had run up to an astronomical figure. And what was the use of it, anyhow? The friends for whom I cared were mostly gone, and for days on end the bell remained silent. Car, lift, water, heating, telephone—it was like *rigor mortis* slowly gaining one limb after another.

I had known that feeling of doom before—in Malaga, Spain, before the town fell into the enemy's hands. The last days of Pompeii. And now one had to live through it all over again, but this time in Paris and in May; as if the dark powers of history had chosen on purpose the loveliest season, and the loveliest town on this planet, to demonstrate their superiority over the powers of light.

III

'. . . *All this destruction is carried out without one's perceiving a living soul. For these insects which are blind, are endowed with the genius to accomplish their task without being seen. The work is done under the cover of silence and only an alert ear is able to recognise the noise of the nibbling of millions of jaws in the night, which devour the framework of the building and prepare its collapse. . . .*

'*Nothing is safe from their depredations, which have something frightening and supernatural about them, as they are carried out in secret and only reveal themselves in the moment of the disaster. . . . Huge trees, apparently in the vigour of life and the bark of which has been scrupulously left intact, crash to the ground when touched. . . . A planter enters his house after an absence of five or six days; everything is apparently as he left it, nothing seems changed. He sits down on a chair, it collapses. He grabs the table to regain his balance, it falls to pieces under his hands. He leans against the central pillar, which gives way and brings down the roof in a cloud of dust.*'

When it happened, I was just reading Maeterlinck's *Life of the Termites*, from which these lines are quoted; I found them an uncannily perfect allegory of the way everything collapsed around us.

The invasion had started on a Friday, May 10th; the following Tuesday morning I had an appointment with Professor Joliot-Curie at the Sorbonne. In the Métro I had been reading Kerillis's leader in the *Époque*; there was a sentence in it which said approximately :

'The spirit of the heroic days of 1916 has returned; yesterday, in reconquering an outer fort of Sedan, our troops have shown a bravery worthy of the glorious days of Douaumont.' I had to get out and left the paper in the train.

'What is the matter with you?' asked Joliot when I came in. 'They are at Sedan.' 'Sedan? You are dreaming. Where on earth did you pick up that *bobard*?' 'Kerillis says so in his article this morning. You know he always gives hints about the real situation in a roundabout way to dodge the censorship.' 'But what exactly does he say?' 'That yesterday we have *reconquered* a fort of Sedan with a bravery worthy of the days of Verdun.' Joliot smiled. 'You have got it all muddled up. He mentioned Sedan as a reminiscence of the war of 1870. I did not know you were such a *paniquard*.'

I felt ashamed and reassured. It was the fifth day since the German offensive had begun and all we knew—we, the French public who read the communiqués and listened to the wireless—was that all went relatively well : the Germans had succeeded in establishing a 'pocket' round Maastricht and advanced somewhat in Holland, but most of the parachutists they had dropped there had been mopped up, and the French motorised cavalry was advancing in the Belgian Ardennes; there was also another 'pocket' somewhere round Longwy, but it was going to be rapidly reduced. All this might, of course, be mere optimistic eyewash, but then Joliot worked in close touch with the War Ministry and he would know. Certainly I must have got that allusion to Sedan mixed up.

When I left Joliot-Curie's laboratory, *Paris-Midi* was just
out. The front page said: 'WE HAVE EVACUATED SEDAN.'

That was the moment when the chair under us broke
down. What came after was just staggering and swaying
about in a collapsing house, where everything you tried to
hold on to turned into a handful of dust under your touch.
Looking back on the week that followed, it all seems a confused, suffocating dream, but without the dreamer's secret
consolation that it depends on his own will to wake up. The
weeks before and after form in my memory a tragic chain,
but those days of the Apocalypse are shuffled together in a
whirling kaleidoscope, without order and sequence, with
only fragments of lurid shape and colour bubbling up in the
grey matter where remembrance is housed.

Reynaud's funereal voice on the loudspeaker: 'As a result of incredible mistakes, which will be punished, the
bridges over the Meuse have not been destroyed. Over these
bridges the German armoured divisions have passed. . . .'

Gamelin's order: 'Death before retreat'; and the retreat
to the Aisne on the same day. . . .

The muddy cars of the refugees from the north—mattresses on top, bicycles on the running-board, bulging with
exhausted people—crossing Paris like a swarm of birds on
their flight from a hurricane; and the people in the streets
staring at them. . . .

The flat-footed waiter from our *bistro*, who had been
mobilised in March, strolling along the boulevard Sébastopol in creased civilian clothes. 'I thought you were at the
front?' 'The front is where the lieutenant is. The lieutenant
has beaten it in his car, so there is no more front for me.' 'But
they will shoot you as a deserter.' 'First they'll have to find
me. And in another week they'll have to shoot half the
Army. Remains to be seen whether the other half is willing to
do it. . . .'

Dinner with André Malraux (or was that some weeks be-

M

fore?). He had volunteered for the *Corps Franc*. '*Si tout est foutu, reste à mourir avec le prolétariat.*' They refused his application; he volunteered for the Tank Corps and eventually got into it. . . .

The avalanche of *bobards*: 'Parachutists land in the Place de la Madeleine.' 'Three children die of poisoned chocolates dropped by the Germans in Belleville.' 'Gamelin has shot himself.' 'Arras was taken by parachutists descending at night from the sky with flaming torches in their hands.' . . .

A smuggled S O S letter from B., the German author of European fame, interned in Roland Garros, to his wife Vera: 'They have taken my strychnine. It was my only protection from the Gestapo. I felt safe and calm as long as it was in my pocket. They have robbed me of the last safeguard of my freedom and dignity.' Vera's visit. She has got hold of a dose of cyanide of potassium from a photographer, and asks me for an introduction to Comte de N., the commandant of Roland Garros. Yes, I can have half of the dose. In her hotel room we decant the yellow powder into two empty aspirin tubes and seal them with candle wax to protect the powder against oxidisation. Vera is frightened of handling the stuff and puts gloves on. In between the radio: the Germans have reached Saint-Quentin and Laon. . . .

Meeting Denise in tears. She had been for fifteen years secretary to Mme. Duprès, a member of Paris society. Last night Mme. Duprès had left for her brother's château at Tours, after giving the sack to her staff: Denise; Thérèse, the cook (fifteen years of service); Marie, the maid (twelve years of service); leaving them a bundle of old evening clothes and one week's wages. . . .

Vera's report of her interview with the Comte de N., who has refused to hand the stuff to B.: '*Quel enfantillage*, Madame. Your husband, as a former officer, should be ashamed to go around with a dose of poison in his pocket.'

'Do you know what happened to the interned German refugees in Belgium and Holland?' 'France is not Belgium or Holland. One should not believe this defeatist talk, Madame.' Next day Vera succeeds in getting the tube with the cyanide smuggled to B. in a piece of cheese. B.'s letter to her : 'Thank God I have received the aspirin you sent me. Now I don't care whatever happens. I am a happy man.'

Bubbles, bubbles, bubbling up in the sore regions of grey matter where remembrance dwells. . . .

The cheerful voice of a young French woman journalist, stopping her car laden with brand-new suitcases on her way out of Paris : 'You still here? They are expected to come in tonight.' . . .

Tea at the P.E.N. Club. Trying to persuade Henri Membré, secretary to the French section, to make a last effort to save Tamàs and Mario from Vernet. Membré's son is with the French Army in Belgium, if still alive; the last news was a telegram from Charleroi, where M. himself had been wounded in 1914. In spite of all this, he still carries on with his efforts to save interned writers—trying to pick needles out of the burning haystack. . . .

Meeting Lieutenant N., in civil life a painter, wounded, left arm paralysed. 'The extended Maginot Line? Never existed. Some blockhouses, that's all.' 'But for years you have known that Hitler has adapted the Schlieffen Plan and that the attack will come through Belgium.' 'So what? To know is one thing, to act another.' 'Even so, since the war began we have had nine months' time to build the extension.' 'You don't say. Suppose they didn't care to. Suppose they didn't want to.' 'Who are *they*?' 'I don't know. I know as much as you do. But suppose I didn't meet one officer— from colonel upwards I mean—whose heart was not with the *Croix de Feu*. Suppose some of the gentlemen in the General Staff preferred Hitler to Blum?' 'You don't mean conscious betrayal?' 'Man—don't you understand : *I don't know.* I only know what I saw. For instance, that the pioneer battalions who were supposed to fortify the Longwy-Montmédy sector had been rotting there since November and never worked more than two hours a day.' 'Why?' 'Ask the General Staff. Sometimes there were no spades and sometimes concrete was short. There is always a reason for everything.' ...

Abbéville gone. The Germans reach the Channel. Boulogne gone. The narrow wedge of steel which pierced right through the body of France until it came out the other side, twisting round in the wound, enlarging the hole, crushing the country's flesh. And again Reynaud's macabre voice on the radio : 'If I were told that only a miracle can save France, I would believe in that miracle. *France cannot perish.*' ...

The onslaught on the railway stations. The disappearance of the buses and taxis. The melting away of the town, as if infected with consumption. The tommy-guns of the *flics* at the street corners. The peculiar glance of the people in the Underground, with the dim candles of fear lit behind their eyeballs.

The parachutist scare. The Fifth Column psychosis. The last round-up—and the long-expected, dreaded ring at the door-bell one morning at seven o'clock. The snap of the lock of the old valise from Vernet. The last glance at the flat— the remaining books, the curtains, the desk—knowing this time it would be really the last. And G., staring after me from the top of the staircase with a frozen, chalky face, as if going to be sick.

IV

Once more the wooden benches in the guard-room of the police station. Exit Jekyll, enter Hyde.

About thirty men were sitting on the benches, all Austrians

and Germans between fifty-five and eighty. It was the last round-up. All those who had been released last winter from the internment camps for Germans had been arrested again a week ago, including the women. The only men left were the ones over the age of fifty-five and the invalids; and now their turn too had come. This time the administrative pogrom was complete. The sick were dragged out of their beds; several of them died during the next few days. The leaders of the anti-Nazi movement, men of European reputation: Heinrich Mann, Lion Feuchtwanger, Willi Muenzenberg, Walter Hasenclever, Ernst Weiss, Carl Einstein, Walter Benjamin—nobody was spared. Of the seven names mentioned, the first two managed to escape; the other five committed suicide.[1]

We sat there from 7.30 in the morning until 3.30 in the afternoon. We were not allowed to move from the benches, nor to get anything to eat. At 3.30 we were packed into a police van. I thought we would be taken to the Salle Lépine, but the car went down the rue de Vaugirard and then followed the *boulevards extérieures*. 'Where are we going?' somebody ventured to ask one of the hostile *flics*. 'Stade Buffalo. There are some nice machine guns there; before the Boches come in, we will stand you all against the wall.'

By this time I was half drunk. For the last three months a bottle of Courvoisier had been packed in my suitcase as an iron ration for this occasion; it lay next to Vera's stuff, at the bottom of the suitcase. During those five hours on the bench of the police station I had discussed with my neighbour, hunchbacked Dr. Pollak, the question which obsessed the minds of all of us: whether the French would be quicker in sending us away from Paris or the Germans in marching in. I tried to convince him that the Germans would stick to their rule: one thing at a time, and first annihilate the isolated

---

[1] *P.S. 1968*. Muenzenberg, the former Communist leader who had broken with Moscow, was probably murdered by G.P.U. agents.

Flanders army; that would give the French a week or ten days' time to evacuate us. But old Dr. Pollak did not believe it: the French needed all means of transport for their retreating armies; the railways were already breaking down; they would not bother about us and would leave us to our fate, i.e. the Gestapo. I looked at him and saw that his forehead was moist with perspiration and that the grey candles were lit in his eyes. Then it got me too. I knew the feeling from previous occasions, and I watched it begin in the region between stomach and heart and grow until the heart got soaked with it like a sponge and then radiate in two directions, down to the bladder and up to the throat; I knew it and detested it more than anything on earth. And I also knew that, whatever people who have never experienced it say, there was only one way to cure it; so I pulled the bottle out and during the next two hours I emptied it in slow gulps. When we got into the car, I was all right—agreeably unconcerned and philosophical about our fate. Then I got into a sort of dreamy state and went through one of the most curious experiences I had ever met with. What happened outwardly was odd enough, for half an hour later I was free; but the really fascinating thing was the inside story of it— the way that bottle of brandy on an empty stomach had brushed away conscious reflection and opened the door for the automatic reflexes of self-preservation. Had I not got drunk, in all probability this book could never have been written.

I have already said that all the others in the car were Germans and Austrians; I was the only one in the category of Non-Enemy Suspects. So far, the 'enemy aliens' had been concentrated in the Buffalo Stadium, a sports stadium in the south of Paris, and the 'suspects' in the Roland Garros Stadium. On that morning, probably because of the shortage of transport, the *Préfecture* had ordered the local police stations to direct *all* arrested men to the Buffalo camp. But,

as it turned out on our arrival at that place, they had forgotten to inform the camp authorities at Buffalo of their
changed dispositions. It was the usual French muddle. I
was the first non-enemy alien to pass through the control
bureau of the camp; when I put my passport on the desk
and saw the official's surprised face, it all came to me in a
flash.

'When and where were you arrested?' asked the official.

'In the Café Dupont, Place de la Convention, an hour
ago.'

I did not for a second consciously think of my answer.
The brandy did it for me—and that sly, hairy super-
ape, the subconscious. The point is that normally I am a bad
actor, and if I try to bluff at poker I am always caught. It
was a very odd experience.

'Where is your *carte d'identité*?'

'At home—10, rue Dombasle, seventh floor. That's why I
have been arrested. I just went down to have coffee after
lunch and left my *carte d'identité* upstairs; there was a
round-up and they took me to the police station. I asked
them to let me go home and fetch the *carte d'identité*, but
they didn't give me a chance even to speak—they just shoved
me into the car and here I am.'

I *felt* that I was absolutely convincing—the right mixture
of polite indignation and honest-to-God stupidity. And all
the time I watched my own performance and wondered.
Normally I am the rather uninspired type of person; when
writing, for instance, I have to sweat out every line with a
conscious effort. It was indeed very odd. In the same dream-
like exaltation in another age, a person would perhaps have
heard voices and produced a mystic vision; now miracles
had to happen at police officials' desks; but it was fundamentally the same process.

The man behind the desk turned my passport over and
looked at my other papers: Press card, the famous letters

from Influential Persons, etc. Over his head, there was a clock on the wall and it marked 4.30.

'All this is a quite amusing experience for a journalist, but the bother is that I have an appointment at five o'clock,' I said—that is, the brandy said, or the hairy ape.

'What sort of appointment?'

'Why—the daily Press Conference at the Ministry of Information.' (I had never been at the Press Conference and I had not written an article since the war started—but I had kept the Press card.)

'That idiot Lamèche is always making a mess of things,' said the man behind the desk to his assistant; he fumbled irresolutely with my papers. Lamèche, I gathered, was the *commissaire de police* of the XVth Arrondissement. Our escort had left immediately after delivering us.

'Look,' I said. 'I have got to be there at five. If you still have any doubts, send a man to accompany me home in a taxi while I fetch my *carte d'identité*. You can give me an armed escort with a machine gun if you think it necessary.'

Opposite the desk was the door that led into the camp—and once through that door there was no returning. I had it before my eyes and I knew it was a death-trap; and I knew that the slightest shadow of a false ring in my voice would finish me. But it was not my own voice and I trusted it entirely.

'No, I don't think that's necessary,' said the man behind the desk and handed my papers back with a smile. 'You are free, monsieur. Sentry, take monsieur to the entrance gate.' And to his secretary: 'Remind me to ring that idiot Lamèche when we are through with the others.' And to me: *'Au revoir, monsieur.* Next time you had better carry your *carte d'identité* on you.'

On the way to the gate I picked up my suitcase which I had left outside the entrance to the office. The sentry did not notice that there was anything wrong about it. At the gate I gave him five francs and asked him to get me a taxi. The taxi arrived. Exit Hyde, enter Jekyll.

But only for a few minutes, while the taxi approached the Porte d'Orléans and the drumming in my chest calmed down. Then the blessings of the brandy began to evaporate and I began to realise the situation into which I had got myself. The camp official would ring Lamèche, or whatever his name was; in half an hour or so the game would be up and the police at my flat—this time perhaps really with a tommy-gun. I knocked at the window pane and gave the driver another address. I knew that I would never see my flat again. Exit Jekyll, enter Hyde.

V

I had either to give myself up to the police or to go to ground, taking the risk of having to face a military tribunal if caught. I decided on the latter course.

I still had some French friends. Who these friends were, how they passed me on in turn, hiding me for one night each, and how they finally succeeded in obtaining for me a travelling permit to Limoges, where a fortnight later I ceased legally to exist, will be an amusing and moving story to tell at a time when the night has gone from Europe and acts of kindliness and solidarity no longer count as crimes. But still it is night; and from the moment when at the Porte d'Orléans I gave the taxi-driver a certain address, the story has to move along a dotted line, until G. and I emerge from an overcrowded train at the railway station at the town of Limoges, famous for its manufacture of porcelain and its retired generals.

Those first days of June in Limoges were like a short coming up for air before the final dive. The Battle of Dunkirk was still in progress, giving France a last respite. Personally,

I felt safe from the police for at least a fortnight. The travelling permit which my friends had procured me was a most respectable-looking document, covered with all sorts of lovely rubber stamps in black and red—my heart jumped with pleasure whenever I looked at it. It enabled me to go to the local police and provisionally legalise my situation; my *carte d'identité*, with the revealing 'E', was officially lost. In due time, of course, the *Préfecture* of Limoges would report my arrival to the *Préfecture* of Paris and would receive instructions to arrest me; but, what with red tape and the administrative chaos, this could hardly be expected to happen for another fortnight or three weeks. So there was time to take a deep breath and think matters over—like a man who, crashing down a precipice and catching hold half-way of a clump of grass, sighs with relief until the roots give way under his weight, and he continues his plunge to the bottom.

Limoges was on one of the main roads along which the stream of refugees flowed down from north to south. My memories of those last days of France are mainly of an acoustic nature : the never-ceasing polyphonic symphony of motor horns, the roaring and humming of the engines, the thundering of the heavy lorries on the roadway, the asthmatic rattle of old Citroëns, the neighing of horses and the crying of exhausted children, as the chaotic stream flooded through the town on its aimless course. Without interruption, all day and all night, the mechanised divisions of disaster passed by and the people in the streets stared at them; some pityingly, some with hostile contempt, some with anxiously thoughtful eyes, wondering when their turn would come to join the Great Migration to the south. For they had watched the growing of the stream from the first days, when it was no more than a rivulet with its sources far away in the north, in Holland and Belgium, and the cars still bore foreign markings; then in the days of Sedan it had suddenly swollen and on the number plates appeared the signs of the

French provinces, M for the Département du Nord, N for the Pas de Calais; and nearer and nearer, X for the Somme, Y for Seine-et-Oise; until the first green buses from Paris appeared and for a few days nine out of ten number plates bore the fatal R of the capital; then even the R's thinned out and new sources of the stream opened in Brittany and on the Loire. The number plates on the cars told the dreadful tale of the steam-roller thundering down over France, and revealed the truth which the official communiqués still tried to hide.

G. and I used to sit on the *terrasse* of the Café de l'Orient facing the Place de la Maire, where the main stream passed through. Most of the time it rained and the mattresses on the tops of the cars became sodden with water. G. was as unsentimental as an Anglo-Saxon female of twenty-two might be, and watched that never-ending procession of misery with a look of reproach, but the sight of the soaked mattresses finally broke her heart. 'Now they are spoilt for ever,' she remarked. 'Think how fussy Frenchwomen are about their mattresses and pillows and *plumeaux*. They'll never get over it. What a revolting war.'

Indeed, these mattresses and *plumeaux* seemed to be the main preoccupation of the people on the road. They tried to cover them with odd bits of oil-cloth and even with their mackintoshes tied on with bits of string. Before the Great Migration started, the stocks of oil-cloth in the Paris shops had been bought up for this purpose to the last yard. Who on earth but a Frenchwoman would have thought of oil-cloth for mattresses in the midst of the Apocalypse? It was a peculiarly sadistic irony of Fate to turn the most *petit-bourgeois*, fussy, stay-at-home people in the world into a nation of tramps. Ten million French people rolling aimlessly along the roads with their mattresses and saucepans, jamming all communications, paralysing every military

movement, smothering like a thick torrent of mud what
was left of the country, until the last twitch of life was
gone.

The Weygand Line collapsed, the Germans crossed the
Somme, crossed the Aisne, the Bresle, the Seine; Reims gone,
Rouen gone, Pontoise gone—and still the stream continued
day and night, pouring down from Châteauroux and on to
Périgueux. Sometimes, while watching it from the café *terrasse*, we were reminded of the day in Roquebillière when the
herds of sheep and cattle had come down from the pastures
near the frontier; it was the same continuous noise of bleating and lowing and barking from the claxons and horns, the
same long, panicky procession with the cars pushing and
jostling each other, as it were, in senseless confusion. And
what cars. Good Lord! As if every specimen of the mechanical fauna, everything that could creep and stink on four
wheels, was hurrying away from the deluge. There were the
giants of the French Air Force with the dismantled material
of the lost aerodromes, and the racy Paris tourist buses,
'*Paris la Nuit*' and '*Excursions à Fontainebleau*' still written
on them; and furniture vans from Brussels and the fire brigade from Maubeuge and the delivery van of a butcher in
Siossons, and of a dairy in Rouen, and of an ambulant ice-
cream merchant in Évreux, and the street-sweeper with
rotating brushes of the municipality of Tours, and, in between, roadsters, sports cars, limousines and the thousands
of tiny Citroëns and Peugeots, five, ten and fifteen years old,
barking up at the mammoth lorries like mangy old fox-
terriers. And everything inside crammed to the last square
inch with a mixture of old men, young women, grand-
mothers, babies, saucepans, bird-cages, sewing machines,
crates, bundles, baskets, cradles, bicycles, cuckoo-clocks,
loaves, petrol cans, spare wheels, gramophones, accordions,
wine bottles, dogs and cats—all stewing together in a sort
of surrealist *goulash*.

Just as G. was philosophising about the mattresses, there passed an extraordinary sight. A rickety motor funeral carriage turned off the road and parked in front of the Mairie, and various small and dirty boys fell out of it, munching cakes; and, as it started to rain, climbed back. It was a shabby, black angular vehicle, as used for poor men's funerals, and, on the black carpet where the coffin should be, an entire family, complete with cousins and mother-in-law, were ensconced, with all the angels carved in black wood over their heads.

On the evening of the same day we listened to the hoarse loudspeaker from a radio shop in the rue Gambetta broadcasting Reynaud's speech with the announcement that Italy had declared war. It was his last speech but one; there was a large crowd in front of the loudspeaker, listening in petrified silence; the traffic in the street had been stopped. Some women cried noiselessly; they had already started crying during the last bars of the Marseillaise before the speech; but when the voice of the little man spoke the words: '*Que les Français se resserrent fraternellement autour de leur patrie blessée,*' several of the men around us joined in with the women. It was the first and last time that I have seen a crowd burst into tears on a political occasion; it was dreadful and yet somehow comforting; there was no hysteria in that assembly in the street. It was a rare moment and it was quickly over; during the last stages of the catastrophe and in the months after it, I have never again seen a French crowd behave with such dignity. A few weeks later Reynaud was arrested and the loudspeaker stammered with the senile hatred of the Old Man, and spat the venomous spittle of his acolytes all over what was left of France, destroying the last moral stronghold of a broken nation: the fraternity of grief.

Two days later, June 12th, I had to send a telegram and when I entered the central Post Office an unknown woman with crazy eyes grasped my arm and shook it as if trying to tear it out :

'Monsieur, monsieur,' she shouted into my ears, 'the Russians have declared war on Germany and Italy. *C'est le miracle*—at last the miracle has come, monsieur !' And out she ran into the street.

Everybody in the Post Office was in a state of hysterical joy. I pushed my way to the telegraph window and asked the girl behind the glass pane whether she knew where the rumour had come from. She laughed with wet eyes and pointed up to the ceiling : 'From up there—from the wireless room. Excuse me, monsieur, but I must see it written myself.' And she ran up the little service staircase behind the windows. Two minutes later she was back, laughing and crying: 'I have seen it with my own eyes on an official telegram form. It is official, monsieur. I have seen it black on white.'

As far as I know, the mystery of the *bobard*, which spread on that day like wildfire all over France, has never been solved. I had been at the Post Office at eleven; at twelve the cafés were overcrowded with people waiting breathlessly for the official news bulletin. At last it came : the last bar of the Marseillaise; the laconic communiqué : 'Enemy pressure south of Seine and Marne. R.A.F. attacks on Genoa and Turin, damaging an Italian warship.' The Marseillaise. Nothing.

But the people still believed in the miracle. 'They are slow in announcing good news to us.' They listened to the news at two; and then again at four. Nothing.

Twenty-four hours later they learned of Reynaud's final appeal to Roosevelt.

Another twenty-four hours later the Germans marched into Paris.

Another twenty-four hours later Verdun was lost and the Maginot Line pierced.

Another twenty-four hours later the British offer to unite

the two empires was rejected and Reynaud ceded to Pétain.

Another twenty-four hours later, the feeble old man's voice, interrupted by dry coughs, whispered for the first time to the loudspeaker: 'With a broken heart I tell you that fighting must cease.'

VI

A few years before, in Paris, I had seen a famous film with Jean Gabin, *Le Grand Jeu*. I remember the story only vaguely, except that Gabin became involved in a murder and was hunted by the police. When all seemed lost, he passed by chance a recruiting office of the Foreign Legion. He went in and signed up for five years under a false name. He was asked no questions and had to show no documents. 'Is it as simple as that?' he wondered when a few minutes later the sergeant handed to him his *carnet militaire*, establishing his new identity. The sergeant smiled: 'Whatever your past has been, from this moment it is dead. Here nobody will ask you indiscreet questions; in the Legion we are all *des morts vivants*.'

When I saw that film the childish idea had occurred to me that if ever France became Nazified and all was lost, this might become a solution. On the day when we first heard Radio Paris play the Nazi anthem, and realised that there was no mistake about the wavelength, I talked it over with G. An hour after the thin old voice had announced the capitulation of France and the surrender of the Continent to Hitler, I went to the recruiting office. I walked in through the gate of the Caserne de la Visitation in Limoges as a man named Koestler, journalist and author, born in Budapest, Hungary; and I came out as one Albert Dubert, taxi-driver, born in Berne, Switzerland. It was really as simple as that. The only price one had to pay for getting one's identity

transformed was to sign up for five years (June 17th, 1940–
June 17th, 1945) with the Foreign Legion.[1]

This time I was neither prompted by Courvoisier nor by
any inspired voice; I had figured it out thoroughly. France,
the last dingy refuge of freedom on the Continent, had gone.
There would either be a total occupation, or a pro-German,
Fascist government with Pétain, Laval and Co.; in both
cases, it was only a question of time before I would land in
the hands of the Gestapo.

I had talked over with G. the possibilities of escape.
The obvious thing was to try to embark to England. In the
first days of the war I had applied for a visa and the permission to enlist in the British Army; it had been refused. When
I was released from Vernet, I made a new application : it
was turned down again. Meanwhile, England had pro-
ceeded, imitating the French example, to the wholesale internment of political refugees. Even should I succeed in getting out of France and crossing the Channel, I would be put
behind barbed wire again.

Anti-Fascists were obviously a great nuisance in a war
against Fascism. We were not wanted. I was through with
offering myself where I was not wanted.

Before the invasion started, and after all hope of getting
into the British forces had gone, I had volunteered for the
French Army. I had never been called up, thanks to the
brand-mark 'E' on my papers. Then I had tried to become a
Front ambulance-driver for the French Red Cross; and was
refused for the same reason. No, they did not want us. Our

[1] This, the 'real' Foreign Legion, should not be confused with the
special units for foreign volunteers in the French Army which had
been created during the war. The latter, called *Régiments de Marche,*
were fitted into the framework of the Legion, but were different in
their structure and human material. They were composed of men who
had volunteered, through political conviction, for the duration of the
war; while the 'real' Legion was composed of the classical type of
mercenary, mainly of 'men with no past', who had signed on for a
minimum term of five years' service in the French colonies.

only contribution to this war, which was our war more than theirs, had been to sit behind barbed wire. They had stolen our war from us. They had stolen it and lost it; now the French were going to wash their hands with Fascist soap while we lay buried under the débris.

Well, some of us still survived, in the physical sense at least. But for us there was no armistice and no 'soldier's peace', and apparently no escape. Try to go to America? G. and I had no visas, no exit permits and no money. Perhaps, if there were no total occupation and if the *Sûreté* did not arrest me beforehand; perhaps then, by pulling wires and writing to Influential Persons and begging fares from Refugee Committees, there was a chance to succeed. But at that time I was through with all that; through with pulling wires and writing to Influential Persons, through with consulates, bureaux, applications; through with asking anybody for anything; through with myself, with ten years of quixotic fights and miserable defeats.

I thought that it would be a great relief to become Albert Dubert, a taxi-driver from Berne, to submerge, disappear, throw off the burden and stigma of the past. I thought they would send me to a nice sunny place in Africa, and nobody will ask for my *carte d'identité*, and I will cease to belong to the scum of the earth. I thought that amongst the Men with no Past one might even discover a vestige of that fraternity for which I had searched in vain in the ranks of the Communist Party. And I also thought that perhaps after a time things might take another turn. Perhaps the fight would even be carried on from Algeria and Morocco. And if not, there were others who had deserted from the Legion.

Anyway, the main thing was to lie low for a time, under cover of the respectable name of Albert Dubert, and see what happened. I thought 'Dubert' sounded very respectable indeed : it was the name of the *Commissaire spécial de Police* in Limoges.

N

The proceedings at the Caserne de la Visitation had not taken more than an hour. When I was shown in, the sergeant and the two clerks in the recruiting office were discussing the capitulation; they looked dejected and drunk. I told the sergeant that I wanted to sign up for the Legion. He went red in the face: *'Sans blague!* Just now when the war is over?' I explained that I did not mean to join 'for the duration', but to sign up with the 'real' Legion for five years.

'That's different,' he said, looking at me searchingly. 'Have you got any identity papers?'

'I have lost them. I thought one didn't need any to join the Legion.'

He looked me up and down. *'Tout de même,'* he said, hesitantly. 'Couldn't you at least bring a letter addressed to you?'

He saw my embarrassed face. The scribes too looked at me. Limoges is a small provincial town and I don't think that recruiting office had seen many people desirous to join the Foreign Legion.

'Are you in such a hurry?' the sergeant asked at last. 'Rather,' I said. 'And just at the moment when we have stopped fighting?' 'Perhaps just for that reason,' I ventured. He looked at me appraisingly, trying to work out what I meant, but I didn't dare to say more. Then one of the scribes asked suddenly: 'Do you mean you want to beat it before they come to Limoges?' I did not say anything, and all three stared at me. Then the sergeant said: *'Enfin—je m'en fous.* If you want it, we can fix it up. You are lucky; the doctor is just in.'

I had to sign four printed forms, which I did not even read, then I passed a medical examination which was a pure formality. Finally, I was shown to the quartermaster's office, where I was to receive my marching orders and the voucher for a free railway ticket, to join the depot of the Foreign Legion. Before the desk stood a timid youngster of seventeen or eighteen who had just been called up, and was to be despatched to his regiment's depot. The sergeant on duty was fixing up his papers. When he handed them over, the youngster stared at him stunned.

'But this is an order for Angers, and Angers is occupied by the Boches,' he stammered.

'*Je m'en fous,*' said the sergeant. 'The orders are to send all conscripts of your class to the depot of Angers, and so far the orders have not been changed.'

'But what shall I do now? How shall I get to Angers if the Boches are at Angers?'

'*Je m'en fous.* What you do once you have left this office is your affair. *Débrouille-toi.*'

The youngster crept out to start his hopeful military career. Then my turn came. My marching orders and railway voucher were for the depot of the Legion at Lyons-Sathenay. The sergeant knew as well as I did that the Germans had taken Dijon that morning and would be in Lyons before me. But I did not say anything. He looked me up and down. 'Good luck for your five years,' he remarked sarcastically. 'Learn quickly to sing the "Deutschland, Deutschland Uber Alles." You'll need it in the future French Army.'

'Couldn't you change my *ordre de marche* for Marseilles?' I ventured. 'The central depot of the Legion is at Marseilles, anyhow.'

'Never mind about your order,' he said. 'All railway traffic in France was stopped an hour ago. And tonight they'll arrive at Limoges. Good luck.'

It was 4 p.m. when I got out of the recruiting office. I met G. at the Café de l'Orient and we had a drink to celebrate the birth of Albert Dubert. The loudspeaker was just repeating Pétain's speech from a gramophone record. The coughing voice and the 'broken heart' sounded even more embarrassing and ghostly. The people in the café listened in a painful silence. Nobody knew exactly what it all meant; they still could not believe that it was really over; they were dazed and looked like an assembly of sleep-walkers drinking *apéritifs*. The radio said that the Germans were still advancing and that resistance would go on until the armistice was signed. Nobody had any idea what this armistice would be—except that they were all convinced that the entire country would be occupied, and that the Germans would arrive in Limoges the same night. But they did not seem really to mind. They sat about on the cane chairs and plush sofas of the café in a sort of apathetic stupor; the only noise was the sharp click-click of the ivory balls kissing on the billiard-tables in the next room. At last the patron said : *'En fin, il fallait en finir.'* Several people nodded approvingly. I paid for our Pernods and we hurried out with a feeling of escaping from a wax-works.

We had no clear idea what to do next, except to get out of Limoges at once and move southwards, following the stream of refugees. Every hundred miles further away from the German advance was so much gained. The next town southwards was Périgueux, so let us try to get to Périgueux; there I would report to headquarters and ask for instructions. As to G., she wanted to know first what would happen to me, and then try to get back to England, or perhaps live with her sister, who was married to a Frenchman in Algeria, if I was to be sent there.

We hurriedly packed some of our belongings into two suitcases and three smaller bags. Before leaving Paris, G. had saved some of the manuscripts and books which the police had not taken away; now these too had to be left behind. Among them were my notes from Le Vernet and my diary covering the last four years. I hardly minded—throwing off the ballast of the past. The material constituents of the late Mr. A.K. were rapidly melting away and *Légionnaire* Albert Dubert began to take shape. In the café I had practised my new signature, and trained G. to call me 'Albert'. I had also begun to grow a moustache—a Vercingetorix-walrus moustache such as can be seen on the advertisements for Celtique cigarettes. In the midst of our despair, we felt strangely exhilarated. Tragedies in France always have a touch of vaudeville; and the place where they play them is called the Comédie Française.

VII

The diary which I had left behind consisted of several bulky note-books, loose pages and newspaper cuttings; it began with the Spanish war and ended on the day before Paris fell.

When my moustache began to grow I also began a new diary, scribbled into an unobtrusive pocketbook. This little red note-book, a black fountain-pen and a blue and white *carnet* of Paris bus tickets were the only possessions which I managed to save from France.

The following pages are copied from that note-book; a few gaps, marked in the diary by cue words, were filled in later, and a few passages reeking of the *sentimentalité de la misère* blotted out.

Monday, June 17th, 1940 (capitulation day).

Packed in a panicky hurry. Left two valises with books, documents, G.'s clothes, etc., with Mme. R., telling her we would come back to fetch them 'some time'. Mme. R., in tears, cheated us out of 30 francs on the bill. Reminds me of the peasants who sold a glass of water for 1 franc to exhausted refugees.

Dragged our two suitcases and three bags to the railway station. Railway station closed. The sergeant was right. All railway traffic suspended all over France. Hundreds of people camping around the station on their luggage. Scenery strangely reminiscent of Spanish civil war. Same fatalistic apathy of the crowd. Same smear-faced children crawling around between luggage heaps like tired flies.

It was late and growing dark. Waiting was no use, so decided to take municipal tram to its southern terminus on the road to Périgueux and then try to hitch-hike. By then it was completely dark, and none would stop. Met a man just arrived from Châteauroux (about eighty miles north of Limoges) he said at 4 p.m. the Germans had not yet reached Châteauroux; so felt reassured that they would not get here tonight and went into a restaurant by the roadside for dinner.

Nice garden restaurant overlooking River Vienne, but crowded with refugees from the north. G. remarked about nuisance refugees. Told her : refugee yourself. In spite of our luggage round the table, she was not yet conscious of having become a tramp among tramps.

Shared table with a medical officer in uniform. Said it was all the fault of Blum and his friends; that it had started with Briand, and that Daladier and Gamelin were the puppets of Blum and the Jews : 'They infiltrate everywhere, they corrupt everything.' We exchanged drinks and he became formal and introduced himself : 'Lieutenant Something'— '*Légionnaire* Dubert.' Funny pang. Did not dare look at G. We had more drinks, discussed probable armistice terms and he said : '*Il fallait en finir.*'

Second time today the same phrase. They explained why they went to war with '*il faut en finir*' and they explain why they capitulate with '*il fallait en finir*'. The tragedy of France in a nutshell.

Tuesday, June 18th.

Slept on tables in the restaurant with eight other people on eight other tables and crawling children everywhere. G.

begins to realise what it is like to be a refugee tramp, but in the morning looks fresh and tidy; just another feat of British hypocrisy.

Listened during breakfast to repetition of new Foreign Minister Baudouin's broadcast of yesterday night: 'It is because we are sure of the French people's spirit of independence . . . that we have asked on what conditions the carnage of our sons might be stopped.' Strange how melodious a self-contradictory sentence can be made to sound in French. 'Because we love independence, we accept Nazi domination.' No information how far Germans advanced.

After breakfast dragged out the luggage, dumped it on the road and tried to stop a car. The other people in the restaurant said they would stay there and wait until armistice was signed, and then go back north to their homes. Did not mind whether Germans caught up with them. Were not afraid of Germans, only of bombs. All relieved that war is over; showed it openly: *fallait en finir*. Thought Germans would take back Alsace, did not care. Alsatians were Boches, anyhow. Mussolini might get Djibuti, perhaps Tunisia. When I suggested he might ask for Nice and Savoy, they laughed: 'Never on your life. We'll kick him in the pants.' Utterly unaware of what has happened. Sparrows chattering on telegraph wires while wire flashes telegram that all sparrows must die.

After an hour's waiting, got a lift to Thiviers, more than halfway to Périgueux. Refugee stream on the road has thinned out, mainly through lack of petrol. All the way saw families camping by the roadside with cars parked off the road, on the spot where last drop of petrol gave out. It is a sort of general stay put. All wait for armistice to be signed and 'everything to become normal again'. They really believe life will be as it was before. Meanwhile, they eat and drink in the sunny meadows and play belotte. The apocalypse as a family picnic.

In Thiviers were told that a bus would probably leave at 1 p.m. for Périgueux. Dragged luggage into a dark little *auberge* and listened to 11.30 news. Some Minister, I believe Pomaret, made a speech asking the people to stop tramping along the roads, stay where they are, keep quiet, trust their leaders and not ask silly questions, there's a good boy. Hitler and Mussolini meet in Munich to discuss terms of armistice. Try to imagine what the streets in Munich must look like compared with streets in Thiviers. Flags, people mad with joy, brass bands, songs. God! why can one never be on the winning side? Since I can remember it has always been explanations why the others had defeated us. It has started to rain. Through the *auberge* window we see a priest standing in the middle of the main street of Thiviers, his wet soutane lifted to his knees, trying to stop a car. More news bulletins. Fighting goes on, but they don't say where. The Russians are massing troops on the Lithuanian frontier. Night over the jungle and the jackals howl; but who has ever seen a jackal posing as the redeemer?

The priest enters the tap-room, discouraged; no car has stopped for him, but they have splashed his soutane with mud. '*Que Dieu soit bénit, faut se débrouiller,*' he says and orders a pint of red wine. A young priest, a French priest, has learnt to be a *débrouillard.* (*Se débrouiller* means 'to wangle it', to obtain a desired end or to get out of a mess by clever and slightly dubious means, by dodging authority and outwitting the bureaucracy and relying exclusively on one's own resources; it is a strictly individualistic and definitely anti-social conception of efficiency.)

Eventually, the bus came and took us to Périgueux. I left G. and the luggage in a waiting-room at the bus terminal and went to the *Caserne* Busseaux. In the orderly-room showed my papers. 'And what the hell do you want?' 'Instructions.' The orderly sergeant stared at me, then he called: 'Hi! Come here, all of you.' About fifteen ragged, unshaven *poilus*, were standing around me. 'Now look at him : This is *Légionnaire* Dubert from Berne in Switzerland, who signed up on the day of the armistice, bound for Lyons and comes to Périgueux to ask for instructions.' Nobody laughed; they shrugged and went back to their benches, dragging their feet. One said : '*Mon vieux*, a fortnight ago I was bound for Brussels and here I sit.' The sergeant rang up the officer on duty : '*Mon capitaine*, there is a lunatic legionary here asking for instructions.' '. . . No, for Lyons.' '. . . Says he could not get a train.' '. . . Told him twice to go to hell, but he insists.' '. . . *A vos ordres, mon capitaine.*' He put the receiver down : 'The captain says we can take you on the establishment. Wait with the others.'

Sat down with the others, found out they were all *isolés*—soldiers who had lost their regiments in the retreat and, following the stream of refugees, had landed in Périgueux. They were all to be taken on the establishment—housed and fed at the barracks until further instructions. The sergeant explained that the captain had decided to treat me also as an *isolé*. Eventually we all got vouchers and went to find the corporal on duty, who was to find accommodation for us, which he did for the others, but refused for me, as I was still in civilian clothes. So back to the sergeant, who, after some cursing, gave me a voucher to the regimental stores. So to the regimental stores, where the store-keeper was asleep, apparently drunk; woke him, he asked for a cigarette, said there were no new uniforms, only used ones, pointed to a sort of rubbish heap of old shoes, trousers, puttees, belts, and field-flasks, all pell-mell; said could take what I needed and went to sleep again. I dug out various items which I hoped would make me look approximately like a soldier. All the tunics bore the insignia of the 15th Algerian Rifles, as this was their depot; so I took one of them; and the only headgear available were red tarbushes with a sickle moon and the number 15 on them, so I put one on my head. Then went to find the orderly corporal who looked a little doubtful, but could not be bothered, so he found me a bed.

Thus, everything being satisfactorily settled, I wanted to join G. in the waiting-room, but learnt we were only allowed to leave the barracks from 5.30 to 9 p.m. So walked round courtyard and climbed over a fence and walked back to bus terminus. Hoped to impress G. by my uniform, but effect disappointing; said I looked like Chaplin dressed up as a Turk. Left baggage in waiting-room and walked to refugee reception-centre to find somewhere for G. to sleep. Met an officer, saluted for first time in my life. Met another one, saluted again, met a sergeant, saluted too. They looked surprised; thought perhaps because I looked so ragged and G. so smart, or that something was wrong with my saluting, so watched how other *poilus* did it. Discovered they did not salute at all, just looked the other way when passing an officer, or even stared at them provocatively and the officer looked the other way. Enjoyed walking in my shabby uniform, felt sort of invisible, for first time since Vernet really safe from police and persecution. Refugee-centre besieged by crowd but they said there is a British ambulance in Périgueux, they might help G., but they did not know where the ambulance is, so said we should inquire at Red Cross, but they did not know where Red Cross is, so should ask a policeman. Asked several policemen, nobody knew where Red Cross was, but one knew a girl at an optician's who worked at the Red Cross. So walked into optician's shop, found tall, dark girl, eyes red with crying; when she heard that G. was British, said she would take her along to her aunt's place; there was a little attic where she could sleep. So fetched luggage, dragged it along to aunt's house. Aunt's name is Mme. Brassard, nice, motherly old woman, was cooking dinner in a big, clean kitchen, shining brass pans and pots hanging all round the walls like a museum of gastronomic art; when she heard G. was British, embraced her in tears: *'Quel désastre, ma petite, quel désastre.'* So arranged to meet G. tomorrow at five and walked back to barracks, very satisfied and again full of love for La France.

Wednesday, June 19th

First night at *Caserne* Busseaux. When I arrived yesterday at 9 p.m., found my bed gone; some *isolé* had taken it, palliasse and all, to another room. But three beds out of the total of fifteen in my own dormitory were empty; room orderly told me I can take one, the owners had not turned up for the last two days. Had brought a litre red wine in my field-flask—field-flask was best thing I had dug out from rubbish in regimental stores; shared it with orderly, the others were already snoring. Orderly's name Cyrano (like *chef de groupe* in Vernet); his father was a Communist *député*, now in jail; he himself believes in 'revolution through love'. He has a glass eye and is a *récupéré*—auxiliary service. Took his glass eye out and gesticulated with it, explaining love and self-sacrifice are the real revolutionary forces, class hatred to be abolished, economics only of secondary importance, etc. Poor fellow, does not know yet that tomorrow he will go Fascist—the fate of his type of well-meaning dilettantes; their nebulous grey matter is irresistibly sucked up by the void of that efficient vacuum-cleaner. The empty red eye-hole and the glass eye staring at me from his gesticulating fist made a perfect allegory.

This morning coffee was brought to the room at six, then everybody went to sleep again. Asked whether there was no roll-call; learnt no more roll-calls for the last few days, too many men missing. Every evening a few do not return from the town. Whoever has his family or a girl somewhere near beats it. *'Nous sommes en pleine pagaille,'* somebody remarked contentedly. (*Pagaille* is, after *se débrouiller*, the most used word in the French Army; it covers anything from slight disorder, mess, muddle to complete chaos.) All snored until about eight; then we loitered about in the courtyards. Two ragged African Zouaves were asleep on the pavement of the courtyard, apparently just arrived from the front; a captain passed and kicked one in the ribs. He jerked up and stared with dizzy eyes at the captain. Captain began to bully : nobody permitted to sleep in the courtyard; they should wait until given beds. Zouave answered back in bad French : 'We waiting for hours, no bed. We marching five days to find regiment. Officers gone, regiment gone, we tired, want sleep.' Captain approached the second Zouave with apparent intent to kick him too. Whereupon the first Zouave went mad, 'You don't touch my comrade. You *salaud*. You *salaud*. All officers *salauds*.' He could be heard all over the vast courtyard. We all gathered round in a semicircle, watching the scene. The captain went pale. 'Give me your cartridge belt—*un-deux,* quick.' (The Zouaves had no rifles.) 'I don't give you cartridge belt. *Salaud*.' He was obviously quite mad. There was a deadlock; the captain turned on his heel and walked away through the middle of the crowd. The Zouave stared after him, calmed down, grinned, sat down and began to undo his shoe. An old lieutenant of the 15th Algerians hurried up and called to him : *'Viens, mon vieux.* Don't start a fuss here. I'll give you a bed.' The Zouave grinned : 'The captain is a *salaud*.' 'All right, all right. For God's sake shut up and come along.' 'My comrade too.' 'Yes, your comrade too. Come, help me wake him up.' They shook him and Zouave No. 1 put on his shoes again very slowly, and the old lieutenant waited until he had finished, then all three went into the building and the crowd dispersed. Asked somebody whether they thought Zouaves will be punished. *'Penses-tu!* The officers don't want any fuss. They've got the wind up.'

Took a sun bath in the courtyard, then went to canteen to listen to wireless news. Germans reply to Pétain's appeal, asking for the nomination of French plenipotentiaries to meet them 'at a place and time to be notified later'. Still nothing about armistice terms; and still fighting goes on and the Germans advance. Total occupation or no total occupation? Nobody at the *caserne* seems to care. They don't even listen to the wireless. Only comments: 'Let's have done with it. We've had enough.'

At five called on G. She has spent the day exploring various old churches in Périgueux. Cathedraling. On the day of the general mobilisation she had to go cathedraling at Avignon. We strolled through the town. Lovely old town. Found a little Alsatian tavern with tables in the open in a little square smelling of lime-trees. Drank dry white Traminer wine and agreed to stay in Périgueux until they send me to the Legion with some transport. Immense relief not to have to plan any more, and to let others decide for us. This is the deluge and we are drifting peacefully on the black waters, Heaven knows where to.

Thursday, June 20th

This morning three more missing from our room. Among them the corporal who slept next to me. His company had been cut off somewhere near Elbeuf on the Seine and captured by a German motorised column. The Germans had collected their rifles, passed over them with a tank and told them to beat it—'We don't need any more prisoners.' Had even given them some tins and chocolate. He got hold of a bike somewhere and pedalled southwards, deciding war was over for him. Was very impressed by the Germans: '*Ils ne sont pas méchants, les boches, tout de même.*' Spent one night in our *caserne*; explained to me yesterday: 'They'll drag on the demobilisation for another six months. I'm going to demobilise myself. At five I'll beat it.' And so he did.

Listened to 8 a.m. news. French plenipotentiaries are leaving Bordeaux today for 'the place designated for the armistice negotiations'. Now the German advance will probably stop. Later another speech by Pétain. That thin voice and that cough. Sounded like a skeleton with a chill. Couldn't understand what he said, except the end: 'Stand by me. The fight still goes on. It is for France.' Impossible to know whether he meant it figuratively or that the fighting is really continuing. Disastrous old gaga. 'Stand by me'—wish he had talked to that corporal yesterday.

Later about twenty of us were taken on a fatigue to another barracks, to sort out boots at the stores. Thousands of pairs of brand-new boots. A bloke with holes in his boots asked for a pair. Lieutenant in command said he was not authorised; bloke should make an application. Bloke—an old *récupéré*—said quietly: 'You are right, *mon lieutenant*. I understand that all these boots must be kept intact for the *Boches* when they come in.' Lieutenant went red, did not answer. When we left, about fifteen pairs of new boots left with us. At 5 p.m. again called on G., and had dinner with aunt and niece in that nice kitchen. They are very patriotic, but very Roman Catholic. 'That unfortunate Israelite Blum has ruined France.' Sad—liked them so much. That kitchen with the shining brass pans was real France. Auntie and niece too will go Fascist without noticing it. Behind each petty bourgeois idyll that lurking horrid grimace.

Friday, June 21st

Morning was peeling potatoes in courtyard when lieutenant called me. It was the old colonial who had talked so gently to the Zouaves. 'Are you the Swiss who enlisted on the day of the armistice?' *'Oui, mon lieutenant.'* 'What is your profession?' 'Taxi-driver.' He gave my hands a quick glance. 'Listen, I don't mind if you hang about here with us until the end of your days, but if by any chance you do not desire to meet the *Boches* you had better beat it. This is strictly private advice.' I must have looked rather flabbergasted, standing there with that potato knife in my hand, for he went on : 'They're coming down along the coast; reports say they've reached La Roche-sur-Yon.' Asked him where he advised me to go. He shrugged. 'I in your place would try to get to Bordeaux and *débrouille* myself to get on a boat. They say there are still boats leaving; for Africa—and perhaps in another direction too. . . .' 'Could you possibly give me an *ordre de marche* for Bordeaux, *mon lieutenant*?' 'I can't, and as for the captain—well, good luck, *et débrouille-toi.*'

Hurried to room, packed my civilian clothes in a bundle, exchanged the red fez for a less conspicuous Basque beret (the blue beret was a tolerated headgear for French soldiers). On way out passed lieutenant's office, he called me in. 'Take this paper.' It was an old soldier's paybook of a certain Jean Rouzier, age thirty, *soldat de deuxième classe,* born in Périgueux, Dordogne. 'If you happen to be captured by the *Boches,* they won't do you any harm if you are a Frenchman. For a Swiss volunteer with that conspicuous recruiting date on your paper, it may be different. Give me your word not to use it except in an emergency, and to tear it up when you are safe.' I promised. Felt moved to my guts. 'Now clear out of here. Maybe we will meet again—in another direction.'

Climbed over the fence, hurried to fetch G. Officially I was a deserter for leaving depot without permission, but did not care. Decided with G. to leave the big suitcases behind and only take the three smaller bags, with G.'s most necessary things and my civilian suit. More ballast overboard; more past left behind; litter strewn on the road of flight. Let the dead bury their dead.

Tramps on the road again. Panicky feeling back again. Wandered out of town to a bridge on road to Bordeaux, then found a convoy of lorries ready to start, tried to get a lift, but soldiers refused, said convoy was on '*mission spéciale*'; tried to argue with them, argument became quarrel, soldiers noticed my accent, asked for my papers, G. deadly frightened, I demanded to see an officer, showed my Dubert papers (Rouzier would not cover foreign accent), soldiers satisfied, said, grinning, 'Thought you were a Nazi parachutist.' Mutual handshakes and shoulder taps, but no lift.

After some waiting, found a civilian car, took us six miles, then walked, then stopped a military lorry with a few soldiers saying they were going to Bordeaux, climbed on happily, but when just starting a car drew up behind us hooting like hell, out jumped a fat adjutant, ordered G. and me to get off the lorry, because G. a civilian and I an *isolé* and all stragglers have to report to the nearest barracks or police station according to new orders. So they drove off escorted by the fat adjutant and we remained sitting on the luggage by the side of the road, in pouring rain, eating hard-boiled eggs. Stream of vehicles on the road now fairly continuous again, but mainly lorries with sleeping, unshaven *poilus* which would not stop, or smart cars with officers looking haughty and unconcerned. At last a puny, ramshackle Fiat stopped, crammed with boxes, bundles and children, driven by a buxom Parisian working-class woman who told us to get on the running-boards. While driving she chattered, said since Paris she had taken lots of people on the running-boards, while the snobbish bourgeois cars never stopped to give people lifts even if half empty—'*voilà le malheur de la France*'.

We did a few miles, then were stopped by gendarmes who told us nobody was allowed to proceed to Bordeaux, except military cars with a 'special mission' order. Sounded pretty odd, as if Pétain feared a revolt. 'Stand by me,' he had said—but don't come near me. So we turned to the left and decided to approach Bordeaux by twisted secondary roads which were perhaps not guarded by gendarmes. Went on for about thirty miles, passed Mussidan, all the time standing on running-boards, our lower halves drenched with rain, keeping upper half dry by leaning into the car in a cramped position. Arrived at Bergerac about five, there the woman said she could not go farther, children completely exhausted; she'd stay here for a couple of days.

Looked up map, saw only road to Bordeaux passes over bridge at Libourne, which would certainly be guarded by gendarmes, hence pretty hopeless to try getting there without special *ordre de mission*; went to military headquarters of Bergerac to try to obtain one. There the usual *pagaille*; crowd of smart civilians queueing up to get petrol for their cars—and actually getting it in spite of stay-put order. Pushed my way through, was sent from one bureau to another, started a row, obtained interview with *Commandant de la Place*—old, grey-haired colonel, looking gentle and helpless. Several other officers chatting in the room. Showed my papers and explained my case. '*Mais, mon petit*, your situation is completely irregular. Why don't you go to Lyons?' 'But Lyons was occupied by the Germans yesterday.' 'Then why didn't you stay where you were?' 'Because as a foreign volunteer I am afraid of being shot by the Germans.' 'But your situation is completely irregular. You can't come to Bergerac with marching orders for Lyons. In these critical hours every soldier has to do his duty and blindly obey his superior's commands' (textually). The other officers were listening, some smiling discreetly.

'But, *mon colonel*, that's what I am trying to do. My duty is to join my unit; Lyons being in the enemy's hands, I am trying to do it via Bordeaux or Marseilles.' 'Who told you to do that?' 'The officer in charge of my last depot.' 'What did he say?' He said: 'The Germans are coming, *débrouille-toi*.' The old man became angry and went red all over his face. 'I do not admit—I do not approve of an officer who tells a soldier to *débrouiller* himself. You are going to stay

o

here. I'll take you on the establishment.' A young lieutenant intervened : '*Mon colonel*, may I respectfully remark that once the armistice is signed the enemy will take control of all ports and this man, being a legionary, will lose the opportunity of joining his unit.' 'I do not admit. The armistice is not signed. How do you know it will be signed at all? Orderly, take this man on the establishment. Dismiss.'

So am writing this on a palliasse in the barracks at Bergerac. Meantime armistice probably signed and trap closed. *Je m'en fous*. Only sleep and stop the mill in my head. G. found a room in an old peasant's cottage. Wished she had gone back to England and left me alone. Wish could escape urge of self-preservation, wish darkness and childhood would come back—dark curtains on all windows, snow outside and a lullaby.

Tuesday, June 25th. Bayonne

Am in Bayonne. G. gone, perhaps dead. Armistice signed. All German refugees to be extradited. Vera's stuff no good, only sick. Germans expected hourly.

VIII

From Friday, June 21st, at Bergerac, to Tuesday, June 25th, at Bayonne, there is a gap in my diary. During those five days the tragedy of France had reached its final stage and I had reached a mood where I felt that there was nothing left to live for. They were the days when my colleagues and friends, to whose memory this book is dedicated, ended their lives in utter despair. I did not know it then; but it was in the air.

We thought that this time the defeat was final; we had been beaten out of one European country after another; this was the *coup de grâce*, journey's end. We did not know that England would carry on the fight alone; nothing in her conduct during the last pre-war decade, nor in the first nine months of actual war, led one to suppose it; and we did not know that, even should she carry on, we would be wanted to help, as was our duty, and be given the shelter, which was our due. Had we known it, had we been given to understand it in time, the men and women who are dead today would still be alive. Oh, we know it would not make much difference to the final issue; we know that others have died without much fuss being made about it; but we also know that it does make a difference how and why a man dies; whether killed by his enemies or driven to kill himself by his friends. Guilt can be forgiven, but it should not be hushed up.

In those days, I, too, did not see much sense in carrying on; but there was G., and there was curiosity stronger than despair, and there was perhaps cowardice and perhaps a rest of irrational hope, and at bottom there was the hairy ape, to whom all of these different terms meant one and the same thing. But above all there was a French N.C.O., whom G. and I met at Bergerac, and who told us that the British had ships at Bordeaux and embarked anybody who wanted to join their Army, without asking for visas or anything. It sounded too good and we did not really believe it, but it was a sufficient incentive to carry on. We found out that, although no private car was allowed to enter the town where the Government had established its seat, the regular auto-bus line Bergerac–Bordeaux still functioned—one of the incongruities of those days of chaos; so on Sunday, June 23rd, I deserted a second time, by leaving the barracks at Bergerac without permission at five in the morning, and G. and I took the omnibus which left at 6 a.m. for Bordeaux.

I was the only soldier in the bus, and people told us that at the entry of the town the gendarmes stopped all soldiers and escorted them to a special camp for stragglers, whereas civilians were allowed to pass; so I put on G.'s mackintosh, which hid my uniform. The bus was actually stopped at the bridge in Libourne, but the gendarmes merely looked through the windows and let the car pass without further formalities. We arrived at Bordeaux about noon—and learnt that the last ship for England had left forty-eight hours ago.

We also learnt that the armistice had been signed the previous day, but still the terms were kept an absolute secret, although almost a week had passed since they had been communicated to the French Government. The only statement by the wireless station of Bordeaux P.T.T. was : 'It cannot be hidden that the conditions are hard.' In the same news bulletin the communiqué of the French high command spoke of 'enemy pressure along the Atlantic coast—St. Malo, Lorient, Poitiers occupied—Italians start offensive in the Alps', while the communiqué about the armistice negotiations said : 'Marshal Pétain's Government took its decision in full freedom, without threat or immediate pressure from the enemy....'

Obviously the Government did not dare to disclose the armistice terms until the German troops were sufficiently close to Bordeaux to protect them against a revolution which they believed to be imminent. The sandbags and heavy machine guns in front of the official buildings, the repeated, almost imploring warnings of Radio Bordeaux to the French people 'to refrain from disorder and violence and to disbelieve all rumours about the armistice terms spread by trouble-makers and *provocateurs*' (whereas the simplest methods against rumours would have been to disclose the terms); the string of gendarmes round Bordeaux and the atmosphere in the streets on that fatal Sunday—all proved that the aged marshal was scared to death by revolution, which in fact was more remote from France than ever.[1]

While listening to the French radio, I was struck by an uncanny feeling of *déjà vu*. Hitler's *coup d'état*, 'to forestall the imminent Communist revolution'; the same pretext used by General Metaxas to establish dictatorship in Greece; the same pretext for the mutiny of the generals in Spain—the fate of the Communist parties in Europe, with all their revolutionary brag and bluster, had apparently been to serve as involuntary midwives for Fascist regimes.

It needed, of course, the imbecility of old Pétain, aged eighty-four, and the political fanaticism of old Weygand, aged seventy-three, to swallow the medicine administered to them by their nurses—Laval and his clique. But they did swallow it; Weygand believed as early as June 12th, when the Government was still at Tours, that Maurice Thorez, the Communist leader, had established a new reign of the Commune in Paris. That story had in all probability been launched by the German propaganda; a simple telephone call by Mandel to Langeron, the *Préfet* of Paris, proved its absurdity; but by that time, Pétain and Weygand were already convinced that 'whereas victory would mean revolution, defeat would save France, for it would, at the cost of a certain loss of territory and prestige, preserve the social order'.[2]

They believed it, those poor, senile, arterio-sclerotic old generals. They also believed that every trade unionist was a Bolshy, that Socialism meant murder and rape, and that Hitler was a gentleman. They had swallowed it all, spoonful by spoonful, while the gangsters tucked their napkins into their collars and their bloodless lips blabbered *honneur*

[1] Cp.: 'A British general, who is also a conservative M.P., returned from Bordeaux complaining that he found Weygand far more concerned about the danger of revolution in France than about the consequences of capitulation to the Nazis' (*Why France Fell—The Lessons for Us*, U.D.C., London, 1940).

[2] *Why France Fell—The Lessons for Us*, U.D.C., London, 1940.

and *gloire* and *Nous, Philippe Pétain*, in majestic plural, into the microphone.

Both in 1792 and in 1870 the French ruling caste had betrayed the nation and preferred the Prussians to revolution. In 1940 there was no danger of a revolution; the proletariat was tired and apathetic; while the bourgeoisie had found its symbolic expression in a living mummy. It was an unreal drama of shadows : the ghost of the French ruling class committing suicide, scared by the spectre of revolution.

The last boat had left Bordeaux forty-eight hours earlier. The Germans were said to be near the mouth of the Gironde and the harbour cut off. The British Consul, too, had left for Bayonne. But Bayonne is a hundred and ten miles to the south and there were no communications.

I suddenly became scared for G. The radio had struck an aggressive note against Britain. 'The attitude taken by Mr. Churchill is inexcusable. . . .' 'Frenchmen cannot listen without protest to being lectured by a foreign Minister.' The last quotation came from another speech by Pétain (the old man seemed to revel in talking into the microphone), and it sounded rather grotesque on the day after the capitulation, but at that moment we did not appreciate the humour of it. This brisk, shameless change in the French attitude towards its ally of yesterday gave the situation a new menacing aspect. It was worse than one's worst expectations. It looked as if France were already *gleichgeschaltet* before we even knew the armistice terms.

So far we had been sad, oppressed, scared; now for the first time we got into a real panic—or I at least. I reproached myself for not having insisted on G.'s going home when it was still time, and felt responsible for whatever might happen to her. We trudged frantically about the harbour and the streets for hours on end, hunting for a boat, a taxi, any means of transport, but it was no good. Then suddenly at the

American Consulate we ran into Edgar Mowrer from the *Chicago Daily News*. He was as grey in the face as we were, and about equally keen on meeting the Gestapo. He said the Germans might occupy the town tonight, and that he had just bought the car which the British Consul in Bordeaux had left behind; he was to leave at 9 p.m. via Bayonne-Biarritz-St. Jean de Luz for Spain and was willing to give us a lift to Biarritz.

It was then 6 p.m. and we spent the remaining hours in a café, listening to the acoustic filth which poured from the loudspeaker, and arguing under a nervous strain. I tried to convince G. that she should go with Mowrer, who would take care of her, and leave me in Bordeaux; I knew that I could not go to Spain, whereas she might get through, and I thought that if there were still boats from Bayonne to England they would take her, but not me, and if I were there she would refuse to leave and thus spoil her last chance; so I preferred that we should separate at once. It was a long and morbid argument. G. cried, and I went to the lavatory and had a sort of nervous breakdown, in the form of uncontrollable weeping, the first in my life; and in between, the loudspeaker went on belching and vomiting, as if the whole ether were being sick in spasms. Finally G. won and we both left in Mowrer's car at nine. He said that, according to his information, German tank columns had crossed the bridge over the Garonne south of Bordeaux, and there was a fair chance of running into them on the road.

But we drove unmolested through the night over the practically deserted road, only stopped now and then by a patrol of gendarmes. Each time they asked for our papers, I half feared that they would take me into custody as an *isolé*, and I half hoped for it for G.'s sake; and finally, this was in fact what happened. It happened in Biarritz, where we arrived about midnight. We were looking for the house of some friends of Mowrer's; he stopped the car and searched for the house numbers with his flashlight; and then a patrol turned up, about half a dozen men with rifles. They were satisfied with Mowrer's and G.'s papers, but not with mine, and told me to come with them to the police. Maybe with some eloquence I could have talked them out of it, as I had done with the previous patrols, but I did not really try. I had to get out of G.'s way, anyhow, and this was as good an opportunity as another to cut things short; I also thought that it was a Heaven-sent chance that Mowrer was there and that he would look after her until she got safely out of the country. So I climbed out of the car and told the patrol that I was ready to go with them. I heard as if in a bad dream Mowrer call to me not to be a damned fool and to get back into the car; I saw through a sort of mist G.'s white face leaning out of the car and we kissed good night. Then I moved along the street between the rifles; I did not turn back, but I knew that she was staring after us, as she had stared when the police had taken me from the flat in Paris for the first time and then the second time; but this time we thought that it was final.

IX

The next four or five days are unreal and dream-like in my memory. There was a constant dull aching, drowned by continuous large doses of alcohol, which contributed to my general feeling of unreality and dizziness. I did not get violently drunk, but lived for about a week in a blurred world, in a sort of thick mental fog which blunted the sharpness of all outer and inner happenings. Now and then an event, like the entry of the German troops into Bayonne, tore the veil of mist with the hard, glaring flash of reality, but after a couple of Pernods the mist closed again and I drifted on through the mercifully unreal scenery.

I remember having spent the night in which the patrol arrested me on the floor of a dirty cell in the *gendarmerie* of Biarritz in the company of a drunken deserter of the French Air Force, who alternately sang and made homosexual propositions. In the morning a police officer escorted me by tram to the infantry barracks of the Château Neuf at Bayonne. At the barracks they told me that a boat was to leave the same day for an unknown destination. I remember going round all day in small circles with a bunch of other soldiers to find out about that boat. We went to the *Bureau de la Place*, which sent us to the *Commission des Transports*, which directed us to the *Commission du Port*, which again sent us back to the *Bureau de la Place*. The others were foreigners like myself, mostly Czechs or Poles, enlisted as volunteers for the duration, scared to death like myself by the prospect of falling into the Gestapo's hands. I remember queueing up at the garden gateway of the *Commission du Port*,which was to issue the permits for our embarkation. There were two gates in the railings and two queues before the gates, one for us and one for civilians; and the civilians passed one by one, but our gate remained closed, guarded by three sentries with fixed bayonets. We shouted for an officer to come and order the sentries to let us in, but no officer appeared. We tried to force the gate and the sentries threatened to charge us with their bayonets. At the row a window in the second floor of the building opened and a woman, probably a secretary, looked out. We shouted to her to call an officer and she shrugged her shoulders and smiled; and then she shut the window again. Everything was bathed in blazing sunlight: the soldiers, mostly from the front, shouting and struggling in front of the closed gate, the sentries with their fixed bayonets, and the smiling woman at the window.

I remember that we stood there for several hours and then ran back to the *Bureau de la Place* and back to the *Com-*

mission du Port again; but no officer turned up and we shouted and shook the gate in vain. The civilian queue had vanished and an old gardener was weeding the flower beds in front of the building, and the sun shone and the bayonets of the sentries flashed. They told us that there were no boats, anyhow, and that all the officers had left the building, for there were contradictory orders from Bordeaux and they feared the responsibility of embarking us. We tried to find that mysterious ship on the quays, or any other vessel, but there was none, and then I gave it up, and strolled back to the Château Neuf. I limped slowly along the quays, for the old military boots from Périgueux had rubbed my feet raw; and I remember a little Polish Jew in uniform hanging on to me and telling me how he had tried to embark on a boat to England a day or two before; there had been a great crowd and pushing, and a Polish officer on the gangway who controlled the Polish soldiers' papers had sent all the Jews back, saying there were already enough of them; and various Jewish soldiers had wept and implored him to take them, and one had gone down on his knees and kissed the officer's hand; but he did not know what happened after that, for he could stand it no longer and ran away. I remember that the Pole and I went to various *bistros* and got drunk, and then I lost him somehow and limped back to the Château Neuf, where they took me on the establishment and gave me a bed; and then I went to sleep for twelve or fifteen hours and did not care any more.

The next two days are completely blurred; there were no roll-calls in the barracks and I remained most of the time lying on my palliasse and did not even go to the canteen to listen to the radio. But there were twenty other soldiers in my room and they brought in all the rumours and news; I learned that the Italian armistice had been signed and fighting had ceased, and that there was a national mourning day, and that Pétain had made another speech and said that all the disasters of France were due to the 'people's love of pleasure'. I also learned that the armistice terms had still not been published, but that the entire Atlantic coast was to be occupied, that the Germans were expected hourly in Bayonne, if not already here; and that somebody had listened to a foreign broadcast which had said that the armistice stipulated the extradition of all refugees to Germany. And I also learned that a last ship had sailed from St. Jean de Luz for England on Monday or Tuesday, that it had been torpedoed and all the people had been drowned; and, as Mowrer had been bound for St. Jean de Luz, I concluded that G. must have been on that boat.[1]

There was a continuous coming and going in that room, but I hardly moved from my palliasse and was most of the time asleep or sick; I did not talk to anybody, but on the second or third evening a soldier sat down on my palliasse and began to talk to me. His face somehow reminded me of Mario's, although it was clean-shaven and round. He asked whether he could do anything for me, as I was apparently ill; and when I said no, he said that this was very regrettable, as for the last few weeks he had looked in vain for somebody whom he could help, being a Father of the Order of the Dominicans, mobilised as an Army chaplain, but this was apparently a time in which nobody could help anybody. He also told me that he was in charge of a convent at St. Zacharie, near Marseilles, a Dominican foundation for ex-prostitutes and female ex-convicts. He was only thirty and reminded me very much of Mario; he had the same peculiar way of smiling; perhaps years of living with a bunch of women in a lonely spot produced similar results in a young priest as years of solitary confinement in a young revolutionary. We had a long talk about Christianity and Socialism

---

[1] This false rumour originated from garbled wireless reports of the tragedy of the *Lancastria* off St. Nazaire a week before; but I did not learn that until three months later.

and 'Render unto Cæsar the things which are Cæsar's', and then I got up and we had dinner at the N.C.O.s' mess. I told him my real name and my story and felt somewhat relieved; I also told him that I thought he had turned up just at the right moment; he said, '*Le bon Dieu est un metteur-en-scène raffiné.*' But at night I was sick again and the fog and mist returned.

There is an entry in my diary which I cannot locate chronologically, but which must date from the next day:

'Strolled through Bayonne, dizzy, looked at Gothic cathedral, thought G. could explain to me all about it. Then saw a nameplate on a house: Maître Lalande, *Avocat à la Cour*. Had sudden idea, when Germans come in tonight, best way to disappear would be to be in prison until war and occupation is over. A man in prison is a forgotten man. So went in, rang at Maître Lalande's door. He was just having his meal, came out with napkin in his hand, elderly, fattish, clever-looking type. Asked him what offence a man should commit to go to prison for about six months. Thought first I was drunk, then understood; was very nice, offered me wine and fruit and money. Accepted wine, but spilled glass over table cloth. Then he explained: if, for instance, I smashed a shop window with a brick, I had to face a military tribunal and would either (*a*) be shot for looting or (*b*) acquitted on account of drunkenness; there was nothing in between. Same thing with any other offence he could think of, as we were under martial law. "*Rien à faire, mon pauvre ami: si on vous fusille, ça ne vous avance pas; si on vous acquitte, non plus.*" Was offended that I did not take money, accompanied me to the doorway, kissed me on both cheeks. Think he was more drunk than I. Limped back to Château Neuf. They are not yet in.'

Next day, or the day after, there was a nervous tension in

the barracks; we were confined to our quarters and there
were rumours that the Germans had arrived in the town.
During the previous days several detachments, mainly of the
younger classes, had left on lorries for non-occupied territory; the armistice terms provided that '. . . the French
armed forces in the territory to be occupied by Germany are
to be speedily withdrawn to territory not to be occupied, and
to be discharged'. But apparently there were not enough
lorries and the unit to which I had been attached—the
22ième *Compagnie de Passage*—was stuck.

We were not allowed to leave the Château Neuf on that
day, but somehow I managed to get out; I wanted to know
and I wanted to see. I limped down the dusty, sunbathed
streets to the bridge over the Nive; and then I saw. I saw
them at a few yards—the dark green tanks, rattling slowly
and solemnly over the roadway like a funeral procession,
and the black-clad figures standing in the open turrets with
wooden faces, and the puffing black motor bikes with men
in black leather and black goggles on their eyes behind them,
and the burning red flags with the white circle and the black
spider in the middle, flapping lazily in the heat. The shutters
of the windows were closed, the streets were empty, the sun
blazing. I leant against a doorway and was sick and looked
at them, and imagined that in passing they all looked at me.
For they had hunted me all across the Continent, and whenever I had paused and stopped, thinking there was safety,
they had come after me, with their slow, rattling, thundering
funeral procession and the lazy black spider on their flag.
They had come after me all the way from Berlin to Paris,
via Vienna and Prague, and down the Atlantic coast, until in
this outermost corner of France they had at last caught up
with me. I looked at the black procession in the sunshine;
there was a tall figure standing immobile in one of the moving turrets; I saw his face, the face of a young peasant lad
from Pomerania, with goggling, cretinous eyes and with a

vague grin undecided between kindliness and brutality, staring at the cathedrals and vineyards of France and licking his pursed lips, like a dog in front of a bone. I could not hate him, hard as I tried, but I wished I had a rifle to shoot at him—not to kill, but to be killed on the level. I had never understood the mentality of Russian and Chinese terrorists, of the Serb and Belgian *franc-tireurs* in the last war, their apparently senseless actions with the certainty of immediate death before them. Now, standing in the doorway, sick, ragged and dirty, and staring at the victorious procession, I understood that a man could kill to cover his aching nakedness.

I limped back, up the sunny, tortuous road, and found my company lined up in the courtyard, ready to leave. I got my kit and fell in with them. There were no lorries, so we had to march; we did not march through the centre, but made a détour all round the town, and stole out of the town like thieves. We crossed the railway bridge over the Adour and gained the dusty highroad, heading east, towards non-occupied France.

AFTERMATH

'The representatives of the people of France, formed into a National Assembly, considering that ignorance, neglect, or contempt of human rights are the sole causes of public misfortunes and corruptions of Government, have resolved to set forth in a solemn declaration these natural, imprescriptible, and inalienable rights.'

Preamble to the Declaration of the Rights of Man and of Citizens of the National Assembly of France, A.D. 1789.

I

THAT night we camped in barns in a little village, only about five miles east of Bayonne, the name of which I have forgotten. We were all *isolés*, and the men were tired, sullen, loaded with luggage and unwilling to march. The next day it became even worse. We dragged along the road like a band of tramps, and in the afternoon over twenty men out of two hundred were missing. They had their homes in the occupied zone and thought that once they got into the non-occupied zone they would not be allowed to return.

The heat was terrible, the roads dusty, the men thirsty and sweaty. Every half-hour or so we simply sat down by the roadside, and the three officers and three N.C.O.s who were with us could do nothing but follow our example. The officers, a captain, an old lieutenant, and a young second lieutenant, behaved with tact and dignity; they were deaf to unpleasant remarks and tried to keep up at least the appearance of military order. Some soldiers still had their combat equipment; during the worst hours of the midday heat, one after the other lagged behind and dropped his rifle and steel helmet into the roadside ditch. Around three o'clock the captain ordered another halt and told us to pile up the remaining rifles, bayonets, steel helmets and cartridge belts next to a deserted farmhouse on the road. We arranged everything in neat piles, and there we left them and marched on. Turning my head, it made a queer impression on me to see those piles of arms in the middle of the lonely landscape, under the blazing sun.

P

Later I found out that the idea had been to take as many arms as possible into unoccupied territory, although the armistice terms stipulated that they should be left behind; but on the road the captain had changed his mind, realising that when we reached the demarcation line there would be no arms left, and also perhaps because he feared that we might run into a German column.

I walked most of the time with Père Darrault, the young Dominican. Rivulets of sweat were running down his forehead and cheeks; his tonsure was burnt dark red by the sun. I told him how I had watched the German tank column and about that lad standing in the turret, and that for the first time in my life I had felt a real urge to kill—to kill without hatred. '*C'est logique*,' he said : 'the only alternative to killing is preaching.' 'Go and try it,' I said. 'Go and preach to those motorised Neanderthal men.' 'What else have you and your friends done during these last years but preach to them?' he said; 'only your preachings and teachings were a little dry. They sounded like the rustling of dry leaves.' He took a long gulp of red wine mixed with water from his field-flask. 'Your results with them were not much better either,' I said. '*Mon cher*,' he answered with his Mario-smile, '*we* can wait. We can wait and wait and wait. But you can't. That is the difference between us.' 'Concretely—what would you preach to those men in the turrets?' 'Always the same simple word which we have preached for the last two thousand years : Love.' 'That is your mistake,' I said. 'Love is no alternative to hatred. They can live perfectly well side by side in compartments of the same mind.' 'Not the love *we* mean. And what is your alternative?' I had waited for this, for I thought that I had a good answer, and wanted to try it out on him. 'The remedy against hatred,' I said, 'is to teach them to laugh and to smile.' He began to chuckle. '*Bon Dieu*,' he said. 'To make a *Boche* laugh—*c'est possible*. But to teach him to smile—that is too much, even for a Dominican.'

In the evening of that second day we camped at Hasparren, a village sixteen miles from Bayonne and still within the occupied zone, the limit of which was roughly twenty miles to the east. As my feet were in a bad state, I went to a pharmacy in the village to have them bandaged, and just then a car with an old couple, a little fat dog, and heaps of luggage in it stopped in front of the pharmacy and the old woman got out to buy some aspirin. I asked her where they were going. She said to Lourdes—she was going to pray for France and at the same time hoped to get cured of her rheumatism. I asked them for a lift, just for twenty miles, to get over the demarcation line; the old woman whined that the car was overloaded, the axles would break, that Coco, the dog, was frightened by strangers, etc.; but finally they agreed to take me to St. Palais, on the border of the unoccupied zone, if I paid them one-third of the petrol—about 6d.

We went off; the old man drove the car at a speed of about fifteen miles an hour along the narrow secondary road to St. Palais. It was already dark, and the road deserted. A mile or two after Hasparren we were stopped by a flash of electric torches and a primitive barricade of branches across the road. I first thought it was a German post; then I saw three soldiers of my company sitting on the barricade. One of them had a shoe off and his foot was bandaged. He limped over to the car, propped up by the two others, and explained that he had been wounded in the foot and that during the march from Bayonne the wound had opened; he too was anxious to get to non-occupied territory, but no car had stopped to give him a lift, so they had built the barricade. His face was livid, but he spoke in a calm and polite tone. The old woman began once more to whine about the axles and Coco, and the old man said he had been an officer in the last war and by God the men had

fought better and had never dared to talk in such an in-
solent way; would they clear the barricade away and let us
pass at once, or else he would report them to the *gendarmerie*. One of the three said we could only pass if we took
the wounded man; while they argued I had opened the door
and dragged the man inside, in spite of his protestations,
for he was rather timid. The old man shrieked that we were
Bolshies and Hitler would teach us a lesson, and the woman
shrieked that her husband had high blood pressure, that the
excitement would kill him and that we were *des assassins,*
and Coco yelped and yapped. In the meantime, the two
others had cleared away the barricade and told the old man
that if he did not shut up and get going they would break
the neck of his *putain d'un chien*, so at last we departed. We
did not speak a word until we arrived at St. Palais, where
the wounded man and I got out in front of the Mairie; I
paid my 6*d.*; the old woman cried, '*Bon Dieu*, these brutes
don't even know how to say Thank you.' I said, No, but did
she perhaps want a tip. They drove off, shaking with indignation, and the old man looked as if he were really working
up a stroke.

The demarcation line was just a hundred yards beyond
the last house of the village, but the Germans had not yet
occupied it; they were expected early next morning. The
boundary was the *Route Nationale* No. 133, running from
St. Jean Pied de Port north-east through St. Palais and
Orthez to Mont de Marsan, roughly parallel to the Atlantic
coast, at an average distance of thirty-five miles as the crow
flies. The *Maire* of St. Palais was an old farmer, who treated
us to hot coffee and wine and offered us beds in the school,
but I preferred to sleep in the fields on the other side of the
demarcation line. Next morning I limped on to Mauléon,
about twelve miles further east, where I intended to wait
for the arrival of my company. But the *Bureau de la Place*
at Mauléon told me that the company had changed its

direction and had marched to Navarrenx, ten miles further to the north. So I trudged on to Navarrenx.

All these picturesque little villages in the Basses Pyrenées were full of stragglers like myself, and the authorities were busy concentrating them in improvised *cantonnements des isolés*, where they were to stay until the demobilisation began; nobody knew when that would be. The cantonments consisted of a few requisitioned barns or cattle sheds, where the men were housed—from 50 to 200 per village—with one or two officers in charge of them. The gendarmes had orders to hold up all isolated stragglers and put them into the nearest cantonment. I could have stayed at Mauléon or any place I liked, but I was anxious to find my Dominican friend again and also my small valise, which I had left with him, containing the last remnants of my earthly possessions —a few letters from G., my civilian suit, etc. But at Navarrenx they knew nothing of the 22nd Company from Bayonne—it seemed to have vanished somewhere on the road between Hasparren and St. Palais.

The next two or three days I wandered about the desolate, burning roads of the Basses Pyrenées in search of my ghost company, alone or with other stragglers, who were visibly transforming themselves into tramps, limping in the sun or getting an occasional lift. From Navarrenx I went to Laas, from Laas to Audage, from Audage I got a lift to Pau, and from Pau they sent me back to Audage. These day-long, dawdling wanderings along the road with the distant screen of the white Pyrenees before my eyes, while the limpid air seemed to boil around me and the asphalt to melt under my heels, had a curiously calming effect; I had no luggage, not even a comb or piece of soap, slept in barns or open fields, had not seen a newspaper for days, and dragged my aching feet in a sort of trance, with the agreeably detached sensation of having lost everything that a man can lose, including my name and even my shadow. Only once or twice, when I found strawberries growing by the side of the road and remembered how G. and I had relished picking them at Roquebillière, did the past come back with a sharp, thin stab; but after a mile or two on the road, the sun had boiled it out of my head again.

After three or four days my feet got into such a bad state that I had to give up the search for my vanished company and look for a nice cantonment in which to settle down. On my wanderings I had discovered a forlorn little village on a hilltop hear Navarrenx. It was in fact a mere agglomeration of about twenty old and ruinous farmhouses with orchards, fields and meadows; there was a minute old church, a minute cemetery, a tiny wooden war memorial, and that was all. Not even a grocer's shop or a *bistro*. The village had about a hundred inhabitants, and about the same number of *isolés* were billeted in farms and stables, with an old captain and a young *aspirant* to look after them. I liked that place; it had a nice name: Susmiou.

The old captain agreed to attach me to his cantonment and to ask for instructions as to what to do with me, as I did not belong to the category to be demobilised like the rest of his men. He said it might take a long time, but I had no conceivable reason on earth to be in a hurry. In non-occupied territory, under the name of *Légionnaire* Dubert, I was safe; I had never felt so safe for years—and had never cared less for my safety. I had no plans, no hope and no expectations, except a remainder of curiosity. I spent two months in the *cantonnement des isolés*, and started again my diary. It is an incoherent, disorderly, scribbled diary, but it kept my mind busy, and it may convey something of the atmosphere amongst the soldiers of the defeated army.

July 3rd, 1940

Found accommodation in a barn where only three others are sleeping on the ground floor: Corporal Gillevic,

Privates Lebras and Moog. Gillevic and Lebras are both
Bretons; Gillevic, a red-haired, freckled giant, rather surly,
Lebras a dark moon-faced sturdy peasant farmer, slow in
speech and gesture, not precisely bright. Moog comes from
Rennes and was in civilian life a tramp, long, thin, with a
squint, and seventeen other bodily defects which he enume-
rates with pride, including a periodically disjointed hip and
'cold abscesses' on both legs.

No straw in the barn; we sleep on a heap of maize stalks,
stored here for pig fodder. The barn has an upper floor
where twenty others sleep. When they trample over the
wooden boards over our heads, flakes of cobweb flutter
down on us. Never saw such giant cobwebs : they must be
decades old, coated with dust and dirt to almost finger-thick
fabrics, which hang down from the beams overhead like
back-cloths from the stage loft.

Borrowed some copies of the *Petite Gironde* of the last
two days. Russians have annexed Bessarabia, Pétain
Government moved to Clermont-Ferrand, preparing return to Paris. Marquet appointed Minister of the Interior;
Pomaret goes. Papa Pétain plays musical chairs with his
Cabinet. Papers appear on only one sheet, more than half
of it advertisements from broken-up families searching for
each other or for lost bikes, cats, luggage. Only print German and Italian communiqués.[1] Rumour in cantonment
that Spain has declared war on Britain.

July 4th, 1940

At night a rat crawled over my arm. Moog flashed his
torchlight on ceiling, saw entire procession of fat rats running along a beam. Moog says his cousin bitten in cheek by
rat died of blood poisoning. CI GÎT LÉGIONNAIRE DUBERT,

[1] The *Petite Gironde* is printed in occupied Bordeaux. Newspapers
appearing in non-occupied territory were allowed to print the British
communiqués too.

WHO BELIEVED IN SOCIALISM AND DIED OF A RAT-BITE.

Morning walked in Lebras' slippers to hospital in Navarrenx (only a mile from Susmiou), had my feet bandaged, bought comb, soap, toothbrush. Only 200 francs left. Shops in Navarrenx empty : no cigarettes, no matches, no cheese, no meat, no vegetables; one pound apples, 8 francs (normally 1 or 2 francs). Greengrocer says all fault of the refugees from the north (about 6 million in the unoccupied zone) and of transport breakdown. '*L'hiver on va crêver de faim.*' Asked 35 francs for safety razor which normally cost 7 francs, saying it is *rasoir de luxe*. Didn't buy it, shaved with Lebras' cut-throat razor (first time for a week). Moustache already twistable.

Afternoon played *manille*, kind of simplified whist, with Gillevic, Lebras and Moog, and drank wine, which the farmer who owns our barn sells us at 2 francs 50 a litre. Farmers unforthcoming, reserved, eagerly waiting for demobilisation to get rid of us. They speak a mainly Spanish *patois* and their barns and stables are very dirty, but the cottages are clean. They hate the Frenchmen from the northern provinces, call them *les boches du nord*. Never knew this hatred was so strong. Similar to the Bavarians and Austrains traditional dislike of the Prussians. *Vice versa*, Lebras says he never saw in Brittany such dirty stables and badly kept cattle. Farmers would like us to work in their fields, but without pay. They say it's a shame to see such a lot of idlers fed for nothing.

July 5th, 1940

Morning great surprise. Condition of my feet improved, so made an excursion with Lebras, in his slippers, to Castelnau (next village on the Mauléon road, about a mile from us). There is a *bistro* next to the church, and in the *bistro* sat Père Darrault, with his red tonsure, drinking wine with water and converting an Algerian Jew. Grand scene. And the vanished company too is in Castelnau, but out of 200 only 60 are left, the rest have simply melted away on the road. '*Que voulez-vous, nous sommes l'armée en déroute.*' '*L'armée en déroute*' has become a popular slogan; everybody uses it as a comic expression without any tragic undertone. Perhaps it is an echo of Hugo's famous poem, the first one learns at school—

> '. . . *C'était un Espagnol de l'armée en déroute,*
> *Qui se traînait, blessé, au bord de la route. . . .*'

Learned from Père Darrault my valise lost: all luggage had been collected on a van at Hasparren and taken to Castelnau, but when the company arrived there three days later, the soldiers who had transported it had looted the contents of the valises, bags and knapsacks, and vanished with the van. As a supreme joke they had excremented into the empty valises and knapsacks, so that everything had to be burnt. So all I have left is my notebook, fountain-pen, *carnet* of Paris bus tickets and 180 francs.

Père Darrault says there is a symbolical meaning in this complete annihilation of a man's past. Asked him sarcastically whether he thought I should throw fountain-pen and bus tickets away too. He said no : God dislikes his intentions being dramatised.

On the back of the bus tickets there is an advertisement:

LOTERIE NATIONALE
Améliorez votre sort. Ne laissez pas passer cette chance.

July 6th, 1940

Saw in *Dépêche de Toulouse* that British Fleet attacked French Fleet at Mers el Kebir; diplomatic relations broken off. Asked M. Pitrel, the farmer who owns our barn, to be allowed to listen to radio; listened for first time since Bordeaux. Very funny, e.g.: 'The Soviet Press condemns severely the piratical attack of the British. Political circles in Moscow are indignant.' Then a quotation from an Argentine newspaper praising French courage. M. Pitrel said it's all German lies; it was certainly the French Fleet which attacked the British. British are as bad as *Boches*, but, anyhow, one cannot change friends from one day to the next, it's indecent, *ça ne se fait pas*.

Broke the news to Gillevic, Lebras and several others, but nobody seems to care. Corporal Jules, the cook, said: 'We should have scuttled that whore of a fleet before the Boches got hold of it. The Germans have always scuttled their warships when they were cornered. *Le Boche c'est un sauvage, mais il a de l'honneur.*' General agreement; that was all.

Nobody here reads newspapers or listens to the radio. They are convinced it is all German stuff (unable to distinguish between direct German propaganda from occupied territory and indirectly controlled Press and radio of free zone, they totally distrust all newspapers and broadcasts). The only thing they care for, which they discuss from morning to night, is demobilisation. But nobody knows when it will begin. Of course they would all beat it and go home without waiting for formalities, but there is a decree saying that whoever cannot show a demobilisation certificate issued by the military authorities cannot get a job and will incur penalties, etc.

Later went to Navarrenx for treatment. Saw several German *émigré* women previously interned in concentration camp at Gurs (four miles away); now released, don't know where to go, what to do. Talked to one in a café; said she is sending telegrams to all concentration camps in nonoccupied France, trying to find her husband; praying that he should not be in occupied territory.

Hundreds of women in her case are living in Castelnau, Population calls them *les Gursiennes*. Peasants lend rooms to Navarrenx, Sus, Géronce and the other villages around.

them or let them work in fields *au pair*. They look undernourished, exhausted, but tidy. All wear turbans *à la mode,*
a coloured kerchief round the head.

July 7th

About one-third of our cantonment had at one time been
captured by German troops, but were let go or escaped.
Jules was in a block-house somewhere on the Meuse; they
had waited for reinforcements which did not come; they
saw the German tanks crossing on rafts at 400 or 500 yards;
adjutant gave order not to shoot, explaining it would be
stupid to get killed pointlessly, Germans having already cut
communications; captain and staff had disappeared during
previous night. So they hoisted white flag; Germans were
very pleasant, collected arms, told French soldiers to walk to
some prisoners' camp around Mezières; said, 'We can't escort
you, have more important things to do. You'll find the way
alone'; gave them a certificate attesting that they were prisoners. Half the company really went to that camp, the others
beat it. Lots of similar stories, monotonous in their sameness.
Rumour says there are about 2 million prisoners, but about
the same number must have escaped or been allowed to go.

Unanimous admiration for German Army's efficiency.
Better tanks, better camouflage, better discipline, better food,
better equipment. They admire precision of German artil-
lery and especially their espionage service. Sergeant Lepetit
alleges they knew not only all our plans but the movements
of every unit down to battalions. Says on Luxembourg
frontier Germans called to them through loudspeakers :
'Welcome, 2nd Battalion of the 51st, we know you arrived
yesterday from Metz. Metz was better, eh?', etc.

Gillevic says during final retreat his regiment was stuck
on the road, chain of lorries at least two miles long, German
'planes had circled over them, but not a single bomb was
dropped. Others have similar experiences. '*Ils ne sont pas*

méchants.' Moog says he was in Rouen under German occupation; praises correctness and discipline of German
troops : 'Any soldier who takes a pin or touches a girl is shot
on the spot.' Whereas later he was in a camp near Bordeaux
and on leaving 'our men looted the stores and even stole
the chalice from the church.' . . .

This was after evening soup, sitting around in the garden
in front of barn, and all competed in admiring the *Boches*
and vilifying the French. Masochism of the defeat. All
unanimous that '*nous êtions vendus*'—have been betrayed.
Betrayed by the generals, by Fifth Column—'there was a
Fifth Columnist in every company staff'—and by politicians. No distinction between Left and Right, Reynaud and
Laval. Accusations against Jews and refugees; Sergeant
Lepetit says his company was attacked by 'a column of
Jewish refugees' near Longwy; all believe it, including Jules
and Gillevic, who are Socialists. No attempt to discrimi-
nate, to discover political motive-patterns; everything is
merde and *pourriture*, one ubiquitous, all-embracing conspiracy of betrayal. When the wine began to act, all spoke at
the same time, accusing all and sundry—the routed army
playing blind man's bluff.

July 8th

Two simultaneous decrees: one, by the local *préfet*,
pinned on the town halls of Navarrenx, Sus, Susmiou,
Castelnau : All ex-internee aliens of the Camp of Gurs have
to leave the *département des Basses Pyrenées* within twenty-
four hours, or else be interned again. Second, from the
Government : No alien allowed to travel or move from his
actual domicile.

Saw Frau Mueller (the *émigré* woman I had met the
previous day) in hysterical state. Advised her to stay where
she was, her farmer patrons would protect her. Said 400 or
500 women are still at Gurs camp; the Gestapo came twice

with lorries to take the Nazi internees home; these Nazi women had been boycotted by the majority and on leaving had shouted: 'You wait. Now it's our turn. We'll soon come back for you.'

Sensation in the cantonment: demobilisation has begun. First lot to be disbanded: all men over forty-five; farmers and agricultural labourers over thirty-five; volunteers for the duration. But only those whose domicile is in non-occupied territory. Most of our men are from occupied territory. Haven't heard from their families since invasion started, don't know whether still alive, whether houses still stand. Sergeant Lepetit says: the Government is sabotaging demobilisation, perhaps because they want to make war on England. He dislikes the English as much as the *Boches,* but 'if the Government wants to start another war, they'd better not count on me'. Lebras says if not demobilised by end of the month will present himself at a German post and ask Germans to demobilise him.

July 9th

Read report of meeting of *députés* at Petit Casino, Vichy, preliminary to National Assembly. Bonnet boasts that on September 2nd, 1939 (when Poland was already at war with Germany), he had 'indefatigably pursued his efforts for peace' and had agreed, in the name of the French Government, that a conference be held during the next weeks (i.e. after Poland was swallowed by Germany). Complains that this settlement was made impossible by 'stubbornness of British and Polish, who demanded preliminary withdrawal of German troops from Poland'.

But the real fun was Spinasse, leading Socialist *député*: 'We must break with illusions of past. We believed in individual liberty, in man's independence. This was an anticipation of a future beyond our reach. . . .' Laval thanks speakers 'in a few words full of emotion'. Then Tixier-

Vignancourt; motion : 'To discover and punish all civilian and military persons responsible for outbreak and pursuit of the war....'

That is beginning of the Terror. Worse than revolution and counter-revolution : the Terror of the Crooks and the Senile. Good night, France.

July 10th

Rumours of landing of British troops in Dunkirk and Boulogne. For the first time the *types* of the cantonment take interest. General discussion of England's chances. Am stupefied to discover more than half believe England will win in the end. Yesterday they sang hymns to German efficiency; now they praise British stamina. Blind man's bluff. But there is something else in it too : They dislike England, but know that an English victory is their only chance of getting rid of the *Boches*. As to taking action, that's another matter. Wonder whether any ideal in the world would induce these men to fight again in less than, say, ten years. But if British landing in Boulogne true (touch wood), things may change as quickly as after Bonaparte's return from Elba. The key of a soldier's morale is perhaps not his belief in the justice of his cause but the promise of victory. An army with the *certainty* of victory is invincible; an army full of enthusiasm, idealism, etc., is not. (See Spain.) If Boulogne is true, even Lepetit will sing 'God save the King'. *Inshallah*.

July 11th

No confirmation of Boulogne; but French parliament's *hara-kiri* accomplished, Pétain gets *plein pouvoirs* to abolish Constitution, to promulgate new Constitution by simple degree. New slogan : *Travail, Famille, Patrie*, to replace *Liberté, Égalité, Fraternité*. Warrants of arrest against Kerillis, Pertinax, Buré, and even against poor Tabouis. Perhaps Pétain believes she is a witch.

Nobody is disappointed about Boulogne not being true; they have apparently forgotten all about it since yesterday. As for the Constitution, etc., nobody cares either. Unique preoccupation: demobilisation. To get home and not be bothered any more by History and such like silly things. I have coined a motto which has become popular at once:

   '*Que l'humanité se débrouille sans moi.*'

July 12th

Frau Mueller still in Navarrenx; discovered her husband at Le Vernet, no hope for his release. She said: 'You, a Swiss, can't understand what it all means.' Tempted to tell her my real name and how well I knew Vernet, but resisted. Most other *Gursiennes* are still here; where should they go, what should they do? Two or three live with their men, released from German camps; but most men are still interned; complete anarchy in their treatment, all depends apparently on local commandant or *préfet*. Saw Dr. A. and hunchbacked Dr. Pollak (who had sat next to me at the *Commissariat du XVième* when I was last arrested). Averted my head and they did not recognise me—moustache very helpful.

Went to Castelnau to see Dominican. They live in barns like us, but Père Darrault has got a nice room with well-to-do *métayeur* (cattle farmer) named Siméon, and another farmer gave him the keys to an empty *ermitage* (tiny summer house) where he meditates during afternoons. Invited me to dinner with Siméon, who treated us to ham, bacon, eggs, sweets, wine—friendly old man, believes that we lost war because Blum and Pierre Cot have personally pocketed all money meant for armaments and aviation. Says Blum arrived in Argentine with sack of jewels—has read it in *Gringoire* or somewhere. Tried to contradict, but hopeless, and Père Darrault not helpful—smiled and nodded to everything. Reproached him for this. Said politics not his domain. Parted on rather chilly terms.

July 13th

Our barn reeks of urine and excrement; everybody uses the back garden; impossible to persuade them to go at least 100 yards away into the fields. In the morning they moisten their hands and faces at the well; in spite of the heat they never strip to the belt.

There are four Spanish former militia men in our cantonment; they had been interned and had volunteered for the duration. They talk bad French, look even more wretched than the rest of us, keep apart. Are sort of boycotted. Sergeant Lepetit says they steal—everybody believes it. Tried to talk to them in Spanish, but they distrust me—scared and fierce. Yesterday they quarrelled with Fontanin, captain's orderly; captain, without inquiring into matter, sent all four to prison in Navarrenx under armed escort. When marched off one cried: '*Libertad, Egalidad, Fraternidad.*'

At night went to Sus with Jules and Lefèbre, both members Socialist Party—workers from Paris suburbs. They called Pétain 'Philippe le Gaga', made fun of the 'national revolution', but lack any positive outlook, except hope for British victory. Asked them whether willing to try to get to England. Lefèbre said no, wants to join wife and kids, doesn't even know whether they're alive. Later—*on verra*. Jules said (after some wine), he would be ready to die, but only if he saw a chance of victory. Fed up with making a fool of himself. 'Might join the Tommies if they manage to come over here, but I wouldn't go there.' Sat in Sus *bistro* until 10 p.m.—in the back room an adjutant from the *gendarmerie* was making merry with three *Gursiennes*—two Polish women and one German Jewess. Made them drink Pernod plus rum. Sort of moderate orgy. Met in the lavatory the Jewish girl, sick and crying; said: 'Do you think he'll give me a travel permit?' When back, Lefèbre asked me whether I had had the girl. Said I was an idiot; yesterday he had had a Jewess from Gurs for 20 francs, and her husband had known about it—'nice old chappy, looked like a doctor or something'.

July 14th

French national holiday : commemoration of storming of Bastille. Captain assembled us at the wooden war memorial in front of cemetery, made a short speech : Reason for defeat was an international conspiracy of plutocrats and Socialists, inspired by Jews.

Later captain called me : said I shall be sent shortly to Camp of Rivesalt, where all colonials are gathered to be shipped to Algeria. But if I preferred to stay until physically fit again, he could easily manage it. I said, no thanks. Asked me whether as a foreigner I agreed with the reasons of defeat he gave in his speech. I said no; plutocracy and Socialists are mortal enemies, and Jewish conspiracy a Nazi invention. He said worriedly : 'I wonder, I wonder.' He is such a decent old man—whose fault, if not ours, that we did not manage to open his eyes? Said proudly he had never read other paper in his life but *Action Française*.

At night in the barn Lebras told stories of ghosts and witches in Brittany. He believes in the evil eye, in killing a man by sticking a pin through his photograph—his neighbour died this way, etc. Said he once had a girl by giving her a love potion. Said there is an old Breton wizard, he lives in Paris, but if anything is wrong, the farmers call him—costs 200 francs, but he cures cattle and men, drives out demons, etc.; he is called the 'Anti-Spirit'. Gillevic too has heard of him.

July 15th

Am not going to Rivesalt—order cancelled.

Read in *Petite Gironde* Carl Einstein has committed suicide; first cut his veins in concentration camp, was saved, released, threw himself in Gave d'Oloron—the river run-

Q

ning through Navarrenx—with a stone tied round his neck.
Yesterday I was bathing in the Gave. Place not mentioned,
but must be close by. Paper said, '*Un nommé* Carl Einstein, *refugié d'Allemagne, neveu du professeur* Albert Einstein'. Saw him last in Café des Deux Magots in Paris,
about 1939; he had been a volunteer officer in Spain, came
back already broken by defeat. Remember what sensation
his first book on Negro sculpture created in Germany.

Thought by becoming *Légionnaire* Dubert and growing a
moustache could escape the ghosts of the past. But there is
no escape; and there should not be. Perhaps no hazard that
wherever I go, in most unexpected places, Frau Muellers
and *Gursiennes* and hunch-backed Dr. Pollaks turn up. '*Le
bon Dieu est un metteur-en-scène raffiné*.'

Went to Castelnau to see Père Darrault. Told him Einstein's death; told him about Frau Mueller, about sick German girl in *bistro*, etc. He said, he goes every day to Navarrenx and Gurs on Siméon's bicycle, he has some protégés
among *Gursiennes* and German refugees, is working hard to
convert them to Catholicism. I said : '*Est-ce que c'est le moment?*' He said : 'Yes, it is the right moment; at the very
bottom of misery their hearts open for grace.' He took me
to his *ermitage* and proved by Isaiah, the Gospels, etc., that
the Kingdom of God will come when the last Jew is converted to the true faith. The remarkable thing is that he is
not a fanatic, but a dialectician—uncanny similarity with S.
in Vernet when he defended the Stalin-Hitler pact; same
quasi-schizophrenic logics : a closed system, perfectly sound
and logical in itself, waterproof against reality; invulnerable
because all counter-arguments fly off at a tangent. Perhaps
deepest cause of Socialists' failure that they tried to conquer
the world by reason. Perhaps Hitler's genius is not demagogy, not lying, but the fundamentally irrational approach
to the masses, the appeal to the pre-logical, totemistic mentality. (Jung's arche-types.) If human brains functioned like

clockworks Utopia would be reached in a year. The correct
metaphor is not a clockwork, but several overlapping mag-
netic fields.

Pétain—Philippe le Gaga—has formed another new
Cabinet.

July 16th

Reportage on atmosphere in Vichy by Raymond Millet
in *Temps*—begins with praising heroic atmosphere created
by Pétain and continues: 'Yet at the same time some aspects of the residential town still remind one of a Vanity
Fair. . . . Petty ambitions abound, also courtesans and intrigues . . . queer mixture of puritanism and frivolity. . . .'
Wonder censorship let it pass.

About twenty of our cantonment have been demobilised;
the others waiting feverishly. Complete indifference to
newspapers, wireless, politics. Only home.

Radio says Britain 'gives way' to Japan, will close Burma
Road. Very disturbing; fortunately nobody here cares. But
perhaps they *feel* that there is something wrong with fighting for liberty and letting the Chinese down.

July 17th

Colonials left tonight for Rivesalt. Invited René for a
farewell drink. He is a *mec* (pimp), a Corsican, very hand-
some, charcoal eyes; served six months' prison at nineteen,
then enlisted in *Infanterie Coloniale*. He 'worked' at Marseilles; told with gusto how it was done: one picked up a girl,
lived with her four to six weeks, then, when she had burnt
her bridges, sold her to a brothel for a commission between
100 and 1,000 francs. He is almost illiterate; told me his
brother-in-law (also a Corsican) has picked up an English
tourist woman at Bastia; she sends him money regularly.
'Her father is a lord—sort of *sénateur*—she says; once he
lent his car to the King. Wonder why the King hasn't got

his own car; perhaps because they are so democratic over there; everybody lends him his, *il se débrouille.*' He got his six months for running a knife into a colleague. '*Quand il s'agit de pognon, la vie ne compte pas.*'

Went to Navarrenx: no cigarettes, no matches, no tobacco—nothing.

July 18th

Found *Le Temps* of 16th: front page (there is only one page) splashes over two columns Churchill's speech, but more than half censored—blank. Headline: 'We'll hold out.' *Temps* really courageous.

Moog tells long story of an *aspirant* who at the front, under very heavy bombardment, shaved every morning and used eau de Cologne. 'This is what our officers were like.' Gillevic and Lebras agreed. Strange—thought that such a show of imperturbability would impress them; in England it would. Then somebody said, during the retreat he tried in vain to get a lift, finally, he stopped a smart officer's car by aiming his rifle at it.

Evening in *bistro,* Jules tells me about some fighting around Rethel which sounds rather different—a company holding a tank column with 75-mm. guns for several hours, killed almost to last man, and similar incidents. Says: 'Don't you believe all this talk. They drag everything into the mud *parce qu'ils en ont le cœur plein.*' Had they not been betrayed by the General Staff, they would have put up a great show. Where the officers were good, the men fought 'like savages'; but only two out of ten officers were good.

July 19th

Radio and paper say invasion of England imminent. Found in village school French edition of British Blue Book on Nazi concentration camps; gave it to captain, told him soon it will have rarity value, when the great bookburning starts. He said: 'You don't believe seriously that such things can happen in France?'

July 20th

Frau Mueller says when the Gestapo came to Gurs to take away the last lot of Nazi internees, a Jewish *émigrée* buttonholed a German officer, asked 'news about her beloved Dresden', complained about bad food the French give them. Same evening the internees of her barrack beat her up and decided to boycott her; next day she was taken to prison in Navarrenx. So far Gestapo only carried away women who asked to return to Germany; but they might come to fetch the *émigrées* any day. And the commandant of Gurs still refuses to release them. Same thing in Vernet. Some women managed to escape from Gurs—from Vernet nobody succeeded.

July 21st

Demobilisation proceeds, but not to occupied territory. Even the restricted traffic across the demarcation line is interrupted. France cut in two—and most French families were cut into several pieces during the days of panicky flight. Now they are searching for each other desperately. Almost half of the space in the *Dépêche, Petite Gironde*, etc., taken up by advertisements in tiny print of this type:

'*André Roure, who disappeared June 17th near Azay-le-Rideau, please communicate with parents via* Le Temps *Clermont-Ferrand.*'

'*Families Combier, Durand, Scholer of Neuilly are at Cusset, Allier.*'

'*5me Cie C.R.M. from Revigny (Meuse) is at Gendarmerie Vichy (Allier).*'

And so on, thousands per day. As if a gigantic explosion had blown fragments of families all over the country.

July 22nd

Franco claims Gibraltar. Pétain sacks a series of civil servants, survivors of *Front Populaire* era. New decree provides that every civil servant is liable to be sacked without pension, during a period of purge from now to October 31st. Another decree : no soldiers allowed to sit on café *terrasses*. Another, in preparation, will regulate length of bathing suits in inches up from ankle down from hips. Brave new world with subtle nuances : Racial-Fascism in Germany, Clerical-Fascism in Spain, Senilo-Fascism in France.

Poor old captain received telegram : his wife is dying. Is leaving tomorrow. Showed me today's newspapers : Laval takes charge of Press, radio, propaganda; read out nauseating bits of comment praising Hitler. I said : 'What else did you expect?' He said : 'Something different. *Je ne comprends plus rien.*'

July 23rd

Ten others left for Pau to be demobilised; all talk, dream, fever about going home. Where is mine? Can't stop myself envying them. The bitterness of realising that ninety-nine out of a hundred of one's fellow creatures wade through the deluge which has drowned one's existence, barely getting their feet wet. I don't mind perishing with others, but I do mind feeling an exception and a fool.

Went to bathe in the Gave at Navarrenx, in spite of Einstein's memory. Dried in the sun and read that Baltic States vote *Anschluss* to Russia, and Hitler's speech. Sham Socialism and sham heroics. Evening sent M. Pitrel's daughter—nervous, jerky little girl of nine, we call her the grasshopper —to fetch a litre of wine; she did not turn up and we had to send a search party with torches, which found her after several hours hiding in a ditch : she had broken the bottle and was scared of returning. She shivered and sobbed in her ditch, under the flashing torches—this was genuine, that child's intensity of emotion and loneliness—whereas mass feelings always seem to move along distorted sham patterns.

July 24th

Mistler writes in *La Garonne* : 'France is busy purging her mind of any sort of ideology. She has been too much lied to.'

Lebras told me a fascinating story why Doriot's Fascist Party was so popular among farmers in Brittany. Up to 1936, the small farmers sold their wheat for 70 francs to the Co-operative, which was a private enterprise run by the big landowners, monopolising the market. When the Popular Front came to power, it created the *Office du Blé*, run directly by the Government, which, by cutting out intermediary profits, paid 180 francs instead of 70. Whereupon Doriot's paper, sent gratis to every small farmer, started a campaign : 'The Government steals your money—ask them for 200 instead of 180.' . . . Lebras (in his slow, stammering manner, smiling slyly): '. . . *Merde alors*, we talked it over and thought, if the Government pays 180 francs instead of 70, there must be something fishy about it, and they could as well pay 200. But Blum and his Jews refused, so we all voted for Doriot' (whose party was largely financed by the landowners' Co-operative).

I had imagined I knew the proletariat—now I realise that those I met at Party-meetings, in C.P. cells, etc., were exceptions, a selected vanguard, entirely untypical. In three weeks here I have learned more about mass psychology than in seven years of Communist busybodying. Good God! In what an imaginary world we have lived. Have to start quite afresh—all of us.

July 25th

Petit Journal (de La Rocque's paper) proposes abolition

of 'offending foreign expression', e.g. 'grill-room', 'lavatory', and 'five o'clock tea'.

New decree creates special commission to revise all naturalisations granted to aliens since 1927; anybody naturalised since that date can be deprived of French citizenship, also his wife and children.

Walking across Navarrenx bridge, suddenly heard my name called—the real one. It was hunch-backed Dr. Pollak; told him for heaven's sake to shut up, but couldn't get rid of him. Told me he had wondered all the time how I had managed to get out of the Buffalo camp. He had been sent a few days later to a camp in Brittany; when the Germans advanced the Commandant and his staff disappeared overnight; the internees scattered in all directions. Pollak and a group of other old men, all over fifty, mainly Jews, set out and followed the road southward. And on the second day ran into a German column. The German C.O. asked what sort of funny procession they were; they had to explain. C.O. said: 'Don't be scared; we in the Reichswehr are soldiers and don't care about race; camp here, be all of you at the Town Hall of M. [nearby village] at five p.m., and I'll see what I can do for you; but five p.m. sharp, mind.'

There were about sixty of them, old Jews, *émigrés*, scared to death, but disciplined Germans: at 5 p.m. they were at the Town Hall, all complete. Waited quarter of an hour in the midst of astonished German soldiers staring at them, but were not molested; then the C.O. turned up, said he had requisitioned a lorry with French driver, who would take them to unoccupied territory; and so it happened. Now P. is here to get his wife out of Gurs camp—regulation is that women internees are to be released if husband with valid papers comes to fetch them; but Commandant of Gurs makes difficulties.

All day distant gun-fire. Germans practise target shooting with French naval guns off Biarritz.

July 26th

New decrees. Jean Zay, Viennot, and two other *députés* in uniform who had sailed for North Africa during armistice negotiations (hoping to continue fight from colonies), to be tried by court-martial for desertion (Jean Zay, former Minister of Education, was one of the really popular figures of Blum's 1936 Cabinet).

Every Frenchman who left country between May 10th and June 30th without 'valid reason' will be deprived of French nationality, his goods confiscated.

Showed decrees to Gillevic. Said: 'That's right, *ils nous ont vendus.*' Hopeless.

Strange how the entire Army has apparently adopted certain expression of Paris underworld slang—even peasants from Brittany, who had never heard them before. E.g. *mec.* Some time ago the current expression used for fellow soldiers was: *copain* (approx., pal); later became *type* (approx., bloke, but with slight derogatory nuance); finally *mec* (pimp). Apparently Le Bon is right in saying massmentality has tendency to adapt itself to the standard of the lowest component as common denominator.

Soldier from cantonment Sus drowned while swimming in Gave. Was to be demobilised tomorrow.

July 27th

Pitrel has a funny little shepherd dog, Médor; this morning Jules, the cook, performed a cosmetic operation on him, chopping off his ears and tail with his carving knife. Médor whined and howled for an hour, the grasshopper had hysterics, and half the cantonment stood around having fun.

The farmers hate us more and more, because only about a dozen agreed to work ten hours on their fields without pay, for a mere *casse-croûte*. Every day they complain to the *aspirant* (the old captain has left) that we steal chickens and eggs, which is untrue; we only steal apples. The apples are of poor quality, they let them rot under the trees and feed them to the pigs, but they have the cheek to ask us 2 francs a pound. We have made long sticks with sharp points, and, leaning over the fence, harpoon the fallen apples on the ground before the pigs get them.

Evening broadcast : Mandel arrested in Morocco under charge of 'plotting against safety of the State'.

July 28th

Maurice Prax summarises in *Petit Parisien* the first month after signing of armistice : '. . . In this short period a marvellous revolution has been accomplished.' Pity we haven't noticed it.

Boredom in cantonment creates new fashions and crazes every week. First everybody played *manille* ; then it was fishing in the Gave; now they have all started to carve walking-sticks, with a serpent creeping up in spirals to the top, leaf-ornaments in between, and an inscription burnt in with a hot nail above the serpent's head : SOUVENIR DE SUSMIOU —GUERRE DE 1939–1940. All sticks are exactly alike. One invented the model, the others imitated it; nobody tries to figure out a pattern of his own.

Two more soldiers drowned in the Gave. Ban on bathing.

Père Darrault to be demobilised tomorrow. Farewell dinner with Siméon. He is very happy at returning to his convent. Told me funny story about Marseilles prostitute who sought refuge in the convent; next week a gang of pimps came in a smart American car, asked Darrault to hand her back. He refused, they came a second time when he was absent, and took her with them. A week later he received S O S letter from girl in Marseilles brothel; she wanted to return, but was scared by menaces. So Darrault made a plot, borrowed a car and chauffeur from pious friends, kidnapped the girl, and sent her to another Dominican convent in the *Massif Central*. Next day, the gang came, furious;

Père Darrault, smiling, invited them to search the entire convent; gangsters departed, convinced girl had joined a rival gang.

Told Père story worth including in *Contes Drolatiques*, but, of course, he had never read them (although allowed to read certain books on the Index). Had to promise that if I got into trouble, I would come to hide in his place. He accompanied me halfway from Castelnau to Susmiou; starry night; then asked me to allow him to give me his blessing—for his own reassurance. I couldn't refuse; had to kneel down on the cart-track, and have Latin words murmured over me; didn't feel ridiculous, but rather moved. Wonder what G. would have thought of that scene.

July 29th

Radio says final attack on Britain only question of days or even hours. Don't believe it; Hitler won't risk spoiling his series of successes by a gamble. Bet 5 litres wine with Fontanin that no invasion attempt within next three months. All traffic with occupied zone again interrupted. Everybody furious, because demobilisation again delayed.

As a consolation, broadcast appeal to staff of Opéra and Opéra Comique to return at once to Paris; special facilities granted. *Le boche s'amuse.*

Am missing Père Darrault—only person to whom I could talk. But he left me the key of the *ermitage*, so went there in the evening with bottle of wine to meditate and try some writing, but no use. This diary is the maximum effort that am capable of.

Got so much into habit of being called Dubert that when old Pollak hailed me the other day on the bridge it sounded eerie. But sometimes feel so lost that I repeat to myself half aloud my name, the real one—conveys a feeling of complete unreality. Had never known what importance one attaches to one's name, and what a queer, amputated feeling it is to lose it.

July 30th

New decree : Everybody who incites a French soldier or
sailor to join an enemy (?) army is liable to be punished by
death.

July 31st

Mass attack on Dover; 160 German planes participating,
but apparently beaten off with heavy losses. Faint stirring of
interest in the barn. Lebras says : '*La Er Ah Ef tappe pas
mal sur les boches.*' Out of eight present in barrack, six believe invasion will be beaten off. But as to reconquering the
Continent, that is different.

New *caporal*, who escaped ten days ago from prisoners'
camp in occupied zone, says women and children evacuated
en masse from bombarded areas in Germany to southern
France. Says whole Ruhr area in shambles. 'We knew more
in that camp than you mules know over here.' Says if
Roosevelt re-elected U.S.A. will declare war and Hitler go
bust. Scepticism and some contradiction, but rather lame.
Had sudden flash of understanding : *These men are afraid
of hoping because too often deceived. They are on the defensive against the temptation of hope.*

Got rather excited about it. Went to *ermitage* to work;
instead fell into day-dreams (as in Seville Prison): stealing a plane, flying non-stop to Croydon. Wonder whether
direction north-west or north-west-north. Realistic end of
dream : landing in Croydon, clapped into concentration
camp. Bless their far-sighted statesmanship.

Some men, too lazy to climb down the ladder at night,
have got into the habit of urinating in a corner of the upper
barn floor. It trickles down along the wall. No use arguing
with them.

August 1st

The four Spaniards back from prison. Even more reserved, distrustful, unapproachable. Remind me of men

from Leper Barrack. But atmosphere now somewhat friendlier to them. Jules gives them double portions of mid-day soup.

Communiqué from Vichy announces formation of Supreme Court of Justice to try all responsible for starting the war. Press comments: 'To the gallows'—'No mercy'—'Wipe them out.' Germany after defeat of 1918 showed more dignity; but, then, there had been a Social-Democratic revolution.

Afternoon *aspirant* announced whole cantonment moving tomorrow to Géronce, eight miles from here on Navarrenx–Oloron road. We are only about eighty now, and the small cantonments are going to be amalgamated as demobilisation proceeds.

August 2nd. Géronce (Basses Pyrénées)

Yesterday at evening soup Jules and Lefèbre invited me to a drink, to celebrate our departure from Susmiou. They had secretive airs, said there'd be a great surprise, wouldn't tell me where we were going. We started after soup and marched several miles to X., a place where I had not yet been. We drank two litres and played draughts; nothing happened. Around 9 or 10 p.m. a fat civilian came in, winked at Jules, then disappeared. We paid and went out. The fat man took us to his farm, closed the shutters; Jules said I was the Swiss volunteer he had spoken of; the fat man was the *Maire* of X. and we were going to listen to a French broadcast from London. The *Maire* offered us wine, fumbled at his wireless for about an hour, we didn't hear a word, everything was jammed, but very exciting—as in the old days, listening in Berlin to the Comintern station. Only for a second did I hear the familiar matter-of-fact voice of the B.B.C. announcer—as if talking to a crowd of intelligent schoolboys, emphasising by his manner that he treats them as though they were grown-ups. We heard a few bars of the

Marseillaise, something about resistance in French North Africa, and 240 Nazi 'planes shot down. Quarrelled as to whether the 240 in one day, week, or month. Felt all very cheerful and drunk.

August 3rd

There are three *bistros* in Géronce; in Susmiou there were none; so everybody drunk. This morning we got tobacco and pay—my first since I am a soldier: 10 francs 50 = 21 × 50 centimes.

Yesterday, on march from Susmiou hither, passed Gurs Concentration Camp. Enormous—about one mile of barbed wire along the road. Saw the barracks, grey and black, same as in Vernet; but women's underwear in all colours drying coquettishly on lines in the sun, and even on the barbed wire; the women all tidy, appetising, many in shorts—a treacherously gay sight. Gestapo was here again day before yesterday.

During march in the burning sun that B.B.C. voice rang in my ear like an old familiar tune—slightly off-hand, bored, blasé, naïve. The fascination of a country where schoolboys behave like grown-ups and grown-ups like schoolboys.

August 4th

Got hold of a bunch of *Paris-Soir's*, printed in Marseilles, completely ghostly. Splash on front page: 'The Marshal and the Peasant—a Modern Legend.' Pétain has received an old peasant 'for a hearty man-to-man talk'. On leaving, peasant said in tears: '*C'est un homme*, an honest peasant like myself.' (Philippe le Gaga has a property on the Riviera where he grows cabbage or something.) Pétain said: 'This interview has convinced me that I have the entire confidence of the peasant class.'

Another splash: 'We want a French Hollywood.' Actors and stars gather on the Riviera, plans of building a French national film centre, gossip about Suzy and Lucy and Marcel and Maurice; 'they go on bikes, leaving their racy cars in the garages; their faces show the consciousness of the grave trial of *La Patrie*, but also the new serenity of the French resurrection, which has already begun. . . .'

Same issue : 'For a French Morality.' General enthusiasm for the new decree making knee-long, two-piece bathing-costumes compulsory for men and women at Nice. 'No more shorts, no more French women disguised as men—*la Révolution Nationale marche.*'

Smaller news items : De Gaulle sentenced to death for treason—every Frenchman serving in a 'foreign army' liable to capital punishment—a new bunch of diplomats sacked—Paul-Boncour appointed to the enviable post of Ambassador in Chile.

Quotation from *La Croix,* the Catholic paper : 'Victory does not always mean what the common man understands by this word. . . . Our victory began probably in June, 1940.'

Wonder what Père Darrault would say to that. Got a postcard from him from Lourdes. Today is Sunday, and everybody even more drunk. Pity can't go listen to London radio again; X. too far from Géronce.

August 6th

Since July 31st, every postal, telephonic and telegraphic communication with occupied zone interrupted. People say it is for good—France will remain cut in two for duration.

Anti-Semitic utterances by Vichy Radio. Labour camps for French youth; every boy of nineteen will have to work six months in a camp. New food rations : 1 lb. sugar; ½ lb. *pâtés* (macaroni, etc.) per month; 3½ oz. rice, 4 oz. soap-7 oz. margarine or other fats—all per month. Suppose this will open their eyes a bit—for the moment they are still sleep-walking. Editorial in *Le Temps* : 'New Order will be based on Continental collaboration; *frontier rectifications are without importance*; nations will understand each other because all will live under corporative, authoritarian, totalitarian regime.'

Morale in cantonment very bad. Chevalier, who was always quiet and gentle, has a *crise de nerfs*. He is a bookbinder from Reims, has not heard from his young wife for months; she is expectant, her time about now. Wanted to run away at night, walk to German post, ask to be sent home. Gillevic calms him down; evening they are both drunk, and Chevalier sick all over the straw. Food now much worse than in Susmiou, rumours that new cooks and new lieutenant cheating us out of potatoes and meat, selling them to peasants. New chief cook is a *légionnaire*, first I have met, Belgian origin, eleven years of service in Africa. Not an encouraging foretaste. Says he will serve four more years, then entitled to pension of £3 a month, will marry a widow and open a *bistro*.

August 7th

This morning a new lieutenant assembled us, read out idiotic instructions from divisional headquarters—blackout to be observed in cantonments. All stared at him, thought he had gone nuts. Everybody furious. They think officers drag out demobilisation in order to get their pay for another month or two.

Paper says new labour law will abolish trade unions, introduce fifty-one-hour week. Abetz appointed German Ambassador in Paris—a slap in Pétain's face. Jules comments : '*Le plus on leur baise le cul, le plus ils nous chient sur la tête.*' *Paris-Soir* (Marseilles edition) gives advice to parents how to find their children lost in the chaos of flight. Says there are thousands of 'globe-trotters aged six and eight years on the roads of France'. Lot of talk about reform of education. 'The French teacher must become a peasant once more and teach little future peasants; the French virgins must learn to cook and sew—not Latin or mathematics.'

Afternoon walked through the hills, met a column of Spaniards, working as woodcutters under escort of gendarmes. They live in Gurs camp (there is a section for men, too), have been interned ever since Spanish defeat, receive no pay for ten-hour day, not even a cigarette. Remember Frau Mueller told me similar fact: all German *émigrés* who joined French Army for duration are now in Morocco, forming labour brigades employed in heaviest work (quarries and road-building) in murderous climate; no pay; at night behind barbed wire; will not be demobilised—kept as slaves *sine die*. The phrase that Europe is sliding back towards Age of Slavery has been so often used as propagandist overstatement that we don't realise it is actually coming true. These labour battalions are in every respect equivalents of slave gangs. Compared to Roman standards of living, the hutments in Vernet and Gurs are worse than antique *ergastulae*. Labour is in part harder than that described by Cato and Varro; food certainly worse. No prospect of collecting a *peculum*. Sex starvation absolute, whereas *servi* married or lived in promiscuity. Complete delusion to believe that school-book horrors of antiquity are worse (relatively or absolutely) than contemporary reality. Facts and proofs abound; but consciousness lags behind; it is easier for the imagination to grasp the past than the present.

Chevalier has another *crise de nerfs*. Strange that our lot in Vernet, with our nerves ground down after five to ten years' persecution, had more self-control than the healthy, relatively unaffected *poilus*. Fontanin told a story: he had bought a couple of eggs in Susmiou, asked the wife of the farmer where he was billeted to boil them for him—and she charged him 5 sous (half a day's pay) for boiling two eggs when her fire was on. Whereupon Chevalier suddenly started yelling: '*Oh, les salauds—les saluds—oh, ils nous emmerdent* ...' and to cry. Most unpleasant.

R

August 8th

Jabo is dead. Notice in *Dépêche de Toulouse* : 'Vichy, August 7th. M. Vladimir Jabotinsky, journalist and author, Chairman of the New Zionist Organisation, died in New York at the age of fifty-nine. He had gone to America for the purpose of raising a Jewish Legion which was to fight on the side of England.'

Exit one of the great tragic figures of this century, unnoticed. Adored hero of the Jewish masses in Russia and Poland; creator of the first Jewish legion which helped conquer Palestine; sentenced to fifteen years' hard labour for organising Jewish resistance against Arab pogrom in Jerusalem; translated Dante and Shakespeare into modern Hebrew; wrote and spoke eight languages; most fascinating orator I ever heard. Striking resemblance to Radek—both Jews from Odessa. One great friend less—there are not many left, at liberty, undamaged. First wondered why Vichy Press agency cares about a dead Jew; re-reading obituary noticed propagandist purpose emphasising that Jews are on England's side, i.e. anti-French.

More talk about educational reform; *inspecteurs* no longer selected by *concours* (competitive examination), but appointed by the Ministry, 'which thus will exercise a direct control on their moral conduct'.

Sport and more sport : 'The new generation will be educated in a heroic climate.'

August 9th

This morning Desmet came from Oloron to visit us. Querulous little man, deaf in one ear and pro-Doriot. He is not *démobilisable*, being domiciled in Zone B (reserved area in the north); so he was sent a week ago to join the newly formed French Labour Battalions at Oloron. We went to the *bistro*, Desmet, Lebras, Sergeant Lepetit, and I. Desmet said the Labour Battalions don't work yet, but if it is true that the pay will only be 75 centimes a day, everybody will desert. Then he said, France had at outbreak of war sixteen aeroplanes, the rest were stolen by *Front Populaire* or sent to Spain. Told him he must be mistaken, perhaps sixteen of one special type—he said no, sixteen altogether, he had read it in paper called *L'Indépendent* published in Bordeaux. Told him he must have seen with his own eyes several hundreds on newsreels, at manœuvres, etc. Said, they were probably English, or the newsreels were faked, but figure 16 is official. Lebras and Lepetit both nodded: 'Yes. It's true. We had nothing. *On nous a vendu.*' Told them: '*Vous êtes une bande d'idiots*'; Desmet said: '*Et toi, tu es moitié boche.*' So that's that. *À la recherche de la fraternité.*

The tragedy is that we move in a vicious circle; without education of the masses, no political progress; but without political progress, no education of the masses.

August 10th

Informed by lieutenant that all alien volunteers to be sent for demobilisation to camp at Septfont, Tarn-et-Garonne; am to leave tomorrow, together with the four Spaniards. Told him am engaged for five years and not *démobilisable*; said *il s'en fout*, alien is alien. I was on his list. I too, *je m'en fous*; am travelling at State's expense and fed up with Géronce. But the *légionnaire*-cook is staying, possibly thanks to some fiddle.

Some *démobilisés* have left their uniforms, all piled in a heap in the schoolroom; so at night broke into schoolroom, found a good, almost new tunic with nice red artillerist stripes, new belt, new puttees, and knapsack; am looking definitely smart.

So once more *en route*. Last night in the barn with Lebras, Gillevic, Chevalier (Moog went to hospital). Leaving without regrets, full of curiosity where journey will lead. Dreamt last night G. was sitting in Mme. Corniglion's kitchen, next to the big stove; I came in very tired, she said in a scolding voice : 'Late as usual.'

II

The journey took exactly three months and when I eventually met G., it was not in the Corniglions' kitchen, but in London; and it was I who spoke the words 'Late as usual' as a first greeting, for she had been held up by some traffic muddle due to an air-raid warning.

It was a long and tiresome journey from Géronce, Basses Pyrénées, to Septfont, Tarn-et-Garonne; from Septfont to Marseilles, from Marseilles to a certain African port, from there to another African port, from there to Lisbon, and from Lisbon to London.

The first stage of the journey from Géronce to Septfont was the shortest in distance, but almost the longest in time. It was rather impressive as a sample of transport conditions in unoccupied France. The distance was about 175 miles, but it took us three days to cover it and we had to change trains five times.

There were eight of us : the four Spaniards; a Turkish pedlar who had married a Frenchwoman in Normandy, a Rumanian student, myself, and the sergeant in charge of our *détachement*. Both the Rumanian and the Turk were Jews, and so debarred from returning to the occupied zone; they had decided to join a Labour Battalion and work for 75 centimes a day—until the problematical date when Jews become human beings again. The Spaniards, on the other hand, hoped to be demobilised, to be paid the bonus of 1,000 francs (£5) due to every discharged soldier, and to find work as navvies. Actually, as I learned later, they were demobilised, but, like most of the Spanish volunteers, they neither obtained their 1,000 francs nor their liberty; instead, they were escorted back to Gurs and various other concentration camps, which they had left nine months ago to risk their lives for hospitable France. Two of our four Spaniards had been wounded.

We arrived in Septfont in the evening of August 13th; at the registration office they told me what I already knew—namely, that the lieutenant in Géronce had been an idiot, and that the place he should have sent me to was the depot of the Foreign Legion in Marseilles. So they typed out a new order and another railway voucher for Marseilles, where I arrived two days later, on August 15th.

It was nine o'clock in the morning when I walked out of the Gare St. Charles, knapsack on my back. The crowd in the streets of the great harbour town made me feel dizzy and excited. Since the armistice I had vegetated in a sort of trance in these forlorn Pyrenean villages; now I felt as if emerging from a long dream.

That first day in Marseilles was full of surprises. Less than 100 yards from the steps of the railway station I heard a voice call out, '*Halt, Genosse Koestler,*' and when I had got over the shock, I saw the conspicuously tall figure of Dr. Breitscheid, German Minister of the Interior in the legendary days of the Weimar Republic, barring my way. He was standing in front of the Hotel Normandie talking to a friend, bare-headed, with his white hair a head above the crowd moving through the street.

'What is this fancy dress?' he asked, looking me up and down, and I saw by his expression that my appearance must have changed. But last time we had met in Paris, his hair had not been white either, and his face had not been that sharp waxen mask. We went to his room, on the third floor of the Hotel Normandie; Mrs. Breitscheid was making coffee on a spirit stove. I told them my story, and then we knocked on the wall of the next room and Comrade Dr. Hilferding turned up in his dressing-gown. Hilferding had been Minister of Finance in those long-vanished days; both he and Breitscheid were leaders of the German Social-Democrat Party and close friends.

We sat on the bed of the little hotel room, and they told me the news.

Feuchtwanger had succeeded in getting to America in some adventurous way. Ernst Weiss, the novelist, had committed suicide by taking veronal in Paris. Walter Hasenclever, the playwright, had committed suicide by opening his veins in a concentration camp near Avignon. Kayser, of the editorial staff of the *Parisier Tageszeitung*, had swallowed strychnine in another camp. Willi Muenzenberg, onetime head of the Comintern's West-European propaganda section, later enemy No. 1 of the Third International, virtual leader of the German exiles, had disappeared from a concentration camp in Savoy during the German advance and nothing had been heard of him since. (News came a few months later. Muenzenberg was found dead in a forest near Grenoble, with a rope round his neck. Whether he was killed by the German Gestapo, the Russian O.G.P.U., or by his own despair, will probably never be established.)

We sat on the bed of the little hotel room, drinking coffee and eating grapes. Both Breitscheid and Hilferding had visas for the United States, but their French exit permits had been refused. The Germans had not yet asked for their extradition, but the French were loyal to the bargain and kept the merchandise ready for delivery. I asked Breitscheid why they did not try to get out without exit permits. Surely there must be ways of obtaining papers under false names, or crossing the Pyrenees at an unguarded mountain pass? I knew that some others had done it and succeeded. But Breitscheid would not hear of it; he still hoped that Vichy would grant the exit permits; he even had promises from some French officials. He and Hilferding had grown up in the traditions of the Social-Democrat Party, the party of strict legality and righteousness, the unique and grandiose product of German democracy. The Social-Democrat Party had believed in Marshal Hindenburg's sense of honour, who sold them out to Hitler; Breitscheid and Hilferding believed in another old Marshal's decency, who delivered them to the Gestapo. Their individual fate reflected that of their nation—the tragedy of credulity and illusion.

When I left the Hotel Normandie an hour later, Breitscheid said : 'So far there have been no demands for extradition and I do not think there will be any. It is unthinkable. The inclusion of Paragraph 19 in the Treaty was a mere formality, to humiliate the French; but they will never execute it.'

This was on August 15th, 1940. Six months later, on February 11th, 1941, Dr. Breitscheid and Dr. Hilferding, together with twenty other political refugees, were handed over by the French authorities to the Germans.[1]

---

[1] How this was done was revealed some time afterwards by a British newspaper.

'. . . On the night of Saturday, February 8th, three high French police officials arrived at the hotel at Arles and took them to the local police station. They declared that the Germans had found out their address and that in an hour they would be there to arrest them. "We, the police, are here to save you," they said. "You will be hidden for a few days; then you will receive a Spanish visa and will be helped to get away." . . . "Where are you taking us?" Dr. Breitscheid then asked. To his horror, the official said that they were to go to special police headquarters at Vichy. "That means you are going to extradite us," declared Dr. Breitscheid. "You have a very low opinion of France, M. Breitscheid," was the reply intended to reassure them. Mrs. Breitscheid, however, insisted on accompanying them and they travelled through the night to Vichy in two cars.

'At Vichy they were detained at police headquarters. Their personal belongings were removed and any article with which they might take their life. They were not allowed to wash or shave. In the evening of the next day they were told they were to be extradited. The Germans had first demanded their extraditions, they were informed, on

The second surprise on that day awaited me at the Fort
St. Jean, the central depot of the Foreign Legion in France.
I arrived there just in time for the midday meal and, after
handing over my papers in the office, was shown to the large
refectory, painted all round with lurid battle pictures of the
Legion's exploits in Algeria, Morocco, Indo-China, and
Senegal. I sat down at a table with fifteen others, all in
civilian clothes; and the first sentence I heard was:

'*There's again no bloody salt in the bloody soup*'—in
English. Then somebody else said: 'Salt or no bloody salt, I
haven't tasted decent soup since I've been in this bloody
country'—in English. The sixteen men at the next table were
discussing a similar subject, in English, and the same at the
tables to the right and to the left. Altogether there were sixty
of them. All sixty had been members of the B.E.F. captured
by the Germans near St. Valéry; all sixty had managed to
escape and were interned by the French in the Fort St. Jean.

They had a large dormitory to themselves, and most of
the ten days I stayed in the Fort I spent with them. Their
stories of escape would fill a *Decameron*; the most famous
was the episode known as 'Lieutenant H.'s crossing of the
Somme'. Lieutenant H. and Lieutenant R., the former a
London solicitor, the latter a student at London University,
had escaped from the German *Gefangenenlager* at night,
got hold of civilian clothes, and were just about to cross the
River Somme in an abandoned rowing boat they had found

December 17th, and had repeated the demand three times since. They
received the terrible news with great courage.

'Mrs. Breitscheid . . . tried to see the Minister of the Interior. On
the admission form, she gave as the reason for her visit "Extradition of
Dr. Breitscheid and Dr. Hilferding." The attendant looked at it and
said. "You don't really think I can give this to the Minister," and
tore up the slip. On February 10th, after waiting for two hours, Mrs.
Breitscheid was allowed to see her husband for the last time. The next
morning, Dr. Breitscheid and Dr. Hilferding were driven from Vichy
in two separate cars to the border between the unoccupied and
occupied zones and handed over to the Germans.'

when two German officers appeared on the river bank. The Germans explained to them in broken French that they wanted to be taken across the river. H., whose French was about as bad as the Germans', said '*S'eel vous play*,' with a suitable gesture, and the Germans stepped in, and were rowed to the opposite bank. When they got out, the Germans said '*Danke schön*,' and H. said '*S'eel vous play, deux francs*', holding up two fingers to make the request clear. The Germans paid the two francs and said '*Bon shour*'; and H. and R. said '*Merci*' and went on their way.

That day of my arrival in the Fort St. Jean proved decisive for me, for a fortnight later H. and R. and myself had succeeded in dodging the commandant of the fortress, the French harbour authorities, the Italo-German Armistice Commission, and set out on our rather devious way to England.

We departed separately, but we met in a certain town in Africa, and on the way we picked up two other inmates of the dormitory in the Fort St. Jean, a Scottish lieutenant of the Medical Corps and a staff-sergeant from the Royal Engineers. By the middle of the autumn, the five of us had safely reached our destination.

The story of this long journey could only be told with so much camouflaging of the facts that it would lose the flavour of reality. But there is an additional reason for not going into it. From the day of his arrival in Marseilles, the author's personal story has to fade out. He has told it at some length as far as his personal adventures were typical for the species of men to which he belongs : the exiled, the persecuted, the hunted men of Europe; the thousands and millions who, for reasons of their race, nationality of beliefs, have become the scum of the earth. The 'I' of this narrative, his thoughts and fears and hopes, and even his incongruencies and contradictions, stand for the thoughts and fears and hopes, but above all for the burning despair, of a considerable portion of the Continent's population.

But this ceases to be the case in the last chapter of his story. The fact that the author escaped, and the way he did it, are no longer typical, but accidental and due to merely personal circumstances. For those who escaped are the exception, and those who perish are the rule for the category of men with whom this book deals.

III

The various preparations for desertion and departure took about a fortnight—my last fortnight in France.

It was the second half of August, 1940; the fortnight when the French trade unions were dissolved in the name of the workers' interest; when people were forbidden to drink spirits at the *bistro* and forced to buy them by the bottle, in the name of anti-alcoholism; when the first Jewish shop windows were smashed in Marseilles and Lyons in the name of the National Revolution; and when the Paris Opéra reopened, for an audience composed mainly of German officers and with Berlioz' *Damnation de Faust* on the stage.

It was also the fortnight during which the mass raids on Britain reached their first peak, and invasion was expected daily. Day by day *Paris-Soir*, printed in Marseilles, screamed in heavy type 'The decisive battle has begun', 'Thames Docks annihilated', 'London a dead town'. It was meant as a kind of consolation and apology, addressed to the French people : 'You see what happens to those who do not capitulate.' But on the back page, and sometimes even on the front page, other items appeared in more modest type : 'Boulogne in flames', 'R.A.F. hits back, bombards Berlin', 'Bad weather causes delay of invasion plans', 'British claim 180 'planes destroyed in one day'.

In the trams and cafés, in the queues at the butcher's, the dairy and the grocer's, the people's comments had slightly changed in tone. It was a very slight change—the people themselves were hardly aware of it—and yet unmistakable. It was brought forth by two facts, which had unconsciously impressed themselves on their minds. The first of these was that Britain was obviously carrying on with the war— whereas two months ago everybody had been convinced she was only trying to gain a few weeks, to save her face before coming to terms with Hitler. The second fact was that, if Britain carried on, there was perhaps a possibility that she might even win; a very slight possibility indeed, but a possibility, nevertheless. And this was the only chance, as far as one could see, of getting the *Boches* and the *Macaronis* out of France.

These two facts were so obvious that even the most blinded, muddled, apathetic mind was bound to perceive them. Yet the emotional sphere of the mind is stronger than its rational sphere, and these considerations would have failed to produce a change in the people's outlook had there not been a previous change in emotional attitude.

The precise character of this emotional change is not easy to define. It was *not* any sort of enthusiasm for British policy, or war aims, or for those Frenchmen who were fighting on the British side. The name of General de Gaulle was known to few people before Reynaud had called him into his Cabinet; these few respected him as an excellent technician and a courageous man; but his name was far from being a rallying call. And it was too early for a rallying call, anyhow. The blow was still too recent.

No, the change of feeling towards England was something less direct and had in fact nothing to do with politics at all. One had to get rid of all 'historical' preconceptions and listen instead to talks in trams and cafés until at last one understood that the feeling which had brought forth this more sympathetic attitude was simply *Schadenfreude*—in other words, the secret pleasure which we all take in our fellow creature's misery. France had seen three invasions within a century—England none. France had suffered every imaginable misery during the First World War of 1914, and the second of 1939–40; England had remained practically untouched, superior, aloof. The German propaganda had exploited this feeling of envy and bitterness with virtuosity; the contact with British soldiers in France, who were paid about twenty times better than the *poilus*, fed better, clad better, who bought up all the chocolate in the canteen and all the available femininity in the village—had largely contributed to it; the accusations of Vichy, that Great Britain had forced France into the war and then left her in the lurch, had officially sanctioned it. But now at last England had 'got it'; now at last, under the shower of incendiaries and high-explosives, *les Anglais* had got a taste of what the French had felt like in 1915 and in 1939; now at last those cold-blooded, dumb, superior islanders had become *human* in the eyes of the French by going through the same misery. Now they were paying the bill; and the women who lived there had ceased to be arrogant tourist ladies who wanted a bath-tub instead of a *bidet*, and had become mothers who hid their children in deadly fear in Underground stations and cellars; and those English children, with their obscene naked knees and ridiculous top-hats, had at last become *des pauvres gosses* who wetted their pants when a bomb crashed close by.

So the French man in the street was moved by pity? No. He had enough to do pitying himself and putting advertisements in the newspapers to find his own wife and children, who had perhaps been left in the occupied zone or perhaps got lost on the road. It was not pity, but the satisfaction of an instinct for justice; and again not justice in an abstract sense, but as the very human desire, that if one's house has been destroyed by an earthquake, the neighbour's should be too. The British had paid, and now one was quits with them. Their penance bought their absolution. This did not mean that one discovered a sudden overwhelming enthusiasm for them, but merely that the emotional obstacle to a more objective appreciation of one's own interest had been removed. Now at last the way was laid open for the discovery that it was in the interest of France that Britain should win the war.

From this realisation to positive action there is still a long, a very long, way. But to realise clearly one's own interest is an important step; perhaps the most important in the psychology of the masses. Had mankind as a whole reached this stage, Utopia would be at hand.

IV

The boat left the Quai de la Joliette in Marseilles harbour about midnight. It was new moon and the stars were bright and their light hard. The coast with its long garlands of gas lamps faded slowly away. The lighthouses emerging from the black water, with their green and red eyes, were the last outposts of France, sleeping under the stars in her enormous, dishonoured nakedness, humiliated, wretched and beloved.

It was a long journey and the night was long on the deck, inviting to futile reflections. Futile, for they all turned on the past, and more precisely on the question of historical fatality. Was the tragedy of France merely accidental, due to an unfortunate constellation? Or was it due to the still undiscovered, secret laws of the rise and decline of races and nations? Could France have been saved?

If one accepted the explanations for the defeat given by the patriots of Vichy, the answer was 'No.' According to them, the reasons were the laziness and greed of the working class and of the lower classes in general—in other words, of the French people; its hatred of Authority and preference for a democratic regime—in other words, the very essence of its historical tradition. In the opinion of Marshal Pétain, the battle of France was lost in 1789 with the storming of the Bastille; and this deplorable event was a proof of the wickedness of the French national character. Further reasons given were: alcoholism, the declining birthrate and the disintegration of the family.

All this, of course, amounted to a confirmation of the German thesis of the degeneration of the French race. Laziness, selfishness, alcoholism, denatality are supposed to be the clinical symptoms of decline. The adherence of the rulers of a defeated country to the victor's philosophy was not surprising; but there was a danger of its spreading to other parts of the world. Indeed, it has since become apparent that a considerable section of public opinion in America, and even in England, seems to adopt the same view of the causes of the French defeat—to believe in that nation's racial decay, to regard the tragedy of France as the fulfilment of biological fatality.

Biology, however, is only the Fascist substitute for sociology. The reason why racialist theories hold such an attraction even for people far from any conscious totalitarian sympathies may lie in the equally unsatisfactory character of their philosophic antidote, the 'economid fatality' of the materialist school. It would be foolish to deny, as the latter practically did, the influence of the racial factor in the long run; and it is quite possible that looking back from, say, A.D. 2941, the future historian might discover developments of a racial-biological order, which give some additional clue

to what happened in Europe in our era. But, for the inter-
pretation of events in short periods, measured in decades or
even a few centuries, racial biology proves a completely unfit
instrument. History has to be written in sociological terms,
and biology confined to developments in the jungle—unless
Fascism is victorious and transforms the history of mankind
into a jungle-book.

Could France have been saved? Yes, of course. It suc-
cumbed, not to racial decay, but to a social phenomenon,
which it might be appropriate to call the 'Chinese Wall
psychosis'.

The Maginot Line, like the Chinese Wall, was destined to
protect and preserve a highly developed and stagnant civilisation against the intrusions of the eager barbarians. Stagnant, because in the second part of the last century, in the
competitive rush of industrialisation, it had fallen far behind both its great neighbours, Germany and Great Britain.
And it had fallen behind them mainly because of the riches
of its soil, which allowed it to remain a country of Bread and
Wine, in an environment of Steam and Steel.

French individualism was a consequence of saturatedness;
French conservatism was rooted in the peasant class, more
especially in the medium-sized farmer, the backbone of the
nation. Thus it was an essentially provincial conservatism,
far from any aggressive imperialist feeling. France had
colonies, but not an empire. She thought in terms of 'La
Patrie', which expressed the peasant's clinging love for the
soil, and lacked entirely the mercantile British empire-
consciousness. Her main interest was to preserve the *status
quo*; a German journalist once described France as travelling happily in a little mule cart, amidst the feverish stream
of locomotives and automobiles on the highway of European
destiny. It was this idyllic backwardness which made French
life outwardly so charming and inwardly so stagnant. The
last grandiose effort to preserve the nineteenth-century idyll

in the midst of an utterly unidyllic twentieth was the building of the Chinese Wall.

For the same money and effort France could have built a modern, mechanised, and three-dimensional army. Why did the warnings of de Gaulle and Reynaud go unheard, who from the early thirties onwards denounced the obsoleteness of the linear fortification system and advocated the system of highly motorised, mobile, relatively self-sufficient and independent units, with an overwhelming air force? The superficial answer is: because the arteriosclerotic French General Staff did not want to be bothered with any new-fangled ideas. But they could only get away with it because the Chinese Wall was indeed the projection of the nation's deep-felt wish to be left alone. De Gaulle's conception of an offensive army might have saved the peace by giving the Polish and Czech alliance a real meaning. But at that stage France no longer wanted to *save* the peace by any constructive effort; it wanted to be *left* in peace—and this psychological nuance made all the difference, and in fact sealed her fate.

Thus, the blessings of bread and wine had become France's curse. If we try to isolate the dominant thread in the complicated weave of a nation's evolution, we are led roughly to these stages: natural riches—saturation—individualism—provincial backwardness—stagnation—isolationism—neurotic fear of being disturbed—Chinese Wall psychosis.

How then could France have been saved? In a world of ruthless imperialist expansion, a mainly bread-and-wine country has in the long run no chance of defending its position against a mainly steam-and-steel neighbour. But in a world of international collaboration and solidarity it has not only the chance but the guarantee of surviving. To change the order of the world from ruthlessness to brotherliness is, of course, the wish-dream of the weaker; and France was the weaker, numerically and in her industrial potential. But in 1918 she had this unique chance. It was forfeited at Versailles. It was not forfeited by the French nation, which gave President Wilson a delirious reception, but by her ruling class. The Marne and Verdun were achievements of a vigorous race; Compiègne and Versailles were the crimes of a degenerate class.

The French nation has no greater responsibility in the suicidal folly of her leaders than the Americans for having supported Coolidge, or the British for having believed in Munich. But it has a better excuse. The fear of a third invasion within one century explains its willingness to accept the policy of *sécurité*. It paid for it by the mental deformation which is the consequence of living behind a Chinese Wall. *Laissez-faire* individualism degenerated to *je-m'en-foutisme, joie de vivre* to hedonism, tolerance to irresponsibility. When the Popular Front came to power in 1936, it was Blum who initiated the Non-Intervention Pact, and thus signed the death-warrant of his comrades in Spain, because he was made to believe that to help the Spanish Government would incite Germany to war. The French Left was more French than Left—it sacrificed the solidarity of the working class to their wish to remain 'behind the wall'.

Yet the *Front Populaire* episode, abortive as it was, had given a mortal shock to the rulers of France, and caused a fundamental change in their outlook. Here was a new menace to their *sécurité*, more threatening than the outer barbarians, because they could not build a Maginot Line against it. But at the same time the barbarians had begun to develop truly civilised ideas : the abolition of trade unions, the dissolution of the Left-wing parties. Hitler's only fault was that he was a German. Otherwise he would be a better 'guarantee of security' for vested interests than an unruly French people in arms.

This dilemma of the French ruling class was as real as

s

the dilemma of the French Communists. Both were faced by two evils and hesitated which was the lesser one; both were involved in the deeper and deeper contradictions of their 'Party line'; both went down the slippery slope of treachery; and in both cases it is sometimes impossible to distinguish between conscious traitors and unconscious accomplices.

In the case of the French ruling class, the main stages on the slope were the Rhineland, Austria, Munich, Bordeaux, Vichy. It was, so to speak, a suicide in monthly instalments. The continuous capitulations, intermittent with bellicose boasts, were an expression of this insoluble dilemma. Only a few went so far as to proclaim openly, as did the *Cagoulards,* the would-be stormtroopers of high finance: 'Rather Hitler than the *Front Populaire.*' They were the *enfants terribles* of the Right, but enjoyed their more or less secret approval and protection. A minority of corrupt politicians and a minority of officers blinded by their class hatred became Hitler's Fifth Column during the war. The majority of the *milieu bien pensant,* of the upper classes, were unconscious tools.

The Parties of the Right had no reason to hate Hitler, and when they were forced into the war they did not fight against Fascism, but for the maintenance of the *status quo.* They knew what they were fighting for, but not what they were fighting against.

For the Left, on the other hand, and especially the working class, the situation was exactly the reverse; they knew what they were fighting against, but not what they were fighting for. Thus, the Right and the Left each had only half their hearts in the battle; and the two halves did not fit together.

For, during the last twenty years, the idea of the Chinese Wall had changed its character; it was no longer meant to protect the national community, but a privileged caste in decay; the wall had shrunk and the majority of the nation was regarded as living *extra muros*. Inside, on a brittle Louis XIV chair, sat an elderly, sharp-faced Marianne, her once lovely chestnut hair replaced by a *toupet*. Scared to death by the noise of the people Outside the Wall, she waited for the barbarian prince to save her. She knew, of course, what price she would have to pay; and while trying to convince herself that he would behave like a gentleman, she waited with a shamefaced curiosity for her dishonour. And when it had happened, and the saviour had knocked off her Phrygian helmet and her wig, she looked into the mirror with horror, and the world looked with horror at her face.

And what comes after?

In one of its last August issues, *Gringoire*, Pétain's favourite weekly, published in non-occupied France, displayed on its front page a cartoon on which Winston Churchill is represented as a tiny doll, hanging on a rubber string from the index finger of an enormous, black-haired, black-bearded, hook-nosed, grinning Elder of Zion.

Industriously, the propaganda of Vichy is building up a new dragon, featuring John Bull, World Judaism, Socialism, and Plutocracy, Blum, Rothschild and De Gaulle, Freemasons, Foreigners, and Free French, all in one; a dragon streaky as a zebra with all this paint and about as fierce in appearance.

It is, of course, dangerous to underestimate the effects of propaganda, even of the stupidest sort, on a despairing nation, isolated from the rest of the world. Certain catchwords have undoubtedly found a response in various sections of the people, such as the anti-trade-union slogans amongst the peasantry and middle classes; and anti-Semitism, the Fascist black magic, is spreading all over France, even amongst the working classes. It will be a long time before the mental depredations of Vichy (and of the decade before) are undone; the view that Hitler's defeat will automatically bring forth France's regeneration is based on an optimistic disregard of social and psychological realities.

But in the main issue at stake, in the French people's attitude to the war, the dangers of Vichy propaganda are limited by the considerations exposed in the last chapter. The motives of the anti-British campaign—self-justification and German pressure—are too obvious; and the man in the street imagines the German influence on the French Press and radio as even more direct than it is; he somehow pictures a *boche* soldier, pistol in hand, standing behind the microphone and the editor's chair. He may believe that the Jews and Freemasons ruined France; but he disbelieves every communiqué and comment on the actual military situation. He is slow to form a definite opinion on anything in this puzzling world, but once it is formed he sticks to it stubbornly; and the simple truth, that in order to get rid of the *boches*, Great Britain must win the war, is a sort of firm rock in the chaotic muddle of his mind.

But mere reasoning is sterile as long as it does not generate action. *When* this will be depends only to a small extent on propaganda, and to a much larger extent on the development of the military situation. As long as they do not receive definite encouragement from hard facts, the French people will remain partial but passive observers. To believe the contrary would be a dangerous fallacy. The French people have been too deeply disillusioned to risk their lives once more without being fairly certain of victory. They have to learn to hope again, as a man after long bedriddenness has to learn to walk. When the scales of success turn in favour of England, the barricades will emerge from the pavement of the towns of France, the snipers will appear behind the attic windows, and the people will fight as in the old glorious days—but not before.

V

The last station on that long journey was Lisbon. I had to wait six weeks for an opportunity to get to England, and during those six weeks, in the late autumn of 1940, I saw for the last time the procession of the outcasts pass by.

Lisbon was the bottle-neck of Europe, the last open gate of a concentration camp extending over the greater part of the Continent's surface. By watching that interminable procession, one realised that the catalogue of possible reasons for persecution under the New Order was much longer than even a specialist could imagine; in fact, it covered the entire alphabet, from A, for Austrian Monarchist, to Z, for Zionist Jew. Every European nation, religion, party was represented in that procession, including German Nazis of Strasser's oppositional faction and Italian Fascists in disgrace.

The most conspicuous part in this tragedy of an entire Continent still fell to the German refugees trapped in France. The information brought by the few who escaped, and the material assembled by the various committees in Lisbon, was too haphazard to allow a statistical survey, but it formed a fairly comprehensive picture.

A considerable portion of the German political exiles were still in concentration camps, such as Le Vernet, or imprisoned for the second and third time, waiting for their extradition to Germany on the strength of paragraph 19 of the Armistice Treaty. As the number of suicides increased, special precautions were taken by the French authorities to preserve them undamaged for delivery.

Another section of the German exiles had previously joined the French Army for the duration of the war. Now that the war was over they were kept in the Moroccan forced-labour battalions to work in mines and quarries, reduced to a state of slavery.

Another part had been called up for auxiliary service during the last period of the war. They were collected into *compagnies de prestataires*, equivalent to the British Pioneer Corps. Their fate varied according to the unit to which they were attached. Several units placed under British command had been embarked with the B.E.F., and had presumably arrived in England. A certain number which could not be embarked were given lorries and petrol by the British before they left, to enable them to gain unoccupied territory. They had arrived on their lorries in Nantes, twenty-four hours before the Germans occupied the town. There the French had dragged them from the lorries, shut them in the local jail and handed them over to the Germans when they came in.

Another unit of *prestataires* had been engaged in trench-digging somewhere near Soissons. They worked under escort, without uniforms and without individual identity papers. One night during the German advance, the escort disappeared—officers, men, lorries and all. The unit, being unable to decide in which direction to go, broke up into several groups. One group was captured by the Germans. A second reached a French village, where they were taken for parachutists and several were shot or lynched. The rest were sent to a concentration camp near Paris. Forty-eight hours before Paris fell, they were still there; what happened to them since is not known.

A considerable minority of the remaining German exiles had by various adventurous ways reached the south of unoccupied France. They were hiding in little villages in the Pyrenees around the Gurs camp, where their women were kept, and on the Mediterranean coast. Their fate depended on the local gendarmes, *maires,* and *préfets.* Any of these had the power to put them back into jail or in a concentration camp, without legal proceedings.

Finally, a few of them had managed to reach Marseilles and to obtain visas for the United States or other American countries. They were the moneyed and intellectual élite, people with connections in the outside world, authors, journalists, scholars, a couple of hundred perhaps out of tens of thousands. The visas to the U.S. were granted to them on the basis of a list of 'outstanding intellectuals', which had been established by committees in New York. Even for this small selection of well-known men, it took weeks and months of waiting, corresponding, queueing up and humiliations, until the magic stamp was put on their passports. And when at last this was done, they had to wait and to queue up for another week or fortnight for their transit visas through Portugal. When this too was obtained, there came the final ordeal of fighting through the red tape, disorganisation, and incapacity of various refugee committees to procure their passage to New York. And when this too was done and the miracle of escape seemed to come true, the French authorities refused their exit permits.

A certain number managed to cross the Pyrenees at unguarded mountain passes. Some of them were arrested by the Spaniards and sent back to France. Some of them were put into Spanish prisons, some handed over to Gestapo agents in Spain. Some reached Portugal and brought the news.

News of more arrests: H., the psycho-analyst, with whom we used to play poker in Paris, arrested in Marseilles at the moment when he tried to stow away on a ship for Indo-China. S., the film critic, arrested when already on the deck of a boat to Oran. D., the architect, arrested while climbing, knapsack on back, over the Pyrenees. The merchandise had to be kept ready for delivery.

And more suicides: Irmgard Keun, author of *After Midnight*, the best satirical novel on Nazi Germany.[1] Otto Pohl, Socialist veteran, Austrian ex-Consul in Moscow, ex-Editor of the *Móskauer Rundschau*. Walter Benjamin, author and critic, my neighbour at 10, rue Dombastle in Paris, fourth at

[1] This, happily, turned out to be a false rumour.

our Saturday poker parties, and one of the most bizarre and witty persons I have known. Last time I had met him was in Marseilles, together with H., the day before my departure, and he had asked me : 'If anything goes wrong, have you got anything to take?' For in those days we all carried some 'stuff' in our pockets like conspirators in a penny dreadful, I had none (Vera's stuff had been no good), and he shared what he had with me, sixty-two tablets of a sedative procured in Berlin during the week which followed the burning of the Reichstag. He did it reluctantly, for he did not know whether the thirty-one tablets left him would be enough. They had been enough. A week after my departure he made his way over the Pyrenees to Spain, a man of fifty-five, with heart disease. At Port Bou the *Guardia Civil* arrested him. He was told that next morning they would send him back to France. When they came to fetch him for the train, he was dead.

And how many unknown? Old Jews and young anti-Fascists, cheating their guardians in an unobserved moment, killing themselves hurriedly, secretly; stealing out of life as they had stolen over barbed wire and frontier posts, after even this last exit permit had been refused to them.

And the procession of despair went on and on, streaming through this last open port, Europe's gaping mouth, vomiting the contents of her poisoned stomach. And they marched past two by two, the Polish aristocrat and the Jewish pedlar, the French patriot and the German pacifist, the Catholic father and the Communist comrade; and they queued up, two by two, in front of the Arks, the sons of Shem and the sons of Japheth, the male and the female, two and two of all flesh wherein is the breath of life. For the fountains of the great deep were broken up and the windows of Heaven were opened. And the flood was forty days upon the earth and the waters prevailed upon the earth; but there was still no rainbow set in the clouds.

EPILOGUE

A

Dear Colonel Blimp,

... Thank you for your letter of welcome to this country, which, as you write, 'stands like a solid rock of freedom and decency facing the shambles of the Continent'. Please excuse the delay in answering your letter, due to certain formalities (six weeks' imprisonment in Pentonville) through which I had to go after my arrival. It did not really matter; we have got into the habit, I and my like. I can assure you that it was the most decent jail I have been in so far; if I should write a Baedeker of the prisons of Europe, I would mark it with three stars.

But the reason why I really did not mind was that all through those nights in Pentonville, in spite of being locked up during the air raids in a pitch-dark, second-floor cell alone, I felt *safe* for the first time since the outbreak of war. I beg you to reflect for an instant on this curious mental phenomenon. For me and my like, 'safety' has only one meaning : to share the collective dangers of war and be safe from individual persecution, torture, and the more humiliating forms of death. The Austrian poet Rilke once wrote this prayer : 'Lord, I don't ask Thee to let me live my own life, but I beseech Thee, let me die my own death.' Amen.

During my stay in Marseilles, after the capitulation, in a country which has reached the bottom of humiliation, on August 15th, at noon, suddenly the air-raid sirens went, after they had been silent for two months. It was only a rehearsal, to prevent the pipes getting rusty, but it gave one a strange, home-sick longing for the good old days of war, when all was not yet lost. I was sitting in a tram and I saw on the faces of the people around me that they had similar thoughts. For a moment they understood that a man might be happier amongst a shower of high-explosives and incendiaries than under the *Pax Swasticana*. For them it was only a question of dignity and bigger food rations; for us it is a question of physical existence.

If you understand this, then you understand perhaps what England means to us. She is the enemy of our enemies; and perhaps one day she may become our ally.

Do not listen to those who pretend that this is already the case; or to those amongst my brother refugees who walk around with leper bells, shouting that the dearest wish of their hearts is to die for the British Empire. They are not lying, but in their distress they have got so muddled that they think Hong Kong is on the Continent. No, I and my like do not wish to die for Hong Kong, nor for a third Versailles (the first dates from 1871) and the perpetuation of the European vendetta; nor for a peace which would be a declaration of war to the next generation. Neither have we any enthusiasm for an economic order which burns the crops which it produces, and reminds one of a certain goose which, instead of golden eggs, lays a time bomb every day and then settles down blissfully to hatch it.

But all this need not disturb you; for in this fight against the common enemy we are tied to you in life and death. If you perish, we perish, and if our brethren on the Continent do not help you, you will not win.

A strange historical constellation has thrown us together, so that we are both in the position of the Indian bride : if one of us dies, the other will be burnt alive with the corpse, on the great funeral pyre of European civilisation.

Yours truly.

B

Dear Comrade Blimp,

... Thank you for your letter of welcome to this country which you call 'an abyss of reaction and hypocrisy', a further proof of which you see in the fact of my imprisonment. Unfortunately your proof is no longer valid, as I have been released unconditionally—partly thanks to a letter of guarantee from your cousin, Colonel Blimp, as I have in the meantime been told.

I must also confess that I have enlisted as a volunteer in the Army, without waiting for the Government to define our war aims.[1] The alternative would have been to follow the example of your step-brother,[2] who refused to handle an Imperialist stirrup pump, whereupon his flat was burnt out by an undialectical incendiary bomb. We have to choose between these alternatives; a third way may exist theoretically, but for all practical purposes there is none.

Of course, I am as unhappy as you are about the fact that our war aims have not yet been defined. Of course, it is ridiculous for us to ask our comrades in Germany to overthrow their rulers without being able to tell them what is going to happen afterwards. We both know that a German

[1] In the spring of 1941, when this was written, the Liberal and Socialist Press were waging an ardent campaign demanding that the Government issue a declaration defining Britain's 'war aims' after the manner of President Wilson's Fourteen Points.

[2] It should also be remembered that at that time the British Communist Party was instructing its members to refuse any participation in the 'Imperialist War', even participation in Air-Raid Defence.

will not commit high treason (for that is what we ask him to do) for the promise of a bigger butter ration, nor for the sake of 'democracy'—which in the memory of the younger generation over there means mainly unemployment plus reparation payments; and that they prefer to march the goose-step to queueing up for the dole. We also know that the German national character is not dominated by sheer wickedness, as your cousin the Colonel believes, but by a sort of aggressive sentimentality, ever since the time of the *Nibelungen*. We know that the whole problem is to fix their political libido on a banner more fascinating than the swastika, and that the only one which would do is the banner of the European Union. We have to teach them to sing '*Europa, Europa über alles*,' or they will never keep quiet. Other solutions have been tried during the past twelve centuries since the days of Charlemagne, and never succeeded. If we do not convince your cousin of this, our grandchildren will have to do it in the next war, unless they miss their chance of being born through lack of available parents.

Yes, by victory we imagine something entirely different from your cousin's ideas, but for the practical purposes of the moment that does not matter. For we both know that the Germans and other people on the Continent will not revolt before the first signs of military defeat. For the moment our situation reminds me of that story about the slum child, whose mother gives him a crust of dry bread to eat and says: 'Imagine there is dripping on it.' Whereupon the child asks: 'Please, Mother, may I imagine marmalade instead?' For the moment we are still choking on the dry crust of war, and if your cousin prefers to imagine dripping with it, let him. We for our part know it will be marmalade.

By the way, how do you define the difference between our marmalade and the Colonel's dripping? We have seen that a Socialist economy can associate with autocracy (Russia), and that Capitalism can be combined with an efficient planned economy (Germany). I am afraid that in a few years our battle-cry, 'Capitalism or Socialism', will have as much bearing on reality as theological disputes about the sex of angels. If, however, we proceed empirically, and extract the tendencies at work in modern history, we come to two pairs of alternatives, overlapping our old one :

In economics: (A) Chaos or (B) Planning (i.e. State Capitalism=State Socialism).

In politics: (1) Autocracy or (2) Democracy (i.e. the rule of the people by representation).

I know that the mark of equation in the brackets after (B) will shock you. But I have not found anybody who could explain to me the difference between State Capitalism and State Socialism in economic terms. The difference lies in the political structure of the State, and is therefore implicit in the second alternative.

Now, if we combine A+1 we get the classical form of tyranny, buried for ever by history. The combination B+1 produces totalitarianism, which we reject. The combination A+2 leads to plutocracy, or the goose that lays the time-bombs. Remains B+2, which has not yet been tried, and which seems to be the only promising one. Of course, it cannot be produced in the laboratory. A new movement will have to arise in a new moral climate where the Means justify the End, and not the other way round. The creation of this climate—that is what I imagine we are fighting for.

But if the Colonel prefers dripping—let him. He laughs best who laughs last. I wish the time of the great, liberating laughter had come. For this is our unique and ultimate war aim : to teach this planet to laugh again. At the moment we are still howling like dogs in the dark. I wish the time of laughter had come.

Yours fraternally.